# KIERKEGAARD'S
# DIALECTIC
# OF EXISTENCE

HERMANN DIEM

# KIERKEGAARD'S DIALECTIC OF EXISTENCE

Translated by
HAROLD KNIGHT

OLIVER AND BOYD
EDINBURGH AND LONDON
1959

OLIVER AND BOYD LTD
Tweeddale Court
Edinburgh 1

39A Welbeck Street
London W1

This book is a translation of *Die Existenzdialektik von Sören Kierkegaard*, by Hermann Diem, first published by the Evangelischer Verlag A.G., Zollikon-Zürich, 1950.

## ENGLISH EDITION

First published 1959

PRINTED IN GREAT BRITAIN
FOR OLIVER AND BOYD LTD
BY T. AND A. CONSTABLE LTD
EDINBURGH

# PREFACE

The external stimulus to the writing of this book was a prize offered by the Søren Kierkegaard Society of Copenhagen for a dissertation on "The Concept of Dialectic in Søren Kierkegaard." I seized upon this opportunity, because I had long felt the need to take issue against the ever-increasing misuse of Kierkegaard's work in present-day theological and philosophical discussion. The first thing to be done was to ascertain once and for all whether Kierkegaard can actually be appealed to in support of the "existential thinking" now so much in vogue.

The misuse in question answers, I fear, to a very widespread need, and hence will not be so easily disposed of. But if I have at least been able, here and there, to bring out that concern for intellectual integrity which lies at the root of Kierkegaard's passion for the existent, and have thereby provoked a few qualms of conscience among his admirers, that will already have achieved something.

For a fuller statement of my position here, especially in the first, philosophical part, I should like, for brevity's sake, to refer the reader to an earlier book of mine, *Philosophie und Christentum bei Sören Kierkegaard*, Munich 1929. Extensive use has been made of the material there set forth. I have likewise felt it unnecessary to duplicate the analysis there contained of the major literature on Kierkegaard. Such additions to it as have since appeared are cited only so far as they serve to throw light on the problems involved. For the rest, the attentive reader will notice for himself that my earlier conception of Kierkegaard's dialectical procedure has since been revised in certain important respects.

The Søren Kierkegaard Society of Copenhagen having awarded me their prize, I hereby thank them for this recognition of my work.

Ebersbach/Fils,               HERMANN DIEM
*August* 1950.

v

# CONTENTS

# SIGLA

*S. V.*    =  *Søren Kierkegaards Samlede Vaerker,* edd.
             Drachmann, Heiberg and Lange.

*S. K. P.* =  *Søren Kierkegaards Papirer,* edd. Heiberg
             and Kuhr.

*Ges. W.*  =  *Sören Kierkegaard: Gesammelte Werke,*
             edd. and tr. Gottsched and Schrempf.

*B. A.*    =  *Der Begriff des Auserwählter.*

*K. G.*    =  *Kritik der Gegenwart.*

*Angriff*  =  *Angriff auf die Christenheit.*

For full details, see Bibliographical Note, below,
p. 218.

## I. THE PROBLEM

The problem of Kierkegaard's dialectic is not a merely academic concern. For years there has existed a so-called dialectical theology which at least in its beginnings was influenced by Kierkegaard. These theologians were dubbed "dialectical thinkers" by those who stood outside their circle, in a way which is not without precedent in Church history, as we see, for example, in the case of the Lutherans or the first Christians at Antioch. Such nicknaming has not always been discriminating; but in any event in the present instance the name stuck, although it soon became clear that the collective description "dialectical" included very divergent types of theological thought. As long ago as 1928 some one made the satirical but by no means pointless observation "that the leaders of dialectical theology were as disunited as the Chinese revolutionary generals."[1] When in 1933 the differences between them became apparent to every one, it had for long been clear to the more perspicacious that these theologians differed from each other not simply in this or that point of doctrine, but that their differences rested upon a disparity in the basic presuppositions underlying their thought. They were "dialectical" in very divergent senses, and this was shown not least in the varying use which they made of Kierkegaard's work.

Let us think, for example, of the opposition between Karl Barth and Emil Brunner, which was disclosed, above all, in the question of natural theology and its implications for a theological anthropology. For Brunner it was a question in this controversy not simply of a single or even central doctrinal statement, but of a whole and far-reaching approach to theological thinking, which he called "existentialist thinking" and which he related specifically to Kierkegaard—whether rightly

---

[1] In *Zwischen den Zeit* (cited below as *Z. d. Z.*), 1933, p. 537.

or wrongly we may for the moment leave undetermined.[2] On the other hand Karl Barth says with reference to the demand for a *theologia regenitorum* as this was voiced in various forms in the nineteenth century: "The anthropologising of theology had been completed," and he goes on: "And now it is a serious question whether we must not say as much with regard to the modern demand for existentialist theological thinking and speaking, which is connected with Kierkegaard, but, above all, is consciously or unconsciously a continuation of the pietistic tradition."[3] Here again we may leave undecided the question whether Kierkegaard can be rightly made responsible for this development, or whether, as Barth seems to suggest, we must see here a pietistic misunderstanding of Kierkegaard. How real is the danger of such a misunderstanding can moreover be seen from the keen interest which has recently been taken in Kierkegaard's work in North America, for this interest has been directed predominantly to the "inwardness" and subjectivity of Kierkegaard without any concern to adopt his dialectical method as a whole.

In all these cases which we have selected only as a few instances among many of the bearing which Kierkegaard's work has on present day theological discussion, it is only possible to make a correct judgement if we do not confine ourselves to isolating some one point from the totality of Kierkegaard's work, but appreciate clearly the presuppositions and the method of his thought in its coherence and wholeness. Since, however, in regard to this thought we are faced not by a system but by a procedure, an enquiry into the idea of "dialectic" in the thought of Kierkegaard must not only furnish us with the key to the understanding of his work itself, but will also help considerably towards the elucidation of the contemporary theological situation.

This is a matter which affects not only the situation within the Protestant world. Since Catholics such as Theodor Häcker, Romano Guardini, Erich Przywara and others have concerned

[2] Cp. E. Brunner, "Die andere Aufgabe der Theologie," in *Z. d. Z.*, 1929, pp. 255 ff.

[3] K. Barth, *Die Kirchliche Dogmatik* (cited below as *K. D.*), i.1 (1932), p. 19.

themselves with Kierkegaard's work, a new impetus has been given to this controversy.[4] For Catholics can always appeal to Kierkegaard's critique of Luther, which is repeatedly expressed in such terms as that "the fact is that Luther was not a dialectical thinker";[5] and on this point Theodor Häcker says that, in point of fact, if we consider certain aspects of Luther, we are tempted to say: "Had he been to a greater extent a dialectical thinker in the Pauline manner, had he not taken over merely one half of the Apostle's dialectic, but the whole, then perhaps the most terrible evil which has ever afflicted Christendom, namely the split in the one faith, might have been avoided."[6] For a genuine settlement of this question we need to understand precisely what Kierkegaard meant by "dialectic." Otherwise there is a real danger that Kierkegaard's objection to Luther's lack of dialectic might, on the part of Catholics, be turned against Luther in an undialectical manner.[7]

Furthermore, this enquiry into the Kierkegaardian dialectic is a matter which has more than a mere theological bearing. For Kierkegaard has influenced contemporary philosophy perhaps even more than theological discussion. We need only mention among many the names of Karl Jaspers, Martin Heidegger, Jean-Paul Sartre. Here again the decisive factor is the concentration of attention on existence and the new orientation which this gives to thought. In spite of the fact that the work of Kierkegaard is thoroughly Christian in its inspiration, and that in the most decisive way it qualifies human existence by the implications of the divine self-revelation in Jesus Christ, it is understandable that philosophers should have

---

[4] T. Häcker, (1) *Sören Kierkegaard und die Philosophie der Innerlichkeit*, Innsbruck 1913, (2) *Der Begriff der Wahrheit bei Sören Kierkegaard*, Innsbruck 1932, (3) *Christentum und Kultur*, and (4) postscript to his translations of Kirkegaard, London 1937; R. Guardini, "Die Ausgangspunkt der Dankbewegung bei Sören Kierkegaard," in *Hochland*, XXIV, pp. 12 ff.; Przywara, *Das Geheimnis Kierkegaards*, Munich 1929; "Kierkegaard-Literatur," in *Stimmen der Zeit*, LIX, Pt. 12.

[5] *Sören Kierkegaards Papirer* (cited below as *S. K. P.*), edd. P. A. Heiberg and V. Kuhr, 11 vols. in 19 pts., Copenhagen 1909-38, x.1 (=VOL. x, Pt. 1), 213; x.2, 312; x.3, 217, 267; x.4, 394; x.5(A), 38, 96; xi.1, 28; xi.2, 266; etc.

[6] T. Häcker, *Christentum und Kultur*, pp. 98-9.

[7] This danger is esp. apparent in E. Przywara (above, n. 4).

fewer inhibitions in dealing with it than theologians. The attack on Christianity which Kierkegaard eventually made with such extraordinary vigour renders it difficult for the theologians to achieve a correct adjustment to his work. Either they must regard this attack as simply an error and a deviation, as a result of which Kierkegaard has revoked all his previous deep and true dogmatic insights; or else they must see in this attack the ultimate logical consequences of his whole life's work, in which case they have to face the question whether this very phenomenon does not prove that his insistence on the subjective appropriation and exercise of Christianity has caused him to lose sight of the objective fact of revelation, and to transform theology into anthropology. In either case the theologian does not see any sound way of using Kierkegaard's work for his own special task, and, in particular, for his dogmatic task.

But for the philosopher these difficulties do not exist. On the contrary, he can even interpret the discomfort of the theologians as an invitation to use the Kierkegaardian dialectic to concern himself all the more thoroughly about human existence and in disregard of the fact of divine revelation. Kierkegaard's work itself seems to justify him in this aim, not only on account of its broad human basis, but also because Kierkegaard himself makes his pseudonymous John Climacus say: "If the meaning of religious existence had been forgotten, then no doubt also the meaning of human existence had been forgotten; the latter had therefore to be emphasised afresh."[8] And at the end of the *Unwissenschaftliche Nachschrift* he explains retrospectively in reference to the whole work of his pseudonymous characters that the latter "had wished to read afresh the original documents concerning individual human relations in their existential bearing, and to reinterpret, if possible in a more inward way, what is old, well-known, and handed down by our forefathers."[9] Why should not the philosophers, whose

[8] *Søren Kierkegaards Samlede Vaerker* (cited below as *S. V.*), edd. A. B. Drachmann, J. L. Heiberg and H. O. Lange, 14 vols., Copenhagen 1901 ff., VOL. VII, p. 210; =Sören Kierkegaard, *Gesammelte Werke* (cited below as *Ges. W.*), tr. and edd. H. Gottsched and C. Schrempf, 12 vols., Jena 1922 ff., VOL. VI, p. 321.

[9] *S. V.*, VII, 548-9; *Ges. W.*, VII, 304.

task this is, allow themselves to be guided in it by Kierkegaard? Of course they must know what they are about if, in so doing, they think they are at liberty to disregard the decisive presupposition of Kierkegaard, namely the fact of revelation.

In this respect the philosophers have taken up different attitudes. Heidegger, for example, has used Kierkegaard's work in the process of his own ontological analysis of existence and it has served him as so much ontic material for the discovery of ontological structural relationships. But in doing this he is very conscious that he is doing something quite other than what Kierkegaard proposed by his existential dialectic.[10] Jaspers uses Kierkegaard as material for the elucidation of a "psychology of world-views."[11] How Kierkegaard is related to Sartre and his existentialist circle is completely problematical. The idea of "existentialist thinking" is just as obscure in its use by modern philosophers as it is in its use by modern theologians, upon whose work it has only had the effect, so far, of blurring all theological categories. Hence philosophy is just as much interested as theology in any enquiry into the idea of Kierkegaardian dialectic.

## 2. A PRELIMINARY APPROACH

In the attempt to find a preliminary approach to Kierkegaard's use of the idea of dialectic, we have the overall impression that this use is very manifold and variable and can with difficulty be reduced to a common factor. For this we adduce a few haphazardly chosen quotations:

"Reality or existence is the dialectical moment in a trilogy, the beginning and the end of which are not there for an existing individual who as such an individual finds himself involved in this dialectic moment. It is abstraction which closes the circle of the trilogy."[1]

"In fact in all obscurity and ignorance there is a dialectical interplay of knowledge and will, and we may go astray in our

---

[10] M. Heidegger, *Sein und Zeit*, Halle 1927, p. 235, n. 1.
[11] K. Jaspers, *Psychologie der Weltanschaunngen*, 2nd edn., Berlin 1925.
[1] *S. V.*, vii, 270; *Ges. W.*, vii, 14.

understanding of man if we emphasise merely knowledge or merely will."[2]

"The dialectical as such does not constitute a point of view which stands in an essential relation to personality."[3]

"Everything depends on making an absolute distinction between quantitative and qualitative dialectic. Logic as a whole is quantitative or modal dialectic, for everything is, and the totality is constantly one and the same. In existence, on the other hand, qualitative dialectic is at home."[4]

"In man there is always this impulse, which is both anxious and desirous of reassurance, to secure something that is both right and firm, and such as may exclude dialectic. This however is cowardice and treachery against the divine.[5] Even the ultimate certitude, revelation itself, becomes *eo ipso* dialectic so soon as I endeavour to appropriate it."[6]

"How far is it permissible to attract men instead of repelling them in order to win them for the truth? But this repulsion must be energetically expressed in action (qualitative dialectic)."[7]

"The dialectical is seen in the fact that he who communicates truth must work against himself."[8]

"The dialectical is seen in the fact that he who communicates truth must always have eyes in the back of his neck as far as the real appropriation of communicated truth is concerned."[9]

"It is easy to see the dialectic in the fact that John Climacus's defence of Christianity is the utmost that is acceptable; for as a result of the dialectical situation defence and attack are within a hair's breadth the same."[10]

"But Luther was not a dialectical thinker. He overlooked the fact that he was an extraordinary person, that perhaps in the last resort he was unique in being able to bear this immediate relation to God. Yet he made himself a measure for others. It was the destiny of Protestantism to declare that all men are

---

[2] *S. V.*, xi, 160; *Ges. W.*, viii, 45, where, however, the sentence is omitted.

[3] *S. V.*, xiii, 141; *Der Begriff der Ironie*, tr. W. Kütemeyer, Munich 1929, 45.

[4] *S. K. P.*, vii(A), 84.          [5] *S. V.*, vii, 440; *Ges. W.*, vii, 191.

[6] *S. V.*, vii, 24 n.; *Ges. W.*, vi, 140 n.

[7] *S. K. P.*, viii.2 (B), 8129.          [8] *Op. cit.*, 31.

[9] *Op. cit.*, 32.          [10] *Op. cit.*, x.2, 163, p. 130.

priests, and the inevitable consequence was either careless lack of balance or sheer deterioration into worldliness."[11]

"But Luther was no dialectical thinker, he persistently saw only one side of the question."[12]

"Yet it has clearly been the misfortune of Christendom that the dialectical aspect of Luther's doctrine of faith has been disregarded; hence the latter has become a covering for mere heathenism and Epicureanism. It has simply been forgotten that Luther emphasised faith in opposition to fantastically exaggerated asceticism."[13]

These examples should suffice for our preliminary orientation. We might just mention further by way of a warning to exercise caution that Kierkegaard concludes this elucidation of his pseudonymous work by expressing the wish: "And may no bungler dialectically touch this work, let it remain as it is."[14]

In these quoted passages the idea of dialectic is obviously used in the first place in the most general and formal sense: to denote the activity of that type of thought which reaches its goal by moving between question and answer or assertion and contradiction in dialogue. In so far as this implies correctness of thought and its technique, this dialectical process may also be called *logic*. Dialectic in this sense is basic to all further and more specific use of the idea.

Such a further qualification of the idea arises at once from the fact that this questioning-and-answering, assertion-and-contradiction, is always directed towards an *object*, the truth about which must be established. *Thought* is related to *being*, and the question of the relation between the two immediately becomes a question of the relation between formal *logic* and *ontology*. In order to answer this question it will be essential to consider *what kind* of being is the object of thought. At this point Kierkegaard opposes to the pure being of Hegel the individual existence of the thinker himself. This produces a contrast in the essential character and aim of the dialectical process on either side, and the implications of this contrast for the problems of logic will have to be clarified. Here it is a question of what Kierkegaard, as we have seen, calls the absolute

[11] *Op. cit.*, x.3, 267.    [12] *Op. cit.*, x.4, 394.
[13] *Op. cit.*, x.1, 213.    [14] *S. V.*, vii, 549; *Ges. W.*, vii, 304.

distinction between quantitative and qualitative dialectic.[15] This qualitative dialectic of Kierkegaard must then be brought out in its bearing on the individual existence of the thinker.

A further point arises when we ask how far, in respect of this existential dialectic, one person can be the *teacher* of another. If, as Kierkegaard insists, it is not a question of knowing the truth but of being in the truth in one's existence as an individual, then we must ask whether and in what way truth so conceived can be an object of communication. Hence to the dialectic by which the thinker probes his own existence there is added the *dialectic of communication*, and it is a question how these two aspects of dialectic are related to each other.

This dialectic of communication is once again qualified when we are concerned with the *communication of the historical fact of God's self-revelation*. In the first place the question arises to what extent revelation is subjected to the dialectical process through its immersion in the stream of historical becoming,[16] and further how it can be imparted to such effect that it becomes for the recipient not merely an object of knowledge, a doctrine of revelation, but something which can be truly received only in so far as it changes the very existence of him who receives it. Then, in connexion with this dialectic of Christian communication, we must pose the questions concerning the significance of tradition, of Church authority and teaching, both in regard to the Apostolic age and the meaning of ordination, the essential character of preaching, and so forth.

By this preliminary approach, we have not yet attained any firm view of the line which we must follow in our study. We have simply tried to gain a clear picture of the relevant problems in their interconnexion. How this complex of problems can best be disentangled and presented in detail must be seen from the course of our study and its intrinsic development.

## 3. DIALECTIC AND DIALOGUE

The most original and simplest form of dialectic is conversation between two persons, or dialogue. In this situation two persons at least are required and neither of them has a complete

---

[15] See above, p. 8, n. 4.     [16] See above, p. 8, n. 6.

command of the truth. The aim is rather to attain the latter
by common enquiry through question and answer. In his
*Begriff der Ironie* Kierkegaard has drawn out the characteristics
of this dialectical type of conversation with reference to the
activity of Socrates and has thus laid the foundation of his own
dialectic. There is no need for us to follow the course of his
argument in detail here, and we propose simply to summarise
those of his conclusions which are most important for our
purpose.

No matter how the historical Socrates was, in point of fact,
related to the picture given of him in the Platonic dialogues, it is
clear, in any event, that the dialogue form was essential to his
mode of thought. This expresses the attempt to allow thought
itself to emerge in its objectivity. In Hegel's dialectical triad
thought questions and answers itself and so effects through
synthesis the unity between thesis and antithesis. In the
dialogue form, on the other hand, it is the object, firmly grasped
and held by both speakers, which establishes the unity between
question and answer.

This questioning has always two aspects. It "implies, in
part, a relation of the individual to the object, and, in part, a
relation of the individual to another individual. In the former
aspect, effort is directed towards freeing the phenomenon from
all entanglement with the limited finite subject. In asking
questions, I assume that I know nothing and adopt a purely
receptive attitude to my object."[1] This questioning on an
assumption of ignorance corresponds to the negative aspect in
Hegel's dialectic. But while, in the latter, this negative aspect
is an element intrinsic to thought itself, here the negative aspect
is extrinsic to the object and lies in the questioning individual,
and an answer follows only in so far as the seeking is genuine.
But the search is not purely arbitrary, for between the ego and
its object there exists a relation of correspondence, just as "a
divining rod mysteriously corresponds with the presence of
water under the earth, and divination takes place only where
water is concealed."[2] The other aspect of the questioning is

[1] *S. V.*, XIII, 130; *Begriff der Ironie*, 31. All further refs. in this section are
to these two works.
[2] 131 n.; 31 n. 24.

concerned with the relation of an individual to another individual. They are reciprocally related to each other but there is no centre of unity between them. The unity between them consists only in the fact that the conversation is constantly directed both to the object and the conversational partner. These two aspects of the quest together form the essence of dialogue.

But Kierkegaard finds in the Platonic dialogues two different modes of questioning. On the one hand, a question is asked in order to receive an answer, and in the course of alternating question and answer knowledge of the object grows ever deeper and more richly significant. On the other hand, questions may be asked in order to overthrow a supposed knowledge and instead of an answer to leave a void. Kierkegaard sees in the first case the "speculative method of Plato," and in the second the "ironic method of Socrates."[3] But in most of the dialogues these two methods proceed concurrently. We shall see later that this distinction is of importance for Kierkegaard's own method of dialectic, and for that reason we must go into it more closely.

The two methods are seen at work with particular clarity in Plato's *Symposium*. The Socratic method of dialogue consists "in simplifying the manifold and complex compounds of life, by reducing them to an ever more abstract basis."[4] Socrates finds he can do nothing with the praises of Eros until he knows exactly what Eros is; and hence in order to clarify the nature of Eros he begins with the question whether love can exist *per se* without an object. In answering this question, "he does not extract the kernel from its husk, but hollows out the kernel itself.[5] . . . Soaring constantly, his reflexion rises gradually above the atmospheric air, until breathing is held up in the pure ether of abstraction."[6] Love is reduced to its most abstract definition as love of something that the lover has not, i.e. it becomes pure desire and longing. "This definition is at the same time the most abstract, or more correctly, it is itself the abstract, not in any ontological sense but in the sense of lacking specific concrete content."[7] The abstract is here a

---

[3] 131; 34.   [4] 137; 39.   [5] 140; 43.
[6] 137; 39.   [7] 141; 44.

description without content, and the study ceases where, according to the general opinion, it should begin. "The result at which he arrives is really the indeterminable description of pure being: love *is*; for the qualification of it as longing and desire is not a definition since it represents merely a relation to a something that is not given."[8] This negative kind of abstractness is the ironic. Such is the standpoint of Socrates.

But then there begins quite a new development with the discourse of Diotima. Here the abstract essence of Eros which Socrates could define only negatively now becomes *myth*. "This negativeness suggesting the eternal unrest of thought, and which both separates and combines, which thought cannot hold firmly since it expresses the onward driving impulse of thought, now ceases and rests and gives place to vision. *This* is the *mythical*." The mythic expression transcends the dialectical procedure of Socrates "by the fact that it exposes something visible which can be contemplated."[9] This means that Eros properly ceases to be the object of the thinker's activity. It is presented now through another medium, namely that of imagination. "The dialectical procedure clears the ground of all that is irrelevant and now tries to climb to the contemplation of the idea; since this, however, fails, imagination reacts. Since imagination has become stiff as a result of the dialectical work, it now sets itself to dream and so produces the mythical. In this dreaming the idea either flies quickly past, or it comes to rest and broadens itself out infinitely in space. The mythical springs from the *enthusiasm of imagination* working in the service of speculation."[10] This mythical element is not the idea, but since consciousness cannot grasp it in any other way, it expresses itself in the form of images and so reflects the splendour of the idea. Thus it develops into a dialectic, which, "proceeding from the most abstract ideas, allows them to unfold themselves in concrete determinations, a dialectic which wishes to reconstruct reality on the basis of the idea."[11] In spite of this, we have here not a dialectic of the idea, such as we have in Hegel, but only an idea of the dialectical. "In Plato, just because it is not an intrinsically logical dialectic, the dialectical movement remains aloof from the movement of ideas, however much it is

[8] 141; 45.   [9] 194; 107.   [10] 189; 101-2.   [11] 207; 122.

amplified intellectually."[12] What it is in search of is something corresponding to Kant's "thing in itself," which is essentially elusive, and which, if it must be apprehended, has to be expressed in terms of the mythical.[13] Thus there is no speculative dialectical movement in Plato, but the impulse to speculation springs from another source: in contrast to the negative qualifications of Socrates, Eros is here positively qualified by receiving as its object the beautiful. And the beautiful in and for itself, which cannot be attained by any constructive dialectical process, can always be "perceived in *vision*.[13] ... The element in which Plato is at home is not thought, but imaginative presentation,"[14] and the latter begins where the dialectical process ends. The mythical is then speculatively interpreted with the help of "a sort of pre-existence of the idea."[15]

For Socrates, on the other hand, "the idea marked the limit,"[16] and he knew nothing of what lay beyond it. "His ignorance expressed an eternal victory over the phenomenon"[17] and prevented him from fathoming the positive, which he glimpsed from afar. Rather, taking the path of the "know thyself," he endeavours to seek plenitude within. For "it is indisputable that in the mind of the ironic thinker lies a primal depth, a *valuta*."[18] Thus his personality is constituted "by a negative attitude towards the idea and by a contemplating of his own navel."[19]

If we have regard to only one single phase of the dialectical process, these two methods possess considerable resemblance, whereas at their extremes they cease to have any further point of contact with each other, as is shown by the difference between the first and the last of Plato's dialogues. In both cases dialectic concludes with an abstraction which does not exhaust the idea. But the difference between them lies in the character and implications of this abstraction and in the attitude of the individual thinker towards it. With Socrates, the abstract is the void, "the indeterminate description of pure being," to which the ego reacts in irony by withdrawing into itself. For Plato, the abstract is something positive, which indeed is no longer attainable by dialectic and which, if we insist on trying

[12] 142; 46.    [13] 195 ; 108.    [14] 191 n.; 104 n.    [15] 193; 206.
[16] 253; 174.    [17] 258; 180.    [18] 148; 31.    [19] 145; 50.

to hold it, leads us into the paths of speculation. The circumstance that, employing the same methods, they arrive at opposite conclusions, results from their contrasted presuppositions. "Every philosophy which begins with a presupposition, naturally ends with the same presupposition, and if the philosophy of Socrates began with the assumption that he knew nothing, he naturally reached the conclusion that men in general know nothing; the Platonic philosophy began with the assumption of the unity of thought and being and remained within that assumption."[20] On the basis of these assumptions Plato inevitably understood the abstract ontologically and Socrates understood it as the pure void.

As regards the relation of the subject to the world, this difference means that for Plato "the ego constantly expresses itself in affirmation of the world" and in so doing "keeps memory straining forwards as it issues forth to encounter reality." Dialectic has therefore a positive liberating effect on the idea, whereas for Socrates this liberating effect operates negatively. The ego expresses itself by its questioning which is destructive of all answers in denial of the world, and maintains itself at the vantage point of irony by keeping memory "negatively retrogressive in opposition to the movement of life."[21]

In this connexion, it is important to notice Kierkegaard's remark to the effect that in the later constructive dialogues of Plato there is no longer any genuine question and answer. "In these dialogues, the question form really represents something that is superseded; the one who replies appears rather as a witness to what is known, as an exponent of common knowledge with his 'yes' and 'amen'; in short, there is no longer any real conversation."[22] It is merely accidental that in spite of this Plato has retained the external form of dialogue and has not chosen a more strictly suitable form of presentation.

## 4. LOGIC AND ONTOLOGY

It is immediately apparent to all readers of Kierkegaard's work that he does not simply take over either the Socratic or the Platonic method of dialectic, as in general he is a very original

[20] 132-3; 34-5.    [21] 210; 126-7.    [22] 147; 52-3.

and individual thinker who can never be explained merely in the light of his historical antecedents. The study which he has undertaken in the *Begriff der Ironie* did however do him the service of enabling him to draw out and clarify the problems latent in dialogical dialectics. In fact, in this study, in so far as it concerns dialectical method, we find indicated nearly all the questions which Kierkegaard endeavours to answer in the course of his own work. In this matter it is everywhere plain that Kierkegaard's sympathies lie on the side of Socratic irony rather than Platonic dialectic. We shall see how he later modifies once more the understanding of Socrates given here.

The realisation which sprang from a consideration of the opposite conclusions of the Socratic and Platonic dialectic, namely that every philosophy ends with the same presupposition with which it began, becomes the central point in Kierkegaard's discussion of the Hegelian dialectic. Hegel, like Plato, though in a very different manner, accepts the assumption of an immediate unity between thought and being. And here, in those logical presuppositions in consequence of which formal logic suddenly develops into ontology, Kierkegaard sees the juncture at which the decisive battle must be fought out. If we concede to Hegel the point of departure by which alone he can bring his dialectic into movement, then it is no longer possible to overthrow him. Since in the course of this debate Kierkegaard secures the logical foundations for his own dialectic, we must first turn our attention to this particular point.[1]

The presupposition underlying the philosophy of antiquity and the Middle Ages, namely that thought corresponds to reality, was rendered so questionable by the Kantian critique of reason that Hegel could not disregard the latter. Hence he aims at overcoming positively this critique, in that, by the aid

---

[1] Apart from the inherent difficulty of the subject, the answer to these questions is further complicated by the fact that although the logical problems involved in them constantly occupied his attention Kierkegaard has nowhere expressed his thoughts about them in any coherent or continuous form. Hence we must try to discover his opinion of them from the statements scattered continuously throughout his work, esp. from the relevant statements in his diary.

of the concept of "pure thought," he endeavours to ascribe a self-conscious reality to thought instead of that which was uncritically assumed. The questions which Kierkegaard asks about this pure thought arise from various sources. But again and again they merge in the one supreme question, whether the Hegelian reality is not a mere reality of ideas.

Hegel does not begin by enquiring into the reality of one specific thing, but enquires in the abstract about reality in general. But "to enquire in the abstract about reality (even if it is a correct procedure to enquire about it in abstract terms, since the individual and the fortuitous belong to the sphere of reality, which abstraction certainly does not), and to answer abstractly, is by no means so difficult as to ask and answer the question what it means to say that this specific thing is a reality. For abstraction discounts the uniqueness of the thing. The difficulty, however, lies precisely in assuming that the specific thing can be equated with the ideality of thought by the mere process of thinking it. Abstraction cannot even concern itself with this contradiction, for abstract thought in fact conceals it."[2] When Hegel suggests that it is the very nature of pure thought to imply an identity of thinking and being, the statement means nothing for Kierkegaard, since as long as we remain within the medium of idealistic thought the disparity cannot become apparent. Such idealism can only assert that thinking and the reality of ideas are the same. But to say so is a tautology. "Had Hegel stated in a preface to the whole of his logic that he was only making an experiment in thought, in the course of which he had at various points evaded certain issues, then he would no doubt be the greatest thinker who has ever lived. But as it is he is simply comical."[3]

And what are the points at which Hegel has evaded the issue? Firstly there is the question of "the *dialectic of the beginning*."[4] The Hegelian system proposes to begin absolutely, and apart from all presuppositions, with the immediate and self-evident. But such a beginning can only be attained by means of reflective thought. However, since it is of the essence of the latter to be infinitely continuous, this infinite process

[2] *S. V.*, vii, 257; *Ges. W.*, vii, 1.  [3] *S. K. P.*, v(A),73.
[4] Cp. *S. V.*, vii, 90 ff.; *Ges. W.*, vi, 193 ff.

must first be stopped in order to make a beginning possible. Now this cannot happen without a decision, and decisions have no place in logic. Nor does Hegel succeed any more with his *dialectic of doubt*. For even if we accept the assumption that all doubt rests on a substratum of abstract certitude, the latter cannot "for one moment be hypostatised so long as I am doubting, for doubt will always free itself from this hypostasis in order to doubt."[5]  Hence one must say that "although the Hegelian philosophy may be free from all postulates, yet it has reached this position by means of one crazy postulate, namely the beginning of pure thought."[6]

Hegel experiences the same difficulty in keeping his dialectic method in motion.  Here the weak point is "mediation," the link which is intended to bind together two ideas, and Kierkegaard asks: "How does this mediation arise?  Does it result from the fact that the two moments strive to unite?  Is it contained in them *a priori*?  Is it added to them as something new?"[7]  In this matter Kierkegaard refers to Trendelenburg,[8] who shows that although Hegel thinks that he is *effecting* movement through logic alone, he is actually *presupposing* it throughout his whole dialectic. "Wherever we turn, movement remains the assumed vehicle of dialectically productive thought."[9]  But Kierkegaard considers that a movement immanent to logic is an impossibility.  "In logic the *becoming* proper to movement can have no place, logic *is*, and all that is logical *is* only, and it is this very limitation of logic which marks the transition from logic to becoming, where individual existence and reality emerge."[10]  At the point where movement begins logic sees merely an interruption of itself, such as can only be overcome by a leap.[11]

There may well be a system of existence which is situated

[5] *S. V.*, VII, 290 n.; *Ges. W.*, VII, 33 n.  Cp. *S. K. P.*, IV(B) 21.
[6] *S. V.*, VII, 270; *Ges. W.*, VII, 13.
[7] *S. V.*, III, 189; *Ges. W.*, III, 137.
[8] *S. V.*, VII, 89, 258 n.; *Ges. W.*, VI, 194, and VII, 1 n.
[9] A. Trendelenburg, *Logische Untersuchungen*, Berlin 1840, p. 26.  On this question of movement in logic, Kierkegaard learnt much from Trendelenburg that was essential for his own method.
[10] *S. V.*, IV, 285; *Ges. W.*, V. 6.
[11] *S. V.*, VII, 296; *Ges. W.*, VII, 40.

only in the realm of possibility and does not attain that of reality.  Only by means of such subterfuges in his dialectic of the beginning and of movement can Hegel falsely present his system of being as a system of existence, and transform his logic into ontology.  When he later asserts that in this system of pure thought the *jerk of contradiction* has been overcome by identity, then that is not surprising.  For contradiction is the hallmark of the real, and it is precisely the real which Hegel has abstracted.  "Hegel is absolutely right in saying that *sub specie aeterni*, in the language of abstraction, in pure thought and pure being, there is no *aut . . . aut*.  Confound it! how could there be, seeing that abstraction itself has removed all contradiction?"[12]

All these objections of Kierkegaard to Hegel's technique of interchanging the real with the reality of ideas appear once more from a different angle when one asks how the empirical subject of thought is to be related to the subject of pure thought.  Hegel asserts that "the absolute is, because I think it," and in order to make this statement irrefragable he turns the matter round the other way and says that "my thinking of the absolute is the self-thinking of the absolute within me."[13]  Between these two poles, pure thought unfolds itself not only as absolute thought, but as the self-thinking of the absolute.  Hence in pure thought the empirical subject, the thinker, coincides with the absolute subject.  But again the question is how empirical thinking can enter into this movement.  "The life of a real man, who is compounded of infinity and finitude, consists in holding together these two aspects, and he himself is endlessly interested and concerned about existence itself.  But this abstract thinker is a twofold being: sometimes a fantastic being who lives on the lofty heights of pure abstraction, and at other times a sad professorial figure, who is laid aside by that abstract being as one would lay aside a stick."[14]  How, by what act,

---

[12] *S. V.*, vii, 261; *Ges. W.*, vii, 5.

[13] *S. V.*, ii; *Ges. W.*, ii, 191.

[14] *S. V.*, vii, 258; *Ges. W.*, vii, 2. Cp. *S. V.*, vii, 287-8; *Ges. W.*, vii, 30-1: "If Hegel had published his Logic under the title of '*Pure Thought*,' without the name of the author or year of publication, without a preface or any learned self-contradictions, without any disturbing explanations of what can only explain itself, had he published it as something accessory to a treatise on the natural phenomena of Ceylon, as the characteristic

does this sometimes sad professorial figure transform itself into the fantastic subject of pure thought? This is Kierkegaard's ever-recurring question, because he is primarily interested in the real existence of the thinker himself. But he finds such an interest absent from Hegel. "Quite a different situation arises when the subject of pure thought tries to explain its relation to an ethically existent individual. In fact, however, it never does this nor even pretends to do so, for if it did it would have to enter into quite another sort of dialectic, namely Greek or existential dialectic."[15]

In attempting to elucidate this other sort of dialectic which Kierkegaard calls the "dialectic of existence" we shall constantly come up against the same logical problems which Kierkegaard finds that Hegel fails to answer or answers falsely and which he himself feels he must try to solve correctly. In this connexion the demarcation of logic over against ontology will be a constant concern of the dialectic of existence.

## 5. THE REALITY OF THE THINKER

The difficulty about Hegel's system is that he cannot reach reality by thinking, because as soon as thought begins to control the real it translates it into the sphere of the possible. "All knowledge of reality is possibility; the sole reality of which an

movements of pure thought, then it would have been a Greek work. A Greek would have acted thus had the idea occurred to him. The artistic element consists in the expression of content through form, and one must refrain from all expressions about it which are inadequate. Now logic, with all its observations, makes as comic an impression as if a man showed a letter purporting to have been sent down from heaven, and yet left in it the rough copy, revealing all too plainly that its origin was on the earth. But in such a work, to attack in notes such-and-such persons who are named, to give knowing winks, what can it mean? It means that we have there a thinker who is thinking pure thought, who is speaking in terms of the movements proper to thought itself, and in fact is even speaking to another thinker with whom he wishes to discuss things deeply. But if it is a thinker who is thinking pure thought, then at this very moment the whole of Greek dialectics, together with the security police of existential dialectics, will seize his person and grip him by the flaps of his coat, yet not as followers, but in order to discover how he behaves in face of pure thought, and at the same moment the whole magic spell is broken."

[15] S. V., VII, 265; Ges. W., VII, 9.

existent individual has not a merely intellectual knowledge is his own, i.e. the fact of his own existence and this reality is the subject of his overriding concern."[1] For this reason Kierkegaard takes as the starting point of his dialectic, not reality in general as Hegel does, but the individual reality of the thinker himself.

Kierkegaard shows how this reality becomes a problem for thought by concerning himself with the further question as to how far the thinking ego is interested in the reality of its own existence. Here the point is that he cannot simply take cognisance of his own specific and characteristic existence. As soon as the reflecting subject performs this act of self-awareness, it automatically differentiates itself as such a subject from its empirical reality as object. It does not make this differentiation without keen interest: rather, in making it, it measures the empirical subject against a conceptual ideal subject. By this act, the ego becomes conscious of itself as an existing ego. It does not thereby become the ideal ego but neither does it remain the empirical ego; the position is rather that as the ego which is interested in its own existence it is a mediator between the two. But it is precisely in this middle term that reality lies, in this *"interesse"* as a mediating activity, in the literal sense of the Latin *"inter-esse."*[2]

As soon as the immediately existing ego attains consciousness of itself this immediacy is suspended by the new awareness of a contradiction between the ideal and the real. In more precise terms this happens because consciousness makes clear its concern about this decisive contradiction, and in so doing affirms itself. Kierkegaard's whole existential dialectic circles around this attainment of self-consciousness by the ego, by which it becomes aware of itself as existent and so wins reality. This is fundamentally its sole and ever recurrent theme, every implicit aspect of which is unfolded. With relentless persistence the ego is pinned down to this position with no possibility of escape into the bypaths of speculation.

At the same time we should note that in this existential

---

[1] *S. V.*, vii, 271; *Ges. W.*, 15.

[2] Cp. Kierkegaard's unpublished essay of 1842-3, "John Climacus," or "*De omnibus dubitandum*," in *S. K. P.*, iv(b), 1-17, 148.

dialectic thought is only one factor among others. Kierkegaard can even say: "The sole ego which is not apprehensible by thought is the existent ego, with which thought has indeed nothing at all to do."[3] But this is said with a polemical intention against Hegel's "pure thought," which of course has nothing to do with concrete existence. In the existence of the self-existing ego thought has its particular function to fulfil within the complex of factors which go to make up existence. To the life of the existent dialectical (or, as Kierkegaard calls him, subjective) thinker, there belong "imagination, feeling and dialectic dwelling together with passion in the inner depths of existence. But first and last passion, for it is impossible to reflect realistically on existence without falling into passion, for existence is one monstrous self-contradiction."[4] The contradiction consists in the fact that existence should be lived from the standpoint of idealism—"which is an extremely strenuous life-work, because existence itself is the obstacle to it."[5] "With his powers of idealistic thinking man shares in infinity, whereas existence keeps him constantly chained to the finite. . . . Only momentarily can the single individual in the turmoil of his existence find himself in a unity of the finite and infinite which transcends the self-contradictions of life. This moment is that of passion."[6] Kierekgaard finds a fitting symbol of this passion in the Eros of the *Symposium*: "This is that child born of the union of the finite and infinite, and therefore ever in conflict. Such was the opinion of Socrates: hence love is ever committed to striving, which means that the thinking subject exists."[7]

But at this point Kierkegaard significantly broadens the Socratic conception. In Socrates the argument between the ideal and the real is carried on essentially by means of thinking, although the conclusion is always reached that thought cannot effect any moment of unity between idea and dialectic. The idea is "that which is in and for itself, ordained by absolute being."[8] Kierkegaard has no objection to make against this

---

[3] *S. V.*, VII, 283; *Ges. W.*, VII, 27. Except as otherwise stated, all further refs. in this section are to these two works.

[4] VII, 303; VII, 47.    [5] VII, 306; VII, 50.    [6] VII, 164; VI, 272.

[7] VII, 73; VI, 179.    [8] II, 201; II, 191.

definition of the idea as the absolutely negative; but in his opinion it must not be a definition which as in Socrates concerns thought alone; for both will and feeling as well as thought participate in the contradiction between the ideal and the real. Because Socrates first isolates thought and endeavours to attain by thought alone an understanding of the ideal, he arrives at definitions which are so abstract that they cannot subsequently be brought into any vital connexion with the other aspects of the ego, i.e. will and feeling. We saw how with Plato imagination then reacts against this failure of abstract dialectic, in that it clothes the abstract in the forms of myth and image and thus gives it the plastic features of life. But this happens as a later reaction to the one-sidedness of the abstracting dialectic of Socrates and hence always in a certain neutralising opposition to the latter. Quite consistently, therefore, with Plato, the reacting imagination gives access to a type of speculation which surpasses the Socratic, and in reality destroys it.

In order to avoid this result, Kierkegaard begins by refusing to isolate thought; rather, in striving to reach the ideal, thought, feeling and will must all work together at every stage of the dialectic process. In this connexion, "imagination" acquires a meaning quite different from that which it has in Plato. It is not a definable mental faculty alongside thought, feeling, and will, but the medium through which the latter attempt to adjust the ideal and the real. "Speaking generally, imagination is the means by which we move in the dimension of the infinite; it is not one faculty among others; but it is, if you like, the faculty *instar omnium*. Imagination reaches out to the ideal and thus provides also a medium of operation for the dialectical *erōs*." Kierkegaard can even go so far as to equate imagination and reflexion, and say: "Imagination is reflexion moving in the dimension of the infinite; wherefore the older Fichte himself rightly assumed in relation to philosophical knowledge that imagination is the origin of the categories."[9] Conversely, as a result of its connexion with reflexion, imagination is prevented from losing itself in the realm of boundless fantasy. "Instead it is turned towards the reality of individual existence which is the proper object of reflexion." "The power of a person's

[9] XI, 144; VIII, 28.

feeling, knowledge and will depends in the last resort on his imagination, on the extent to which his feeling, knowledge, and will are able to reflect; hence upon imagination."[9]

Thus imagination is not only the means by which the various aspects of the ego attain the dimension of the infinite, but also the means by which they attain a correct balance. Feeling, will and knowledge mutually condition and correct each other. "Knowledge is led astray through excessive reflexion on the self, it has no power to stop itself—for this the will must come into play—and if the will is misguided, it is checked by the counteraction of feeling, etc."[10] Nevertheless thought is the superior element, for we must master life by the power of thinking.[11] The perception of universal truth attained by reflexion must normalise feeling and will, and in such a way that at every moment of life we reflect critically on feeling and will. All these faculties are directed towards the infinite κατὰ δύναμιν latent within them as soon as they are emancipated by the movement which *erōs* effects in them.

It should however be noted that critical reflexion combined with imagination is not yet the dialectic of existence, but furnishes merely the possibility of the latter. "The self grows out of reflexion, it is self-awareness in which lies the possibility of personality."[12] The possible self must become the real self, the action that is conceived must become a real action, if the ego is to exist. "If I think that I would like to do such and such a thing, such thought is not yet act and is eternally qualitatively distinct from an act; but it is nevertheless a possibility, in which the question of reality and action is already reflected."[13] One can hardly distinguish any longer action as conceived and action as effected, and "perhaps there is no difference between the thought and the deed from the point of view of content; but from the point of view of form this difference is essential."[14] As regards the form of the action, which here means the will that sustains it, this distinction is a qualitative one. Between the thought and the deed lies the act of choice, not as something which can be temporally fixed, but as a qualitative modifica-

[9] XI, 144; VIII, 28.
[11] S. V., VII, 304; Ges. W., VII, 48.
[13] VII, 293; VII, 36.

[10] S. K. P., IV(B), 212.
[12] XI, 144; VIII, 28.
[14] VII, 295; VII, 38.

tion of the will effected in every moment of true existence, and as a result of which the ego chooses itself as existent.

## 6. MOVEMENT IN DIALECTICS

For Hegel the problem of the beginning of the dialectical movement was to discover how the empirical ego was to become the subject of pure thought; and the question of the continuation of this movement implied the problem of "mediation." With Kierkegaard, on the other hand, the question was how the existent thinker should enter the stream of conscious existence in which his potentiality is realised in the dynamism of reality. As we have seen, this is brought about by the act of choice with which the ego chooses itself into conscious existence.

But this does not mean a unique and temporally definable act. The reality of the ego existentially realised at any given moment of time is at the next moment immediately seized upon by reflective thought and transformed into possibility in order to be expressed once more existentially. In this process there is no beginning and no ending.

If in this connexion we consider the relation of thought and existence, i.e. of action as conceived and as effected, thought is no doubt logically prior to existence and hence the presupposition of the latter. Nevertheless, this priority is not temporal. "We should give to the question about the logical and temporal priority in thought and existence the same answer as John Climacus gave to the question about the relation of immediacy and mediacy in *De omnibus dubitandum* which he set aside by referring to the reply that Thales is said to have given to the questioner who asked whether day or night was first: "Η νύξ, ἔφη, μιᾷ ἡμέρᾳ πρότερον."[1] In the life of self-consciousness the ego finds itself involved in the circle where thought and existence, knowledge and will, are inseparably mingled in the thought of the existent man.

Thus, for Kierkegaard, the question of the beginning of the dialectical process coincides with the question of movement in the dialectical process. It is a question of the impulse which enables the ego to accept responsibility for its vital existence

[1] *S. K. P.*, IV(B) 1, 146.

in order that it may, by an act of conscious choice, become in reality what it is already in possibility. In these specific terms is posed, for Kierkegaard, the problem of the transition from possibility to reality.

It is clear that this transition is not completed in thought itself. For an act of will is needed in order that it should be carried out. But again the will operates only within the conditions which are determinable by thought. Hence we must first enquire what these conditions are, and, further, how thinking and willing are related to each other in this act of transition. But the specific terms of the problem must always be carefully borne in mind: in the process by which the concretely existing ego becomes a self and acquires a history, it is a question of the transition from possibility to reality, from non-being to being, from failure to exist to fullness of existence.

In any attempt to define the character of this movement, we must first keep well in mind the truth that what becomes is continuously the same being. There can be no question of a change in the *essence* of the being which is in the process of becoming, otherwise the subject of becoming would no longer be the same; the change lies in its *mode of being*.[2] This consideration makes it clear—and this emerges in contradistinction to Hegel —that we are not here faced by any necessary process. In the sphere of necessity the mode of being and its essence coincide. It is of the essence of *a* being to be. Necessity characterises *a* being, whereas possibility and reality characterise being.

Thus the transition with which we are here concerned cannot take place in necessity, it must take place in freedom. "Nothing that becomes becomes for a reason, but always for a cause. Every cause issues in a freely operating cause."[3] This applies also to the becoming of the ego. In so far as this is a purely naturalistic becoming, it is conditioned by specific reasons, and hence is necessary. "Nevertheless becoming may contain a dual aspect, a potentiality of becoming within intrinsic becoming."[4] This second type of becoming, which Kierkegaard calls "historical" as opposed to "naturalistic"

---

[2] On the following, cp. the interlude in *Philosophische Brocken*, S. V., iv, 235-51; *Ges. W.*, vi, 66-78.

[3] *S. V.*, iv, 239; *Ges. W.*, vi, 69.    [4] *S. V.*, iv, 240; *Ges. W.*, vi, 70.

becoming, is of course always entangled in the latter. Therefore its causes operate only with relative freedom, for they can be effective only within the naturalistic becoming produced by necessarily operative reasons. But, conversely, neither can this necessity destroy the freedom which operates in the act of choice.

Although that which has historically become is immobilised in the past and thus is unchangeable, it is not for that reason a product of necessity. Its unchangeability only means that its real mode can now no longer be otherwise, but this does not exclude the possibility that it might have been otherwise. But this unchangeability of the past is dialectically related not only "to an earlier change from which it proceeded, but must also be dialectically related to a higher change by which it can in effect be cancelled (as, for example, in the matter of repentance, which operates to change the character of actualised reality)."[4] Only if this is true can the individual really assume responsibility for his historical becoming. Further, what is true of the past is equally true of the future. If necessity could enter the stream of becoming at any one point, if the past were in any sense necessary, then the future would be necessary too, and it would be fundamentally the same thing to prophesy the future as to understand the past.

Kierkegaard's principal argument for this freedom of the dialectical movement is: "In logic the *becoming* proper to movement can have no place; logic *is*, and all that is logical *is* only, and it is this very limitation which marks the transition from logic to becoming, where individual existence and reality emerge. . . . Every movement (if we admit the term for one moment) is in logic only an immanent movement, and of this we are easily convinced when we consider that the idea of movement itself is something transcendent which can have no place in a logical system."[5] This means merely, however, that by logical thought about the limitations of logic, Kierkegaard has only found the point at which movement can take place, and he must now define the character of this movement more

---

[4] *S. V.*, IV, 240; *Ges. W.*, VI, 70.

[5] *S. V.*, IV, 284-5; *Ges. W.*, V, 6-7. Cp. Kierkegaard's observation: "The eternal expression of logic is the point which, through a misunderstanding, the Eleatics applied to existence: 'Nothing arises, all is.' "

exactly. For this purpose he goes into far-reaching logical considerations in discussing Hegel, Plato and Aristotle, and in the course of these surveys Trendelenburg is a great help to him. But even in the latter he finds only logical connexions, in which transition is to be noted, but there is no real insight into the significance of this idea which marks the boundary of logical immanence as a whole. Kierkegaard has to solve the problem of transition not in abstract terms but in concrete terms of the thinker existing in the moment of choice. From this point of view his objection to Trendelenburg is easily understandable: "Trendelenburg recurs far too much to examples drawn from mathematics and the natural sciences. Hardly ever does he give an example of the ethical in the logical (so much the worse) and according to my ideas this awakens a suspicion against the logical and serves to confirm me in my theory of the leap belonging essentially to the sphere of freedom, though it should have its prototype and intimation in logic; above all it should not be lied away, as it is in Hegel."[6]

Kierkegaard finds such a prototype and intimation of transition in the logic of Aristotle and Plato, and by reference to them he tries to further elucidate the problematics of the subject. In Aristotle he finds the idea of κίνησις as implying transition from possibility to reality and comments thus: "*Kinēsis* is difficult to define, for it belongs neither to possibility nor to reality, it is more than possibility and less than reality."[7] What interests Kierkegaard in *kinēsis* is chiefly its character as such a mediating term. He attempts to define movement more explicitly by bringing it into relation with space and time "which presuppose movement, unless it be that movement presupposes them."[8] Since Kierkegaard's interest is directed not to the knowledge of nature, but above all to the historical becoming of the individual,[9] unlike Aristotle he

---

[6] *S. K. P.*, v(c), 12.    [7] *Op. cit.*, iv(c), 47.    [8] *S. V.*, vii, 296; vii, 40.

[9] Kierkegaard wishes to be (*S. K. P.*, iv(b) 177, 290) a "philosopher of life," and, as such, is not concerned with the knowledge of nature. In this connexion, he refers (*op. cit.*, 116) to Socrates, "the only world-historical philosopher of life there has ever been," and to his words to Phaedrus (*Phaedr.* 230 c-d): "My dear, forgive me, for although I am very eager for knowledge the countryside and the trees teach me nothing, but men in towns teach me much."

is less concerned with the question of space than with that of time.[10]

Time, which in the abstract is an "unending stream of successiveness,"[11] takes on concrete reality as soon as we wish to fix a point in this flux in order to show the transition from the before to the after. By this means time is brought into connexion with movement, either because we explain movement in the light of the original successiveness of time, or because, on the contrary, we suppose that movement from the before to the after forms moments which in their succession constitute time. In contrast to Kant, Kierkegaard adopts the second approach, and in so doing he uses the dialectic of being and non-being as expounded in Plato's *Parmenides*.

If a thing is first at rest and then in motion, a transition between the two states must have taken place. But this transition cannot be defined as lying in any given point of time, for that would imply two contradictory facts about such a point of time. The point at which the transition took place cannot, in fact, be derived from the time-stream at all. Plato calls it the moment (τὸ ἐξαίφνης), but can say nothing more about the character of his idea except that its φύσις is ἄτοπος, μεταξὺ τῆς κινήσεώς τε καὶ στάσεως, ἐν χρόνῳ οὐδενὶ οὖσα.[12] The moment in which something comes to be does not itself belong to time, but alone makes it possible for something to enter the time-stream and so to be. For by definition being is "participation in being through present time" (τὸ δὲ εἶναι ἄλλο τί ἐστι ἢ μέθεξις οὐσίας μετὰ χρόνου τοῦ παρόντος;—151 E).[13]

The moment in which this transition from non-being to being is effected Plato also calls τὸ νῦν. That which is to become cannot skip this "now" between non-being and being. But as soon as it has arrived at this point, it desists from becoming, and is now what previously it was in the process of coming to be. When that happens, the τὸ νῦν becomes the present instant of the time stream (ὁ χρόνος ὁ παρών), "it is non-being from the point of view of time."[13] Again, strictly speaking, it is

---

[10] On the following, cp. *S. V.*, IV, 350-60; *Ges. W.*, V, 78-87.

[11] *S. V.*, VII, 296; VII, 40.  [12] Plato, *Parm.* 156 D; cp. *S. K. P.* V(B), 72.

[13] *S. V.*, IV, 351 n. 2; *Ges. W.*, V, 79 n. 2. All further refs. in this section are to *S. V.*, IV, and *Ges. W.* as cited.

not itself a point in time, but merely distinguishes the point at which that which is coming to be enters the time-stream, while itself standing outside the latter as the moment of transition between non-being and temporal being, as the abstract moment—μεταβολή.

Kierkegaard comments on this: "In all this, Plato acquires at least the merit of making the difficulty clear to himself; but this moment remains none the less a mute atomistic abstraction which is not explained by being ignored. If, now, logic will grant that it cannot deal with the question of transition (and if it has this category, then it must find room for it in its system and say whether it operates therein), then it will become all the clearer that the historical dimension, and all knowledge which moves with in it, has this moment of transition. Such a category is of the highest importance for discrimination against heathen philosophy and against equally heathen speculation within Christianity."[13] Within the abstractions of Platonic dialectic there cannot be a concrete understanding of this moment. Kierkegaard points out that the description τὸ ἐξαίφνης brings it into relation with the invisible and sees here the attempt to define something alongside time and in contradistinction to time, something which he himself would term eternity. But in Plato the idea of the eternal remains as abstract as the idea of time, for which reason he has to content himself with the category of the invisible, without being able to define the latter in its relation to time and eternity. But what does Kierkegaard mean when he says that the historical dimension has this moment?

We have seen that becoming can contain a dual aspect: within naturalistic becoming and entangled with it is achieved the becoming of the individual whereby the latter chooses himself in freedom. "Here we see the historical in the stricter sense, dialectic in its relation to time."[14] "The subject of this historical becoming, the thinking (and, through thought, existing) ego is a synthesis of the temporal and the eternal".[15] "Where then is the third term? If there is no third term, then, properly speaking, there is no synthesis either; for a synthesis

---

[13] *S. V.*, IV, 351 n. 2; *Ges. W.*, V, 79 n. 2. All further refs. in this section are to *S. V.*, IV, and *Ges. W.* as cited.

[14] 240; VI, 70.         [15] 355; V, 80.

which contains a contradiction cannot come to be as a synthesis without a third term; if the synthesis is a contradiction, then it is not a synthesis."[16] If, on the other hand, time and eternity are to meet, then this can only happen in time—and this brings us to the character of the moment.[17]

If we isolate a point in the process of historical becoming and examine how it comes to be, we see that it has already become and at the same time is in the process of becoming. As something which had already come to be, it is a part of temporal succession, but as still in the process of becoming it lies in the moment of *kinēsis*, and hence is outside time as "the moment of transition." As something which has already become, it is a point in time, which has a history; as still engaged in becoming it has no history, but yet is. It derives its being, not from temporal successiveness, but from the being of the eternal, for "the perfection of the eternal consists in the fact that it has no history, and is the only thing which is and yet has absolutely no history."[18] At the point of becoming, the eternal enters temporal successiveness, and time and eternity touch each other in time. The transitional moment "is that ambiguous something wherein time and eternity touch each other, and this gives us the stamp of temporality in which time constantly clashes with eternity and eternity constantly penetrates time. Only from this point of view does the division which we have been discussing receive its full meaning, the division of time into present, past and future."[19]

### 7. THE CATEGORIES

Hence, for Kierkegaard, the problem of the relation of thought and being thus concretely presents itself as follows: How can something be actualised in temporal successiveness, or, to express it in another way, how can something come to participate in its ideally conceived being, and so in reality be what formerly it was only in possibility? We found that this transition from thinking to being was completed in the moment of *kinēsis*. Kierkegaard again and again describes this moment

---

[16] 355; v, 81.    [17] 357; v. 84.    [18] 239; vi, 69.    [19] 359; v, 86.

as a category, even as the decisive category on which all other categories depend.[1] What, now, does he mean by a category? The question cannot easily be answered, for neither does Kierkegaard himself give any definition, nor does he draw up a table of categories. He desiderates such a definition in modern philosophy, especially in Hegel,[2] and says that he would like sometime, in opposition to Hegel, to study the question "in what sense the category is a summary of existence, and whether the logical is an abstraction from existence, or is abstract without any relation to existence."[3] In any event, he has not done this explicitly and in regard to the idea of the category. The matter itself however occupied his mind a good deal. Questions and observations about it are found constantly in the diaries, especially in the course of debate with Hegel. Also it soon becomes clear to him that the single point of view from which categories as conceptual abstractions from being are to be attained can only be the moment of *kinēsis* because nowhere else do thinking and being come into contact with each other. Later he finds a confirmation of his own thoughts in Trendelenburg, who likewise proceeds from the moment of *kinēsis* as the factor which unites thought and being and who sees in it the original creative deed from which stem fundamental concepts. "When thought considers movement and its productions and relationships, then the categories emerge."[4] From this point of view Trendelenburg proceeds to unfold the categories of causality, substance and quality.

For the sake of brevity we will summarise here those of Trendelenburg's conclusions which Kierkegaard considered

---

[1] In his "Lecture on the Greek Sophists, based on the Sources," Kierkegaard says: "The category which I was anxious to make central, i.e. the category which, as it were, is latent in Greek sophistry, is that of movement (κίνησις), which perhaps forms one of the most difficult problems in the whole of philosophy. In modern philosophy it has been expressed differently, i.e. as transition or mediation" (*S. K. P.*, iv(c), 97).

[2] "What is a category? So far as one is aware, the moderns have given no definition. At least, Hegel has not done so; by means of his inverted method he always leaves it to the skill of the reader to do the most difficult part—i.e. to gather up the manifold into the concentrated energy of a single thought" (*S. K. P.*, iv(c), 63).

[3] *S. V.*, vii, 90; *Ges. W.*, vi, 195.

[4] Trendelenburg, *Logische Untersuchungen*.

most important, and show in what direction he amplifies them. Above all, Kierkegaard is interested in the category of *quality*, or, more precisely, in the transition from quantitative to qualitative descriptions which he sees Hegel perform so unconcernedly. But it is "sheer superstition if in logic you suppose that from the continuation of something specifically quantitative something qualitatively new will emerge; and it is a quite intolerable subterfuge, if, while not concealing that in fact this is not quite the case, you nevertheless conceal the consequences of this principle for logical immanence as a whole, and assimilate it to the logic of dialectic as Hegel does."[5]

The qualitative which is supposed to emerge from this quantitative category is said to imply a statement about being. But being as such is not qualitative. We can define it as qualitative only in so far as we define it through itself, i.e. as engaged in existence. In this qualitative description of being, being itself is presupposed or expressed; and this qualitatively defined being—being as existent—can then further be described in quantitative terms. With Hegel the inference from quantity to quality can be made within the boundaries of logic because the being with which he is concerned is only a product of immanentist thought and is not real being. One might also say, on the other hand, that because he can without more ado conclude from quantity to quality, it is impossible for him with his deductions to break through the circle of merely conceptual being and to penetrate into the sphere of real being. At this juncture Kierkegaard finds that his views are confirmed by Trendelenburg and Aristotle. The question is how being itself is first engendered before the qualitative category can be applied to it, or how, in the application of qualitative terms to being, being itself is at the same time either expressed or presupposed. This problem can be solved by means of Aristotelian concepts.

Trendelenburg shows how the classification of being itself according to its various modes must precede all application of categories to being modally defined in a certain way, i.e. as possible or real. Such classification takes place by means of the

[5] *S. V.*, IV, 302; *Ges. W.*, V, 24-5. On this cp. the note, and, further, *S. K. P.*, IV(c), 37 and 68.

κίνησις in which being κατὰ δύναμιν passes into being κατ'
ἐντελέχειαν or κατ' ἐνέργειαν.  This *kinēsis* interpenetrates all
the categories, or rather it procures the presupposition for all
categories by distinguishing first in being itself what is expressed
according to potency and what is expressed according to act.
The categories as predicates can be applied to being modally
defined in a certain way.  But in order that being may be
modally defined in a certain way, it is first necessary to classify
being itself κατὰ δύναμιν καὶ ἐντελέχειαν by means of the κίνησις
in which a transition takes place ἐκ τοῦ δυνάμει ὄντος εἰς τὸ
ἐνεργείᾳ ὄν.[6]

If for these Aristotelian categories we substitute Kierkegaard's ideas, we find here the description of being as possibility
and reality effected by means of the use of *kinēsis* as a category
of transition.  Possible being cannot be qualitatively described,
and all statements made about it Kierkegaard would consider
to be quantitative.  Only by means of the transition of *kinēsis* is
being to be described in terms of the self-existent, and hence of
the qualitative.  The being which is here engendered is
qualitatively determined being, because as being it is determined only by its quality of having come to be.  This determination becomes effective at the moment when it ceases to be
*possible being*, and also when it ceases to *become real*, since it
now *is* what according to possibility it *was*.

Thus, for Kierkegaard, this transition from the quantitative
to the qualitative takes place through the "leap" of *kinēsis*.
Kierkegaard of course fails to find this expression in Trendelenburg,[7] although the latter, too, considers that *kinēsis* is not
simply an act of thought but points rather to a break in the
process of immanentist logic.  We must now examine more
closely the nature of this break.[8]  Aristotle distinguishes between
an active and a passive moment in *kinēsis*, reflecting its character
as mediating between possible and real being.  It effects
something (κινεῖν), but only that which already is in the
sphere of potentiality and therefore is at the same time effected

---

[6] Cp. Trendelenburg's *Geschichte der Kategorienlehre*, 1847, 159-63.

[7] "Trendelenburg does not seem to be at all aware of the leap" (*S. K. P.*,
v(A), 74).

[8] *S. K. P.*, vii.2(c), i.  Cp. Trendelenburg, *op. cit.*, 99 ff.

(κινεῖσθαι). Where *kinēsis* is manifested in the category of quality, as κίνησις κατὰ τὸ πάθος, it is distinguished by ἀλλοίωσις. "Aristotle says that πάθος is the quality as a result of which it is possible for a thing to suffer change (ἀλλοιοῦσθαι). In the quality of πάθος it is necessary to distinguish, following the distinction between κινεῖν and κινεῖσθαι, between ποιεῖν and πάσχειν as active and passive moments in the category of transition. This is important for Kierkegaard for the reason that ever since 1844, and hence before he became acquainted with the doctrine of categories in Trendelenburg, he had made a distinction between the "dialectic" and "pathetic" transition.[9] Trendelenburg finds in Aristotle no real conceptual definition for πάθος. "Nevertheless it is important that here a reference to the senses, which in their characteristic working operate as forces rather than as *quanta*, is made a measure of the qualitative."[10] This is precisely the point on which, for Kierkegaard, every-thing depends. If, in the transition from the quantitative to the qualitative, the sensuous affective element is made the criterion of the latter, and if, in this matter, it is specifically established that the senses operate as forces, not as *quanta*, then it finally becomes clear that the transition is effected by means of an element which lies outside thought. As the same time Tren-delenburg's doctrine of categories shows that this transition, as Kierkegaard maintains, "has a prototype and intimation in logic."[11]

It can now, further, be shown how the individual categories explicated by Trendelenburg come to have importance for Kierkegaard. Firstly, there arises as the relationship between productive activity and its end-result the category of *causality*, since movement places products after each other according as they are conditioned by what precedes.[12] "The effect is only an arrested movement, a product isolated from the flux of phenomena and examined in itself. In seeking for the cause

---

[9] *S. K. P.*, v(c), 1; cp. vIII. 2(c), 1: "It is incredible what profit I have derived from Trendelenburg; I now find the technique for what I had thought on my own several years ago."

[10] Trendelenburg, *op. cit.*, 100.

[11] *S. K. P.*, v(c), 12.

[12] On the following cp. Trendelenburg, *op. cit.*, 282 ff.

of the phenomenon we are restoring the isolated thing to the movement which engendered it."[13]  This causality is the same thing as the becoming on which Kierkegaard lays stress, and since Trendelenburg thinks that implies the deduction "*ex hoc, ergo post hoc*," but not the deduction "*post hoc, ergo propter hoc*," such causality constitutes no objection to Kierkegaard's idea that this becoming happens in freedom. To employ Kierkegaard's own terminology, the "*ex hoc*" is only a cause not a reason for the becoming.

If we isolate a product of movement and regard it as thus detached, in a state of rest or persistence, then we are confronted by *substance*, in its original sense of οὐσία or *substantia* as persistent being in contrast to becoming. "The productive movement has come to rest in the thing which it has produced. The arrested product of the movement of causality is substance."[14] This substance as being which has come to be through transition and is now persistent is for Kierkegaard the existing ego of historical becoming, when it comes to self-awareness as an existing ego and so attains continuity of being. In such a moment it acquires being in the sense of existence.

This detached product of movement, namely substance, becomes now the source of its own movements; causality clings to it too. "Such a causality inherent in substances we call quality."[15]  The existence of the ego is qualitatively determined being and as such becomes once more the cause of a process of becoming; for in this being there can be no persistent state as opposed to the process of becoming. But since causality inheres in substance not only as the cause of a forward movement but also as the link with a backward movement, since substance itself is the product of a movement, therefore the ego as something which has come to be is likewise qualitatively determined. In this connexion we should note Trendelenburg's observation to the effect that this quality can also be referred to activities such as the will which is formed analogously to substance. This is of special importance to Kierkegaard on account of the great significance which he attributes to the element of will in existence. This gives the will also its special place within the scheme of the categories.

[13] *Op. cit.*, 286.        [14] *Op. cit.*, 290-1.        [15] *Op. cit.*, 291.

We now understand why Kierkegaard does not speak of the categories as abstractions from *being*, as is usually done, but as abstractions from *existence* in conceptual form. All the categories emerge in that dynamic process where existence and reality are manifested. This is for him the conclusion of all his strenuous endeavours to define the relation of the quantitative to the qualitative. "Everything turns on making absolute the distinction between quantitative and qualitative dialectic. Logic as a whole is quantitative or modal dialectic, for all is and the totality is constantly one and the same. In existence, on the other hand, qualitative dialectic is at home."[16] It is this distinction which Kierkegaard has in mind when he says: "Even if I were a better dialectician than I am, I would still be limited and at bottom it is just this immovable adherence to the absolute and to absolute distinctions which makes a good dialectician."[17] Such adherence however is not merely a concern of thinking. Kierkegaard's categories are not those proper to being and logic, but existential categories, i.e. categories in which one not only thinks, certain as it is that one does that, but within which one moves and exists. "I compel myself with all my might to keep my life within the categories. One may die, I know that; one may be slowly tortured to death, I know that too; but at all events one can adhere immovably to the categories. That is what I intend to do, what I require from every one whom I admire and whom I am to honour: I demand that all such should think of the categories of their life by day and dream of them by night."[18]

## 8. BEING IN TRUTH

Truth consists in the coincidence of thought and being. Whether we approach this "more from the empirical angle as the coincidence of thought with being, or more from the idealistic angle as the coincidence of being with thought, we must in any case pay careful attention to the question as to what

---

[16] *S. K. P.*, VII(A), 84.
[17] *S. V.*, IV, 270; *Ges. W.*, VI, 99.
[18] *S. V.*, VI, 284-5; IV, 275.

exactly we understand by 'being.'"[1] From the course of our previous investigation it is clear that by "being" we can now understand nothing other than the concrete existence of the individual thinker, who as a concrete ego thinks the universal abstract ideal and at the same time exists through his thinking of it. Hence the point is not to think truth but to live in the truth. This means that truth is no longer to be conceived as an objective statement about certain relations of being, but as a form of existence in which such relations are actualised. Hence truth is "not something objective suggesting that the knowledge of it is concerned with what is to be found in existence as an object, but implies rather that knowledge is something related to the knower, who is essentially an existing individual, and that all real insight is essentially related to that which exists and to existence itself."[2] Being in truth therefore implies a process which is never complete. Man always remains in the position of one who strives, and the complete coincidence of thought and being hovers before the existent individual as a "creaturely longing"[3] only. This longing finds its most forcible expression in moments of passion when all aspects of existential subjectivity, raised to their utmost intensity, are most fully exploited. Here lies for man the utmost attainable expression of truth, and in this way Kierkegaard arrives at his famous thesis, formulated in the most polemical fashion. "Subjectivity is truth,"[4] the terms of which can equally well be inverted: "Truth is subjectivity."[5]

Every aspect of the ego participates equally in this being in the truth. Since however life "is to be mastered by thought,"[6]

---

[1] *S. V.*, VII, 157; *Ges. W.*, VI, 265. Except as stated, all further refs. in this section are to *S. V.* and *Ges. W.*

[2] VII, 165; VI, 273.          [3] VII, 164; VI, 272.

[4] VII, 171; VI, 279.

[5] VII, 157; VI, 265. The greatest possible misunderstanding arises when from his inversion the conclusion is drawn that K. "sought truth in the subjective (psychological) sphere," and "made it the object of personal feeling." So H. Höffding, *S. Kierkegaard als Philosoph*, 1922, pp. 74 ff. To be able to say any such thing, one must completely disregard all that Kierkegaard ever said about the problems of logic, the categories, thought, truth, etc.—in fact his whole dialectic.

[6] VII, 304; VII, 48.

we shall attempt to clarify further the special task of thought in this connexion.

We have seen that imagination as the power of reflexion reaching out to infinity grasps the ideal world and thus becomes the medium of the dialectical *erōs*, reflecting the contribution of will, knowledge, and feeling. In this respect Kierkegaard has widened the dialectic of Socrates, which isolates thought, in such a way that at every stage of the dialectical process thought, will and feeling are equally engaged in reaching the ideal. But from another angle, too, Kierkegaard later corrected the picture of Socrates given in his *Begriff der Ironie* . According to the provisional edition of the *Unwissenschaftliche Nachschrift*, he writes: "Magister Kierkegaard has certainly attempted to discover the Socratic in his dissertation, but does not seem to have understood this, presumably because with the help of Hegelian philosophy he became over-subtle and objective and positive, or did not have the courage to understand the force of negation. From a finite point of view, of course, the continued and constant striving towards a goal without ever reaching it is something to be rejected, but if we look at it from the point of view of infinity, life itself consists precisely in such striving, which indeed is the very hallmark of the life of man, who is compounded of the finite and the infinite. The conception of positive completeness is chimerical. No doubt it is possible that logic has such completeness, though this should be more clearly elucidated than has hitherto been done; but subjectivity is existential, hence consists in contradiction and becoming, and if it exists at all exists in striving."[7]

Kierkegaard had at that time still regarded it as a defect that man should exist only in striving and that Socrates should have attained no kind of positiveness. He had explained this limitation on the part of Socrates by suggesting that, from the point of view of world history, Socrates represented "a magnificent pause in historical development,"[8] thus clearing the way for speculation by the succeeding generation. "The enthusiasm of his standpoint is energy making itself felt in the manifestations of positiveness which succeed him."[9] Thus Socrates is essen-

[7] *S. K. P.*, IV(B), 35.
[8] XIII, 279; *Begriff der Ironie*, 205.    [9] XIII, 297; *Begriff der Ironie*, 225.

tially an exceptional phenomenon, an idiosyncratic personality. This is shown, too, in the special gift of his *daimōn*, which is linked up with his mission of irony and is not yet what Kierkegaard means by conscience: "The mystery of conscience, which is locked in the secret recesses of the individual life, is that at one and the same time it represents the individual and the universal, even if not immediately so, yet in potentiality."[10] Only when the Socratic *daimōn* broadens out into this conscience can it be applied to aspects of life from which Socrates kept himself detached.  Kierkegaard had indeed correctly understood, even at that date, and in contrast to Hegel, that Socrates was not concerned about the definition of the good, but that his whole life consisted in a movement of aspiration towards the good.  "The point of this is not that, let us say, towards the end of his life he reached the good, but rather that his whole life consisted in a constant aspiration towards it and in persuading others to so aspire.  But in this sense also we may say that he attained the knowledge of the true (i.e. the truth in and for itself), of the beautiful, (i.e. of the beautiful in and for itself), and in general, of being in and for itself, as reflected in the world of ideas.  This he constantly attained, without question."[11] But at this earlier date Kierkegaard was hesitant in his appreciation of this attitude: Socrates "allowed individual reality to become absorbed in the sphere of the ideal, and the infinity of the ideal world as a negative infinity was nothingness, in which the whole world of reality in all its manifoldness became engulfed."[12]  The fact that Socrates could remain at this stage is however explained by alluding to his significance as a "divine missionary."

Kierkegaard now drops this attempt to explain Socrates as an exceptional phenomenon and gives a different evaluation of the negativity to which he had formerly objected.  "The fact that several of Plato's dialogues achieve no positive conclusion has a far deeper reason than I had formerly thought.  For this in fact shows the influence of the Socratic intellectual midwifery, which brings the reader or the hearer into effective personal

---

[10] II, 229; II, 219.
[11] XIII, 311; *Begriff der Ironie*, 242-3.
[12] XIII, 312; *Begriff der Ironie*, 243.

co-operation, as a result of which the dialogue ends not in a positive conclusion but in a stinging remark. This is a splendid satire on our modern methods of drawling things out, by which we prefer to state everything at once, the sooner the better, and which awaken no active co-operation in the reader but merely cause him to imitate our drawl, parrot-like."[13] In its dialectic this point of view illuminates Kierkegaard's thesis about being in truth as consisting in a continued aspiration. Kierkegaard's own dialectic grew out of the dialectical practice of Socrates as it is most clearly expressed in the first so-called dialogical dialogues. It is a dual dialectical movement, as contrasted with the single ones of Hegel or of the later Plato, for the firmly maintained dual relation of the enquirer to the object, on the one hand, and to the conversational partner, on the other, results in a twofold dialectical movement. For Kierkegaard its object is the individual ego, which must be set free for effective action based on its own private existence. This is the dialectical movement which arises between the conversational partners themselves and in which they bring into play their own individual existence. The other movement arises between the two partners as they mutually free each other from all assumed positive knowledge by calling in question every affirmed conclusion.

## 9. THE DIALECTICIAN'S IRONY AND HUMOUR

Although Kierkegaard does not write in the dialogue form, everything which he makes his fictitious characters say moves within the sphere of dualistic Socratic dialectic. In truth he did not renounce the dialogue form, but made one single sustained dialogue of the entire work of his pseudonymous characters. The reader takes the place of the conversational partner. Kierkegaard does not confront this reader as a teacher demonstrating some particular point of view, but through the medium of the pseudonyms he experimentally and dialectically puts before him points of view towards which the reader cannot have any definite reaction, because the attitude of one figure is ironically cancelled by that of another, so that

[13] *S. K. P.*, vii(a), 74.

the reader can nowhere find any conclusion which Kierkegaard himself would guarantee. Moreover Kierkegaard says about himself: "I prefer to regard myself as the *reader* rather than as the *author* of the writings,"[1] in order to preclude the misconception that he might have something to teach. And to prevent the same misconception he makes Climacus say, for example, in the preface to the *Philosophische Brocken*: "If, on the other hand, anybody should be so polite as to attribute to me a point of view, and if he should carry his gallantry so far as to accept this point of view because it is mine, then I regret politeness, for it is thrown away on some one who does not deserve it, and I regret his point of view, if he has no other point of view than my own. I can pledge *my own* life, I can stake *my own* life in all seriousness, but not that of another. I can do this, and it is the only thing that I can do, I who have not any learning to offer . . ."[2]

In such expressions we may not regard irony as a mere mode of speech; it is rather a specific attitude which is an integral part of this whole dialectic. The aim of the conversation is to free the participants to live in their own right. But this cannot take place by a direct transmission of the existence of the one to another. The reality of the experience proper to the one can only furnish the possibility of existence for another. Hence all existential communication must take the form of possibility. "An expression in the form of possibility is the clearest mode of communication between man and man compatible with an existential basis."[3] Every direct relation between man and man by which the one might immediately assimilate the experience of another, without its being first conveyed in the form of possibility, must be prevented. It can be prevented by communication in the form of irony, for which Kierkegaard supplies the general definition "that the phenomenon is not reality but the opposite of reality."[4]

Everything can be concealed under the veil of an ironical statement; it fetters neither the speaker nor the hearer to what

---

[1] *S. V.*, XIII, 501; *Ges. W.*, x, 166. Except as stated, all further references in this section are to *S. V.* and *Ges. W.*
[2] IV, 178; VI, 6.
[3] VII, 310; VII, 54.          [4] XIII, 322; *Begriff der Ironie*, 253.

is stated. It may provoke the other to reveal himself; it may entice him on to a false track in order consequently to trip him up, and so to awaken his insight. But it will use all these means only in order to release the individual negatively. In this matter it can direct its destructive activity either simply to one particular point of view or to the whole of existence as such. In the latter case it is no longer a question of particular expressions of irony, but of irony *sensu eminentiori*, which is used not in the service of some standpoint or other but becomes itself the standpoint. "Irony *sensu eminentiori* is directed not to this or that particular form of existence; it is directed against the whole of reality as it presents itself at some particular time and under certain particular conditions. Hence it contains a certain *a priori* element, and this consists not in destroying one aspect of reality after another in order to arrive at its own total point of view, but rather in the strength of the latter it destroys particular things. It is not this or that phenomenon, but the whole of existence, that it regards *sub specie ironiae*."[5]

Behind this activity which gives negative release, there stands of course a certain positive element. "For irony is, like the law, a challenge; it despises the actual and demands the ideal."[6] But the question is how this positive element is manifested. In the *Begriff der Ironie*, where, under Hegel's influence, Kierkegaard still regards the Socratic irony as a "pause in world-history," he alludes to Hegel and sees Socrates exercising his activity as a thinker in the service of "world-irony."[7] But once Kierkegaard has broken, finally and completely, with the "dialectic of the idea" which realises itself in the course of world history, he assigns to irony the function of eliciting ideality in the existence of the conversational partner.

---

[5] XIII, 328-9; *Begriff der Ironie*, 261.

[6] XIII, 293; *Begriff der Ironie*, 221.

[7] Cp. XIII, 336; *Begriff der Ironie*, 270: "But in so far as he destroys reality itself, he is serving the idea of world irony. In his *History of Philosophy* (VOL. II, p. 62), Hegel observes: 'All dialectic accepts things as they claim to be, and thus allows their inner destruction to work itself out—which is the universal irony of life'; and in this respect the idea of world-irony is correctly thought out. Just because every historical reality is only a moment in the process by which the Idea is realised, it bears within itself the seed of its own destruction."

Only so can it carry out the part which Kierkegaard had already ascribed to it in the *Begriff der Ironie*: "Irony limits, sets bounds, confines, and thus imparts truth, reality, and content; it disciplines and punishes, and thereby gives stability and consistency. Irony is a disciplinarian feared only by him who is not familiar with it but beloved by those who know it."[8]

Thus irony becomes the incognito behind which the complete transformation demanded by the ideal takes place. It is "a mode of existence, and there is nothing more absurd than to suppose that it is a manner of speech, or for an author to congratulate himself on having here and there expressed himself ironically. Whoever essentially possesses irony possesses it as long as the day lasts, and it is fettered to no form because it is the expression in him, of infinity."[9] This implies that irony is only justified where there is latent in it an intense passion for existence, and Kierkegaard counsels us as to how to avoid allowing irony to lapse into frivolity and wantonness: "If we want to go through a good school we restrain ourselves for some time from laughing (for laughing arouses the passion of antipathy, whose demonic power can so easily lead us astray), and we learn to see the comic aspect of things or people with a desire to be indulgent, to exercise sympathy, concern, and love, which are the best safeguards against folly."[10] Irony is *eo ipso* spurious where it is practised not by an individual but by the crowd. In his struggle against the satirical journal *Korsars*, Kierkegaard was concerned with spurious unjustified irony, at a period when Copenhagen, owing to its influence, had become ironical *en masse*, with the result that irony had degenerated into mere vulgarity and coarseness. "Irony presupposes quite definite intellectual culture such as is seldom found in any generation; and this rabble of men called themselves masters of irony. Irony is absolutely unsocial; irony wielded by the majority is certainly not irony."[11] In taking up the struggle against this false irony, Kierkegaard thus had to fight single-handed, and in order to unmask this coarseness he had personally to expose himself to it; nor could he carry through the struggle directly, but only ironically, not by appear-

---

[8] XIII, 392; *Begriff der Ironie*, 338.    [9] VII, 438; VII, 189.
[10] VII, 452 n.; VII, 204 n.    [11] XIII, 550; X, 39.

ing on the scene armed with moral indignation but by challenging men to the struggle against themselves. The ironical personality may not allow his own inner values to be directly recognised in order to persuade men of some truth, but he must use all his talents in order to prevent any direct relationship with himself and to arouse the other to exist as an individual. Even though by this means he were to incur the reproach of frivolity, lack of seriousness, and so forth, yet he can do no other if he is "to train himself in the truth and guard himself against the most terrible of all untruths—against a follower."[12]

As regards *humour*, considered as a means of protecting the existential thinker's own individual uniqueness and enabling him to express himself, the same considerations apply as in the case of irony. It is distinguished from the latter only by the fact that it has to maintain a different kind of paradox. The ironical personality guards himself against attributing to any action in its external aspect the absolute value of the ethical ideal in order to remain on the height of an absolute ethic with passion and inwardness. But the religious man masquerading in the guise of a humorist must prevent God from being perceived or apparently disclosed in any purely outward reality, because God can be truly present only in the inner depths of existence. "The religious consciousness under the incognito of humour is, therefore, the unity of a passion for the absolute (rooted in the inner depths through dialectic) and of intellectual maturity which recalls the religious mind from the external to the internal and thus proves itself as relentless and passionate religious awareness."[13]

As in the case of the ironical personality it cannot be decided by outward observation whether a religious mind is latent in the humorist or not. He uses humour not merely as an incognito in his relation with others in order to prevent them from fostering any religious relation to what is external, but in the

---

[12] VII, 220-1; VI, 337. A good example of this is when, during press controversy over the *Korsar*, K. himself talks with Goldschmidt, its editor, in the street, thus abandoning pseudonymity, about the ideal right of Frater Taciturnus. Cp. E. Geismar, *Sören Kierkegaard*, 1928, 355.

[13] VII, 440; VII, 191.

first instance he takes up a humorous attitude towards his own thoughts and ideas in order to protect his inexorable religious passion. Up to the last he must be able to regard humorously both himself and his greatest religious exertions, for "to shorten one's sleep at nights and to make the very most of one's day and never to spare oneself, and then to realise that all this is a joke —that is what I call being serious."[14]

## 10. THE SOCRATIC PARADOX

It is also true of Kierkegaard's dialectic of existence "that every philosophy which begins with a certain presupposition naturally concludes with the same presupposition."[1] All that is possible by means of this dialectic which is disintegrating to all positive knowledge, is to refer man back to himself, if we assume that man will find in himself that positive element on the basis of which this negatively emancipating dialectic works. We can only release man, in the interest of truth, from all objective knowledge, and refer him back to his own existence, if we assume that by a dialectical searching of the depths of that existence he will stumble on the truth. We can only bring to bear the absolute distinction between quantitative and qualitative dialectic, if we assume that only by holding fast to this distinction do truth and reality come to light. The fact that all these (fundamentally identical) presuppositions become themselves the object of dialectical investigation makes no difference to the truth that the latter runs in a circle where the presupposition is apparent again as a conclusion.

The question is, however, in what way the existent ego comes to grips with the truth presupposed within it. Both Socrates and Plato assume that the man in search of truth must already have a relationship to the truth, otherwise he could not seek it. For both it is true that "all knowledge is recollection,"[2] but each applies this principle differently. Plato investigates this

---

[14] VII, 410; VII, 160.
[1] S. V., XIII, 132; Begriff der Ironie, 34-5. Except as stated, all further refs. in this section are to S. V. and Ges. W.
[2] VII, 172 n.; VI, 280 n.

recollection, and although by means of dialectic he attains truth only as an abstraction, yet for him by the help of the imagination truth attained by recollection can be contemplated in the form of myth and represented and interpreted plastically. This capacity for visual contemplation through recollection frees Plato positively for the speculative reconstruction of truth.

Socrates, too, proceeds on the assumption that behind his negativity there lurks something positive; but for him this itself can only be apprehended negatively. With him the abstract result of dialectic is sheer nothingness, "the indefinable determination of pure being."[3] He too needs recollection in order to discover this, but he does not investigate this recollection. Instead, he (as it were) constantly dismisses it, because he wishes to plumb the depths of existence. It does not occur to him to explore recollection speculatively because he realises that he can know nothing positive about the eternal truth concealed within it. He knows only *that* there lies truth at the foundation of all but *what* this truth is he does not know. Hence he renounces all attempt to establish what absolute being is and rather makes his life a movement orientated towards absolute being. As Kierkegaard says, he firmly believes that recollection "is a negative retrograde movement in opposition to the movement of life."[4]

This means that Socrates, "from an intellectual point of view, was engaged in a movement reaching out to infinity. His ignorance is infinite resignation."[5] This movement also implies that the Godward relation of mankind culminates in ignorance. "He had no knowledge of that which lies at the ultimate ground of all things, he knew *that* it was, but he did not know *what* it was; he was aware of it, and yet he was not aware of it, inasmuch as the only thing which he could say about it was that he knew nothing of it."[6] But this ignorance must not be equated with scepticism, it is rather the beginning of a true relationship with God. "The heavenly hosts of the gods rose from the earth and vanished from the sight of mortals, but this very

[3] XIII, 141; *Begriff der Ironie*, 45.
[4] XIII, 210; *Begriff der Ironie*, 174.
[5] III, 18; III, 66.          [6] XIII, 256-7; *Begriff der Ironie*, 178.

disappearance became the condition of a deeper relationship."[7]
Of course this movement of infinite resignation is not confined
to the intellectual sphere but embraces the whole of ethical and
religious life. Kierkegaard's various pseudonymous figures
express this with a wealth of concrete illustration drawn from
life as a whole. We point this out specifically because in our
essay we must limit ourselves as much as possible to the intellectual aspect of the matter and in view of this abstraction
cannot give the faintest idea of the abundance of living concrete
forms in which this attitude is manifested. Any one who has
any conception of the dialectical passion which is here at work
will naturally observe that it is impossible to be content with
the mere reflexion of it in terms of abstract thought.

Thus Socrates attained no objective knowledge of the divine,
but in spite of this clung to the passion which arises from the
negativity and inwardness of dialectical conclusions. Now this
is precisely the way by which Kierkegaard comes to the
absolute. For Kierkegaard dialectic is "a friendly serviceable
power which discloses and helps you to find where lies the
absolute object of faith and adoration—there in fact where the
difference between knowledge and ignorance is resolved in the
sheer adoration of the unknown—where the resistance of objective uncertainty only results in the release of the passionate
certitude of faith, where the strife between right and wrong
is suspended in surrender to unbounded adoration. Dialectic
itself does not perceive the absolute, but (as it were) it leads the
individual up to it and says 'It must be here, I guarantee that;
if you worship here, you will be worshipping God. But
worship itself is not dialectic.'"[8] Hence the existent person
must simply dare, in spite of all objective uncertainty, to enter
on the relationship with God. "In that moment he possesses
God not in virtue of any objective consideration, but in virtue
of the boundless passion of inwardness."[9] But on no account

---

[7] XIII, 256-7; *Begriff der Ironie*, 178. Here K. gratefully refers to an
observation in H. T. Rötscher, *Aristophanes und sein Zeitalter, eine philologisch-
philosophische Abhandlung zur Altertumsforschung*, Berlin 1827, 253: "From his
point of view it becomes clear how the Socratic ignorance is so frequently
misused, and so often serves people both as a good apology for their own
ignorance and as an excuse for refusing to recognise true knowledge."

[8] VII, 426-7; VII, 177.                    [9] VII, 167; VI, 275.

must this be taken to mean that one renounces the method of objective thought and leaves the path of objective reflection, in order to withdraw into the uncertainties of the world of subjective inwardness. In defining truth as the subjective the conclusions of objective thought must at least be taken into account. "If subjectivity is truth, the definition of truth must at the same time contain a reflexion of the reaction to mere objectivity, a recollection of that parting of the ways, and such allusions would suggest the tension of true inwardness. Here is such a definition of truth: *objective incertitude, clung to and appropriated with passionate inwardness, is truth,* the highest truth that there can be, *for one who exists.*"[10]

This definition of truth is subjective only in the sense that it does not claim to state objectively what truth is, but is content to establish what the character of subjectivity must be if it is to be anchored in truth. In this connexion—but only in this connexion—we may now enquire what truth is objectively, and this means what objectively corresponds to that which the subjective thinker expresses existentially as truth, and this must be done solely by those resources of thought which are at the disposal of such a thinker, and without any attempt to reach a standpoint outside such an existence. If "from such a point of view we enquire about the truth objectively, then we see that truth is a *paradox.*"[11] "The eternal essential truth, i.e. truth which is vitally related to an existent personality, because it essentially concerns existence (all other knowledge is from a Socratic point of view contingent and its ground and extent a matter of indifference) is paradoxical. Nevertheless the eternal essential truth itself is by no means a paradox, but becomes paradoxical through its relation to existence."[12] "Paradox constitutes the real pathos of the intellectual life."[13]

Kierkegaard, of course, very well knows that this account of truth as paradox is not without its dangers. As soon as we neglect the precise dialectical connexion in which alone this idea is reasonable, it can only too easily be misused as a *refugium ignorantiae*; and Kierkegaard foresaw that this would indeed happen: "Gradually the word 'paradox' has gone out of

---

[10] VII, 170; VI, 278.
[12] VII, 171; VI, 279.
[11] *S. K. P.*, VI(B) 40.26, 127.
[13] *S. K. P.*, II(A), 755.

fashion; but people will soon begin chattering about it and in consequence the παράδοξον itself will soon become an ἔνδοξον. How absurd this is with people who once for all have freed themselves from the bother of thinking what they are talking about and who are merely eager to get hold of a new word in order to bandy it about."[14]  In opposition to this attitude Kierkegaard stresses with all possible emphasis that paradox is a category which like all his categories is an epitome of existence in conceptual form for the use of the existential thinker. "Paradox is a category: everything turns on this point, really. People have been accustomed to talk thus—to say that one cannot understand such and such a thing does not satisfy science which insists on understanding. But it is this point of view which is wrong. One should say, rather, just the opposite: if *human* knowledge will not admit that there is something which it cannot understand, or, to speak more precisely, something about which it clearly realises that understanding is out of the question, then all is confusion. The problem for human knowledge is to see that there is something which it cannot understand, and also to determine what that something is. Human knowledge is normally in a hurry to understand more and more, but if it will at last take the trouble to understand itself, then it must frankly confirm the fact of paradox. Paradox is not a concession but a category, an ontological description expressing the relationship between a personally existent spirit and eternal truth."[15]

14 *S. K. P.*, v(A), 79.                    15 *S. K. P.*, VIII.1(A), 11.

## PRELIMINARY PROVISIONAL ACCOUNT OF THE
## DIALECTICAL METHOD

"That subjectivity, inwardness, truth, existence, is the decisive factor, that we should steer our course in life towards Christianity, which means precisely interiority (though not, let it be noted, every sort of interiority, wherefore the previous stages must be firmly kept in view)—such was my idea." These words Kierkegaard puts into the mouth of John Climacus in the *Unwissenschaftliche Nachschrift* where he makes the latter comment ironically on the underlying purpose of pseudonymity in the continuity of the author's work, and with special reference to a similar effort in contemporary Danish literature. In this connexion, he also assigns to the *Philosophische Brocken* their correct place in this context, and says of them that "they decisively approximate to Christianity without ever explicitly referring to it or to the name of Christ."[1]

At this point we must ask a few questions about Kierkegaard's dialectical method. In the *Brocken* the Christian revelation becomes for the first time the dialectic's central theme. This does not mean that in the earlier writings—even if we leave out of account the *Erbauliche Reden*—the Christian theme had played no part and that Kierkegaard's interest in it had been concealed. What possible or personal reason could Kierkegaard have had for concealment and for speaking unambiguously as a pagan philosopher? Not only did he live in a "Christian" world, but even when he was speaking as a philosopher, he was not concerned with those philosophers who—as was still the case with Kant—endeavoured to delimit philosophy strictly as against revealed religion. His philosophical colleagues of the school of Hegel were, on the contrary, much more concerned to assimilate revelation to their own systems and so to prove themselves to be Christian philosophers.

When Kierkegaard wishes to speak as a Christian also, he

---

[1] *S. V.*, VII, 241-2; *Ges. W.*, VI, 354. Unless otherwise stated, all further refs. in this Interlude are to *S. V.* and *Ges. W.*

feels embarrassed at sight of so much Christianity in the world. For this reason he does not write a dissertation about the relation of philosophy and Christianity in order to make the two quantities systematically cohere with each other, but simply treats the problem which the Christian revelation sets for philosophical thought, and which is formulated as follows on the title page of the *Brocken*: "Can there be a historical point of departure for an eternal consciousness? How can such a thing be of more than historical interest? Can eternal felicity be built on historical knowledge?" He does so in the main without placing the problem in its real historical setting and without specifically mentioning the Christian revelation, but he discusses his problem rather as an experiment in thought. But when Climacus says that the pseudonyms are steering towards the Christian, this might be taken to mean that existence as understood by the pseudonyms postulates the Christian revelation as its fulfilment and completion. The further observation "that the previous stages must be firmly kept in view" might be supposed to point in the same direction. And then retrospectively we might consider and elucidate the whole Socratic existential dialectic as being, from the point of view of the Christian revelation, the necessary *ordo salutis* constituting the path of Christian existence, just as theologians have again and again been accustomed to construct a particular philosophy to underpin their theology, and form an approach to it.

In point of fact, this has constantly been attempted. Kierkegaard's splendid consistency of thought, which means that not the smallest fancy can remain outside the comprehensive conception of his dialectical method, greatly tempts every systematic thinker to do so. The preference which certain theologians show for Kierkegaard—theologians who are, above all, concerned to seek out the natural man in his own sphere and to demonstrate to him from his own point of view the necessity of taking the step towards faith—obviously is connected with the fact that they have succumbed to this temptation. But in adopting this approach they have prematurely eluded Kierkegaard's dialectic and have overlooked certain essential aspects of it.

Kierkegaard does indeed say: "If the meaning of religious

existence had been forgotten, then no doubt also the meaning of human existence had been forgotten; the latter had therefore to be emphasised afresh."[2] And therefore by means of his pseudonymous characters he "wished to read afresh the original documents concerning individual human relations in their existential bearing and to reinterpret, if possible in a more inward way, what is old, well known, and handed down by our forefathers."[3] Thus he did, without a doubt, seek out the natural man on the ground of his own characteristic type of existence. But he did not do so in order to point out to him that you cannot remain on this ground and to urge that you must advance to the higher level of Christian living, but simply in order to help him in the task of existence. Of course he does so with a constant consideration of Christianity, but not in order to prove the truth of the latter, or to prepare the way for an advance towards faith, or to invite his partner to make such an advance. On the contrary, his purpose is to free from all materialistic self-deception those who are already convinced of Christian truth and think they have made the decision for faith, and this he does by instilling into them a passionate concern about existence itself as the unavoidable preliminary condition for Christian living. For "to exist subjectively and passionately (and objectively one can exist only in distraction) is in general an absolute prerequisite for having any sort of opinion or understanding of Christianity."[4] In this respect Kierkegaard can even feel free to find at times the children of darkness wiser than the children of light and to make Climacus say: "That one can exist with interiority outside the sphere of Christianity has sufficiently been shown by, for example, Greek civilisation; but in our day it is typical that while we are all Christians and know a lot about Christianity, very rarely do we find a person existing with such passionate concern as a heathen philosopher possessed. It is no wonder that the question of Christianity is so easily settled when we begin by putting ourselves in a condition in which there can be absolutely no question of our ever acquiring the faintest idea what Christianity truly is."[5]

[2] VII, 210; VI, 321.     [3] VII, 548-9; VII, 304.
[4] VII, 238; VI, 351.     [5] VII, 237-8; VI, 350.

But in this dialectic of existence by which Kierkegaard wishes to help man in the business of living is there not latent an *anthropology*, which can be established as a general anthropology from a Christian point of view, or, on the other hand, may need or be capable of broadening or modification in a Christian sense? Of course such an anthropology of one sort or another could be extracted from Kierkegaard's dialectic, and both theologians and philosophers have done this. But if this is done, one has only an excerpt from Kierkegaard's work— an excerpt which, moreover, leaves out the decisive thing, namely the dialectic, and which can for this reason be directly imparted, the very thing which Kierkegaard forbade himself to do.[6] If this is done, then the conscientious exactness of the scholar must prevent him from appealing to the name and work of Kierkegaard.

Climacus says, for example, about the *Stadien auf dem Lebensweg*: The meaning of the writing, "if it has one, will be found to lie in the existential interiority of the various stages, manifested in diverse ways as passion, irony, pathos, humour, and dialectic. This sort of thing does not, of course, interest the lecturer. Perhaps it is not inconceivable that, in the last resort, a lecturer would carry his politeness so far as to say, *en passant* and subordinately in a note to some paragraph, that this author represents the quality of interiority. By this sug-

[6] J. Climacus says something about a reviewer of the *Philosophische Brocken* that would, even in the more favourable circumstances, be applicable to an anthropology so abstracted from K.'s existential dialectic: "The report is exact and on the whole dialectically reliable, but now comes the difficulty; although the review is so accurate, every one who reads it alone will get a completely wrong impression of the book . . . the review is academic, utterly so. And this is why it gives (in my opinion) the most utterly wrong impression. The reader of such a review gets not the slightest idea of the antithesis in the form of the writing, of the mystifying contrast of the experiment to the content, of the brazen inventiveness (such as even Christianity invents) in the single attempt that is made to go further than speculative constructions, of the indefatigable activity of the ironic faculty, of the whole parody on speculation in the design of the work, of the satirical purpose which is shown in that efforts are made as though something quite extraordinary and new is to be brought forth, whereas constantly everyday orthodoxy appears in fitting respectability: of all this indeed the reader gets no idea" (VII, 233 n.; VI, 346 n.).

gestion the author and an ignorant circle of readers have come to know everything about it. Passion, pathos, irony, dialectic, humour, inspiration, and so on, are regarded by the lecturer as something of subordinate importance, something which everyone has at his disposal. Thus when it is declared that the author represents interiority, with this brief word which any one can say, everything is said and much more than the author has said."[7] The latter, in fact, does not represent the quality of interiority neither by allusion to his own interior existence nor by speaking about interiority as an attitude, but his purpose is through the avoidance of any direct communication to provoke his interlocutor to explore the inner depths of existence.

But did not Kierkegaard utter that famous expression about his intention being to "cheat men into a knowledge of the truth"?[8] And if the truth lies (as in his case we must presuppose) in Christianity, must that not mean that, though provisionally concealing his real intention, he wishes to urge upon them the Christian way of life by deepening their own natural self-understanding? This is for example how Emil Brunner understands the matter when, thinking of Kierkegaard, he makes a plea for an "eristic" theology to take the place of classical apologetics, and says about such an eristic theologian: "He must know the language of the world and of his own time, he must even talk in terms of it and only indirectly and furtively express Christian truth. In fact as a rule he should not express it but have it constantly in the background only, as a secret accompaniment of knowledge, while driving the 'enemy' into a tight corner."[9] And speaking of the eristic activity of the theologian as a preacher, he says that the latter should seek "to press the considering mind of the hearer until he finds himself in a narrow pass where there are only two possibilities: the empty, despairingly defiant negative of reason, pressed against the wall, or entrance through the narrow gateway of faith."[10] We shall see later that Brunner is here

---

[7] VII, 256-7; VI, 369.　　　　[8] XII, 541; X, 28.

[9] tr. Brunner, "Die andere Aufgabe der Theologie," in *Z. D. Z.*, 1929, 272.

[10] Brunner, *op. cit.*, p. 259.

requiring of preaching the very thing which Kierkegaard absolutely forbids it. Our immediate concern is to consider whether this whole programme of an eristic theology is consonant with the spirit of Kierkegaard.

In any event we shall look in vain in Kierkegaard's work for anything akin to this driving into the "narrow pass" or the bringing of reason to bay and "pressing it against the wall." Kierkegaard would certainly have mocked at such enterprises and their "dreadful solemnity,"[11] for the simple reason that they are undertaken in such an utterly humourless spirit; and he would strongly have felt that this would have been a sufficient material argument against them. Perhaps he would have concerned himself with that "considering mind" and, in the interest of clear ideas and distinct categories, enquired what really is in despair, whether a process of thinking or the thinker's weariness of mind and heart, and how these two are related to each other. In any case, he would have taken to task the eristic theologian himself, and would have asked him how he himself felt when driving his hearer into the narrow pass, whether he himself had already come through it, and whether, assuming that he had left the pass once for all behind him, he had not exchanged the scandal of faith for a simple *sacrificium intellectus*, and for this reason was now exercising his preaching activity so undialectically, so utterly without irony and humour, and was thus finding it possible to argue against the natural man with a lecturer's forthrightness, without feeling the sting of his own remarks. And Kierkegaard would assuredly have said that he did not in any case understand how the eristic theologian could suppose that such an undertaking had anything to do with his own work.

On the other hand Brunner could say, in justification of his eristic idea: "Classical apologetics did not err by engaging in this debate" between naturalistic and Christian self-understanding, "but rather by the fact that it carried through the debate on false ground, namely that of theoretical speculation. It did not err in making the conflict explicit, but in cutting it adrift from the spirit of faith and its creative decisions, in

[11] VII, 240; VI, 352.

watering it down to a mere confrontation of opposing world-views."[12]

Kierkegaard would no doubt have seen the error in the fact that classical apologetics not only conducted the debate on false ground, but that it conducted the debate at all and that the new eristic method goes on conducting it, and, despite all assertions to the contrary, on essentially the same ground. And, further, for the clarification of ideas, he would perhaps have asked what exactly was this "spirit of faith and its creative decisions" and how it could be grasped in terms of categories, because he would have feared that in this argument all categories and all distinctions between thought and being were becoming hopelessly confused. This is just the sort of confused thinking that Kierkegaard allowed nobody to get away with.

But what did Kierkegaard himself mean by his expression about his intention to cheat men into the knowledge of the truth? In the posthumous work *Der Gesichtspunkt für meine Wirksamkeit als Schriftsteller*, Kierkegaard explains this point in connexion with aesthetic authorship. His point of departure is that he is speaking in a situation where all are entangled in the illusion that they are Christians, and which makes it difficult, therefore, to convey a direct impression of what it means to be a Christian. In such a situation Kierkegaard's object is to make men alert to what is characteristically Christian. For this purpose he needs quite a new technique of persuasion, a technique which must wholly depend on arousing men's powers of reflexion. "The whole matter can be expressed in a single word, namely that the method must be indirect. To carry through this programme, work is needed, day by day and year by year: an unbroken attention at every hour of the day; unremitting daily finger exercises in dialectical method; and a 'fear and trembling' which know no rest. Hence the method must be indirect."[13] Thus this new technique of persuasion is exactly the opposite of classical apologetics, which sought to justify or extol Christianity before a circle of non-Christians. "The entire classical technique of persuasion,

---

[12] E. Brunner, *Das Gebot und die Ordnungnen*, 1932, p. 569.
[13] XIII, 539-40; X, 28.

E

the whole paraphernalia of apologetics, serve only, to put the matter bluntly, to betray the essence of Christianity.   Our tactics at every moment and every juncture must be to insist that we have to struggle against a conceit, against an illusion."[14] Such an illusion can only be unmasked by deception.   "Yes, in reality there is only one way of bringing a man who is involved in such conceits to the knowledge of the truth, namely by deceiving him.   If any one thinks otherwise he is only betraying the fact that he is not a remarkable dialectician, which for this business it is essential that you should be."[15]

This conceit or illusion consists in the fact that a man thinks he is a Christian and yet lives on an aesthetic level, thereby making interchangeable the aesthetic and the Christian. "What then in this connexion is the meaning of cheating?   It means that you do not begin *directly* with what you propose to impart, but rather you begin by assuming that the ideas of your interlocutor are the genuine goods.   Hence you do not begin (to confine ourselves to the essential theme of this work) by saying, 'I am a Christian, you are not,' but rather by suggesting, 'You are a Christian, I am not.'   Or, again, you do not begin thus: 'What I preach is Christianity, whereas you are living on a purely aesthetic level.'   No, you begin thus: 'Let us talk about aesthetics.'   The deception consists in the fact that you employ these subterfuges in order to come to the essential religious point."[16]

Using this new technique of persuasion, Kierkegaard writes his *Philosophische Brocken*.   The fancy which is here in question is the synthesis achieved by speculative thought between philosophy and the Christian revelation.   But he does not directly attack this synthesis; he shows that he is alluding to its dubiety merely by the motto of the book: "Better well hanged than badly married."   Then he begins simply with the question as to how far truth can be taught and asks what it would mean to suggest that God himself has appeared as teacher.   He describes this experiment in thought as a "poetic essay" and the "absolute paradox" at which he arrives as a "metaphysical whim" and the offensiveness of this paradox as an "acoustic illusion."   Like the preface, which has already

---

[14] XIII, 540; X, 28.      [15] XIII, 541; X, 28-9.      [16] XIII, 541; X, 29.

been mentioned,[17] all these expressions are by no means to be regarded as witticisms of no material significance. They are intended to suggest that Kierkegaard for his part is not attempting such a systematic synthesis, but wishes merely to make an experiment which of course he carries out with complete systematic thoroughness and consistency.

[17] See above, p. 42, n. 2.

## 11. THE ABSOLUTE PARADOX

In the Socratic paradox, eternal truth itself was not paradoxical but only became so by the fact that it entered into relation with a mind existing in time. But the position is otherwise when God Himself appears as a teacher in history by becoming a particular man. This means that eternal truth itself becomes paradoxical. It then repels the one who wishes to assimilate it, no longer, as in the case of the Socratic paradox, by its objective uncertainty, but by its absurdity and self-contradictory nature. "What then is the meaning of the absurd? The absurd is the fact that eternal truth has come to be in time, that God has appeared on the plane of history, has been born and grown up, etc., that He has become utterly like any other individual man and indistinguishable from any other."[1]

This absolute paradox shows the greatest possible intensification of the Socratic paradox. If man attempts to enter into relation with the absolute paradox, he cannot go back behind the Socratic dialectic in order to gain an immediate relation to eternal truth. Man must be expressly warned against any such attempt, for "there is in man a tendency anxiously desiring satisfaction to acquire something really firm, such as will exclude all dialectic; but this is a cowardly betrayal of the divine. Even the firmest truth of all, that of revelation, becomes *eo ipso* dialectical when I have to appropriate it; even the firmest thing of all, the endlessly negative decision which expresses the infinite and the divine in the individual, becomes immediately dialectical. So soon as I remove the dialectical, I become superstitious and cheat God of the effort to acquire at every moment what has once been acquired."[2] Revelation cannot spell the end of dialectics because it means that eternal truth becomes historical and receives the predicates of the

---

[1] *S. V.*, VII, 176; *Ges. W.*, VI, 284. All further refs. in this section are to *S. V.* and *Ges. W.*

[2] VII, 24 n.; VI, 130 n.

historical. In this matter it is not a question of whether God is—"the supposition that God is defines God as He is in His eternal being, not as He is in His historical manifestation"— but of "whether we will agree that God has become, which means that the eternal being of God is disclosed through the dialectical determinations of the world of becoming."[3] What are these determinations?

We have seen above (Sect. 7) that Kierkegaard distinguishes historical becoming from merely natural becoming, as a doubling of the latter and taking place within it. But whereas natural becoming is dialectical only in relation to space, historical becoming is dialectical in relation to time also. If, then, God becomes a specific historical man, He becomes a fact of history; and if any one wishes to enter into relation with this fact he needs in the first place the general organ for the apprehension of the historical which Kierkegaard calls "faith." By this is not to be understood anything specifically Christian.

Every happening can be directly perceived either by the direct perception of the eyewitness or on the basis of the report of contemporaries which can be directly apprehended. But what can thus be directly known is not the historical, for "the historical in relation to present being is characterised by the fact that it has become, and in relation to the past that it was present being by its becoming."[4] In order to know the historical in this its essence, there is needed an "organ for its perception appropriate to its nature," and one which can grasp "the uncertainty of all becoming."[5] This means that he who wishes to appreciate correctly what has become cannot be content to appreciate the certainty and reliability of facts, but must also at the same time reflect on the possibilities of the "how."

"The sphere of potentiality from which there emerged the possible which became the actual always forms the background to what has become and remains with the past, even though we are removed from it by millennia; as soon as one of later times repeats that a certain thing has become, he is reaffirming its background of potentiality without taking into account whether a more particular description of this potentiality can be given

[3] IV, 251; VI, 80.     [4] IV, 248; VI, 78.     [5] IV, 245; VI, 74.

or not."[6]   Thus the historian, who sees the past in its free process of becoming, must realise, from a subjective point of view, the uncertainty which lies behind the certainty.   He must have, not merely by direct perception, a means of grasping the certainty of its real happening, but also a means of understanding the uncertainty implied by its potentiality and mode. For there is no means of knowing directly that the historical has come to be as the effect of a cause.   It can be immediately realised how doubtful it must always be whether it has become thus by necessity or by a freely operating cause.   This question cannot be decided by knowledge and the accompanying doubt cannot be argued away.   If the historian supposes that what he immediately perceives is the effect of a certain cause and therefore might have been quite different, he is drawing a conclusion against which doubt must protest.   In order to preclude this doubt, therefore, the statement must take the form not of a conclusion but of a decision.   And for Kierkegaard this decision is *faith*.   By his decision the doubter reserves all conclusions in order not to fall into error.   "When he decides to believe he takes the risk of erring, but in spite of this he wishes to believe. In no other way can you believe; if you wish to avoid all risk, then you want to be sure that you can swim before you enter the water."[7]   "He believes in what has become and thus suspends within himself the uncertainty arising from the background of nothingness and non-being;  he believes that the thing has happened thus, and so has resolved within himself any doubt arising from the potential modality of what has become and without denying the possibility of a different mode;  for faith the mode of the thing as it has come to be is the most certain point."[8]   Faith therefore is the means for the apprehension of the historical.

What all this implies concretely only becomes clear when we ask why Kierkegaard is so concerned about this means of grasping the historical.   The historical is an alien reality to which the individual must take up an attitude.   His attitude may be aesthetic or intellectual, and if so, he is indifferent to the question of its reality.   "If I understand a thinker, then in proportion as I understand him his actuality (that he exists

<hr />

[6] IV, 249; VI, 78.        [7] IV, 246 n.; VI, 76 n.        [8] IV, 247; VI, 76.

as an individual man, that he himself has *really* understood the matter thus, etc., that he himself has realised its truth) becomes a matter of indifference. In this philosophy and aesthetics are absolutely correct and we must above all note this point."[9] But it is a different matter if we approach an alien reality from an ethical standpoint. We then enquire into it in order to grasp it in its inmost reality. But man has no means of grasping directly an alien reality as reality. He must first see it in the reality of its becoming in order to apprehend and realise its background potential and the decisive steps by which it has come to be. In thus interpreting an alien reality in terms of its potentiality he is dissolving it in ideality. This latter cannot be directly perceived, for "ideality as the animating principle does not simply enter into history. What can be conveyed to me is not ideality, but a number of facts."[10] We must think out ideality for ourselves, otherwise we can know nothing of it. "If I know that Caesar was great, then I know what greatness is and see it exemplified in him, otherwise I do not know that Caesar was great."[11] Even the most precise reporting cannot convey what is ideal; on the contrary, the latter must be brought to the task of interpreting the report. "Whether the event really happened in the way it is said to have done is something that can only be checked by idealistic thought; it cannot be bottled and sealed historically."[10] "The historical is always only so much raw material which only he who truly apprehends it knows how to dissolve into a *posse* in order to assimilate it as an *esse*."[11] Thus ethically all mere contemplation of the historical is excluded. If from an ethical standpoint we enquire into an alien reality, then just as in the case of aesthetic and intellectual questioning it appears first only as possibility, "only this possibility no longer leaves us cold as it does on an aesthetic and intellectual level, but becomes a thought-out reality related to the reality of my own life in so far as I intimately realise it."[12]

The question of the factuality of an event is on the other hand of minor importance, for it contributes nothing to the understanding of the historical. It may even hinder such an

[9] VII, 280; VII, 23.    [10] VI, 409; IV, 406.
[11] VI, 408; IV, 405.    [12] VII, 278; VII, 21.

understanding by concealing the essential beneath inessentials, and Kierkegaard can see in the mere effort to reconstruct historical facts a training in stupidity. "The sensible thing is to ask two questions: (1) 'Is what is said possible?' and (2) 'Can I do it?' But it is senseless to ask: (1) "Is it actual?" and (2) 'Has my neighbour Christophersen really done this?'."[13] When God reveals Himself as man, we have in the first place to do with a historical fact like any other historical fact: namely, the God-man as man. On this level belongs everything that can be directly known about Him and conveyed as so much historical information, susceptible of ideal interpretation. In this sphere all the traditional detail about the "historical Jesus," His teaching and His deeds, has its place and brings Him into line with all other historical phenomena, as a man among men, within the comparative classification of historical factors. And the instrument by which man becomes related to Him on this level is faith considered as the means of apprehending the historical in general. Hence both contemporaries and posterity are related to the God-man as man in a merely Socratic way.

From this revelation of the God-man as man which yields us a general historical fact, or, as Kierkegaard says, the historical in elementary potency, is to be distinguished revelation as an eternal fact, the God-man as God or the historical in two dimensions. When faith as the instrument for the apprehension of the historical enters into relation with this two-dimensional historical fact, it undergoes an involution. Here we are confronted by "faith in a quite pre-eminent sense, in a unique sense and a unique relationship."[14] The reason for this lies in the object of this faith, viz. revelation, which is not a simple historical fact. Inasmuch as it states that God has entered into the process of becoming, it contains a self-contradiction, for it predicates historical becoming of God although the very nature of God is that He is eternal and is not subject to becoming. By this self-contradiction, the Christian, absolute paradox, as we have seen, repels us not merely by dint of its objective uncertainty but also because of its sheer absurdity. And faith, addressing itself to this absolute paradox, must

---

[13] VI, 410; IV, 407.     [14] IV, 250; VI, 79.

not only overcome the objective uncertainty, but also this very absurdity. How can this be?

The fact of revelation has "no immediate contemporaries in so far as it is historical in elementary potency (faith in the general sense). But neither has it any immediate contemporaries in its two-dimensional aspect, where it is based on a contradiction (faith in the pre-eminent sense)."[15] In this connexion contemporary nearness to the event is a matter of complete indifference. In such a matter there can be no immediate knowledge or perception, which the eyewitness might transmit to posterity, for that this fact is what it declares itself to be is something which cannot be directly perceived but even by eyewitnesses only believed. The eyewitness can only report: "I believe and have believed that this has happened, although it is folly in the eyes of reason, and a cause of stumbling to the human heart."[16] Thus the eyewitness has no advantage over his successor nor has the latter any advantage over the eyewitness. The results of the fact which he has before him are the results of a paradox and hence are just as paradoxical as the fact itself. They can only arouse his attention as happened with the eyewitness and do not bring him any nearer to understanding itself. Thus revelation is equally near to every epoch. Faith in the Christian sense is only possible in the situation of contemporaneity. For Kierkegaard this solves the whole question of historical factuality in relation to revelation. "Had the contemporary generation left behind them nothing but these words: 'We have believed that in such and such a year God manifested Himself in humility as a servant of mankind, taught and lived among us and then died'—it would have been more than enough."[17]

No doubt this argument shows how man faced by revelation deals with the question of historical factuality. But another and more difficult question remains to be answered, namely how man is to come to terms with this absolute paradox. The eternal has disclosed itself in the particular and has appeared at a specific point in the time series. Following the New Testament, Kierkegaard calls this special moment of history "the fullness of time." Now such a moment, as is the case with

15 IV, 251; VI, 80.    16 IV, 264; VI, 93.    17 IV, 266; VI, 94.

any other historical phenomenon, becomes for man an occasion and cause of self-recollection if he is to assimilate the fact in its ideal bearing. But here he comes upon a twofold difficulty. Firstly, it is impossible for him to conceive the self-contradictory idea that God has become subject to the process of becoming; and, secondly, he cannot imagine that eternal truth confronts him as a fact of history, since he thinks that he already possesses it in recollection. Hence he must re-examine his presuppositions according to which he believed himself to be in possession of the truth, if he is to do justice to the claim which this fact makes. If such a fact *is* the truth, then the only conclusion must be that man himself lives in untruth. If God becomes a teacher in this manner, then prior to this man's being was rooted in untruth, but only now, when stung by revelation, does he become conscious of this. "What the teacher can arouse the learner to realise through recollection is thus merely this, that he dwells in untruth. But in proportion as he reflects on this, the learner is completely excluded from the truth more than in fact he was when he did not know that he dwelt in untruth."[18]

Now this means that the whole Socratic dialectic, as up to now we have found Kierkegaard expounding it, is called in question at the decisive point. In its two aspects, the dialectical plumbing of the inner depths of one's own existence as also the dialectic of debate with an interlocutor, it depended essentially on the supposition that man can find the truth in himself and therefore by the exploration of his inner depths can dwell in the truth. Thus the introduction of the absolute paradox means that this whole notion of dialectic must be revised.

### 12. BEING IN UNTRUTH

Kierkegaard finds in Socrates himself an ultimate intensification of his search for the truth which brings him to the very edge of the recognition that in spite of everything he is not in possession of the truth. The fact that he is not capable of thinking about the divine being introduces confusion into Socrates's self-

[18] IV, 184; VI, 12.

knowledge. "Thus the suspected paradox of reason has its repercussions on man and his self-knowledge, so that he now no longer knows for certain whether he may be perhaps a still more curiously compounded animal than the typhon or whether he has a gentler and divine side to his being."[1] Socrates did not take further this final point which threw doubt upon the whole of his self-knowledge, but he always adhered steadfastly to the idea that man can know himself and in that self-knowledge has the criterion of the truth. Since Kierkegaard observes this and yet does not himself remain at this limit, we must consider in detail how he deals with this borderline problem, because this is of fundamental significance for certain essential questions which we have yet to pose in reference to his dialectical method.

In the first place, it is to be noted that he does not use the doubt thrown upon the Socratic method by this last confine of knowledge in order to show man how natural knowledge itself postulates the need to overstep this border. The position is rather that eternal truth spells for man a limit which he has no means of recognising because it signifies the absolutely other. But reason cannot even say this from its own resources, "for reason cannot even conceive the absolutely other, since it cannot negate itself absolutely; in attempting to do so, it uses itself and conceives of the wholly other from within its own scheme of thought; it cannot absolutely transcend itself and therefore thinks only of that which is superior to itself according to its own ideas."[2] Reason cannot dare to make any sortie beyond this limit. It cannot succeed in doing so either by the *via negationis* or by the *via eminentiae*. In fact it cannot even establish this limit as such, without surrendering itself completely. Any attempt to do so leads to the "self-mockery of reason."[3]

This confusion can only be ended when we realise that through the fact of revelation and inasmuch as God becomes our teacher, this limit is fixed and at the same time we can recognise its significance. If this fact is the truth—and let us

---

[1] *S. V.*, IV, 206; *Ges. W.*, VI, 36. All further refs. in this section are to *S. V.* and *Ges. W.*

[2] IV, 212; VI, 41.

[3] IV, 213; VI, 41.

remember that up to now it has been introduced only in an experimental dialectic—then man dwells in untruth. No other possibility remains. The eternal truth which man thought he possessed in the depths of self-recollection has become historical at a specific point in the time series. This means that man does not now learn something which he might have known had he only thought sufficiently deeply about it, but that he had not searched for the truth in this direction, that rather by his seeking in the wrong place, namely in recollection, he had moved ever further and further away from it.

Now let us suppose further that man was created by God— and the fact of revelation does indeed imply this—then the being of man must have had the primal capacity to know the truth. If now he no longer possesses it, then he must have lost it, and that by his own fault. "Thus our teacher is God, who operates upon us in such a way as to bring us to the realisation that we dwell in untruth, and that through our own fault. But this condition of being which causes us to dwell in untruth, and that through our own fault, how shall we describe it? Let us call it sin."[4]

It is no part of our purpose here to expound fully and in detail, as Kierkegaard does, the qualification of human existence by sin and the overcoming of sin through faith. This must be studied in Kierkegaard's own writings. We can only do so in so far as it is necessary for an understanding of Kierkegaard's dialectical method. As previously, we shall have to bring out the specifically intellectual aspect of this existential dialectic and into the bargain be content with giving a rather colourless summary of the sequence of his thought. The central question still remains how the dialectical thinker, whose personal existence receives a totally new meaning as a result of this paradox, can come to terms with the latter. The means by which this is done is still faith, the organ by which we apprehend the historical, exactly as it is within the Socratic framework. But in this instance faith has to contend with the opposition of reason quite otherwise than on the simple level of history where it had to resolve doubt by decision. For the absolute paradox signifies the submergence and defeat of reason. "Thus reason

4 IV, 185; VI, 13.

has many objections to raise in this matter of the absolute paradox, and yet on the other hand in its paradoxical passion and concern it wills its own destruction. This destruction is of course the very thing that the paradox requires and in this way they come after all to an agreement; but this agreement comes to pass only in the moment of passion."[5] This passionate affirmation of faith has always to contend with the resistance of reason, which is scandalised by the paradox. And this shock of scandal must always first be experienced if man is to attain faith. "The possibility of being scandalised is the parting of the ways or is like standing at the parting of the ways. From the possibility of this crux we turn off either to scandalisation or to faith; but we never reach faith except through the possibility of scandalisation."[6]

## 13. SCANDAL AND FAITH

In regard to the Socratic paradox we emphasised the point that the crucial issue where the subjective thinker abandons the path of objectification may not be simply left behind once for all, but must always be kept in view as a constant reminder of objective incertitude. Exactly so must it be with regard to the triumph of faith in the paradox; such faith must always contain an echo of the scandal that has been traversed. The believer cannot once for all have decided for faith and against scandalisation, but at every moment in which he believes he must still overcome the possibility of scandal.

This distinguishes the experience of scandalisation from a mere *sacrificium intellectus* which is made once for all, and as a result of which the difficulties are decisively overcome. In the latter case one is moving throughout in the sphere of objective thought. The objective contradiction is removed on an objective plane in that the antinomy is accepted as something objectively insoluble; and the thinker who has once made this sacrifice of his understanding goes on thinking and exercising his reason within the area which has been cleared by this sacrifice, as though nothing had happened. There can be no question that his existence has been utterly reorientated by this crucial

[5] IV, 215; VI, 43-4.  [6] XII, 78; IX, 68.

decision, however much he may assert this and thus make himself out to be an "existential" thinker. This misunderstanding, to which the work of Kierkegaard has not seldom been subject, must be avoided.

For the offensiveness does not consist merely in the fact that man is to believe a self-contradiction and thus hold something senseless to be true, but in the fact that all the presuppositions of his being as an existence anchored in truth are called in question. Were he to make the *sacrificium intellectus* on an intellectual level and thus consent to the negation of his understanding, it would not help him in the least. By the aid of this understanding he has of course ordered his life up to now and "has mastered it by thinking." And it is this very thing which has now become impossible, since it has proved to be the case—or rather has once been accepted as true—that man does not already possess truth in the depths of his recollection, but, on the contrary, that truth confronts him in the divine self-revelation at a particular point in the historical process.

Further, in the description of this scandalisation and its overcoming by faith, thought must not be isolated in contrast to the other aspects of existence, as we have repeatedly insisted in our study so far. It is the whole of human existence from every angle which in its confrontation by the absolute paradox is revolted and shocked by the latter and resists the consequent new orientation of life which this paradox brings. Let us enquire first how the change in existence brought about by revelation works itself out in concrete detail.

Through revelation the eternal becomes historical and enters the time series at a specific point. But did not this already happen in that moment of the dynamic process of historical becoming when existence became meaningful through time with the result that "time constantly clashes with eternity and eternity penetrates time?"[1] This is no doubt true, but there is needed a more exact consideration of the eternal such as will take us beyond the Greek conception. The Greeks understood the character of temporality "naïvely" and since they "had

[1] *S. V.*, IV, 359; *Ges. W.*, V, 86. Except as stated, all further refs. in this section are to *S. V.* and *Ges. W.*

no idea of eternity in any deeper sense, neither had they any conception of the meaning of the future."[2] For them eternity lies behind man; it belongs to the past and appears retrospectively, as in Platonic recollection. Time has no direction, it is merely a passing away of all things, and life in time is not a question of the relation of the present to the past and future. "It is as though I should allow a man to travel a certain road without giving him any directions, in which case the road behind him will appear as ground already covered."[3] The mistake in all this is that eternity is conceived too abstractly for it to be manifested concretely in time and to impart to temporality the stamp of direction from the past to the future. It touches time everywhere and therefore nowhere and the life of personal existence is still subject to the "metaphysical authority of the idea of eternal recollection."[4]

Through revelation, on the other hand, eternity is particularised at a special point of the time series, and relationship to the eternal, thus localised, becomes of decisive significance for existence. This effect of the absolute paradox is as paradoxical as the latter itself, and thus from the point of view of Socratic thinking can only be understood as a scandal. But it is just so and not otherwise that the paradox itself insists on being understood. Reason has discovered the ground of scandal just as little as it has discovered the paradox itself. Rather the position is the reverse: the paradox does not allow reason to entertain any opinion of it, but as truth it is itself *index et judex sui et falsi*. What offended reason asserts is quite right, what is wrong is its supposition that this is an objection to the paradox discovered by itself, whereas in reality it is the paradox which has provoked that very objection. "All that the offended reason says about the paradox it has learnt from the latter, even though it maintains that it has discovered it for itself, because it is under an acoustic illusion."[5] If the claim of the absolute paradox, as we have suggested, is correct, the question can only be what such a relationship to the eternal (as thus appearing in time) signifies for the character of temporality.

The eternal thus appearing through revelation is described in

[2] *Ibid.*  
[3] IV, 360; V, 87.  
[4] VII, 230 n.; VI, 343 n.  
[5] IV, 219; VI, 49.

Christian terms as "the fullness of time." And according to Kierkegaard, "the idea on which everything in Christianity turns, and which made all things new, is the fullness of time; but this idea implies the moment as the eternal, and this eternal is both the future and the past. If we do not heed this point, we cannot rescue a single idea from heretical and perfidious appendices which destroy the idea itself."[6] What does this rather abstract and even speculatively sounding idea really mean in the concrete? "The eternal is the future"—thus at times our common speech identifies the eternal and the future, and it is right, inasmuch as the future is in a certain sense the whole of which the past is only a part. Furthermore, the eternal as the future means the endlessly free and open possibilities of the future as contrasted with the fixity of the past which has completed its becoming. "The future is the incognito under the mask of which the eternal—incommensurable with time—nevertheless wills to maintain its connexion with time."[7] But the allusion to common speech cannot be adequate in this matter, and more precise conceptual definitions are needed.

In the present in which man encounters the revelation of the eternal, the past, as a result of that present experience, becomes distinct from the future. As contrasted with the fixity and finality of the past, the eternal contains the seeds of all creative development in the future, for it seals off the past and so prevents it from hindering by its deadness the free vital possibilities of the future. But at the same time the creative present moment establishes a continuity between the future and the past, for, as we have been told, "the eternal is both the future and the past." What comes to be in the future is not an utterly different story from that which has been in the past. "Once the creative present is realised, we have with us the eternal which is at the same time the future, reverberating too in the past."[8] In this way the past lives again, and yet it is no longer the same, since as it passes through the creative present it becomes transmuted by eternity. We must describe more closely this qualitative transmutation.

Kierkegaard regards man as a synthesis of body and soul,

[6] IV, 360; V, 87.         [7] IV, 359; V, 86.         [8] IV, 360; V, 87.

held together by the spirit as the third factor. But the same point can be expressed as follows: man is a synthesis of the temporal and the eternal held together by the creative present. In both these syntheses it is a question of one and the same thing. "The synthesis of body and soul must be established by the spirit; but the spirit is the eternal and operates therefore only when it establishes the first synthesis as identical with the second, that of the temporal and the eternal."⁹ This happens through the moment in which revelation comes putting an end to the *naïveté* of the Greek outlook on the body and time and qualifying both as *sinfulness*.

We should note at this point that Kierkegaard does not deduce this description of sin from the nature of the body and time, but argues rather from the standpoint of faith in revelation. The condition in which the self stands on the heights of faith and has overcome its scandalisation, is described thus in the *Krankheit zum Tode*: "In that it becomes related to itself and wills to be itself, it is clearly rooted in that Power which ordained its being."¹⁰ And sin stands out in contrast to this faith: "It is of the very essence of Christianity to affirm that the opposite of sin is not virtue but faith."¹¹ For "whatever does not proceed from faith is sin" (Rom. xiv.23). Hence sin can only be understood as a stage on the way to faith which hinders the attainment of that goal. How sin is to be expounded from this point of view, so that its bearing on dogmatics, ethics and psychology is brought out, Kierkegaard has shown above all in his *Begriff der Angst* and his *Krankheit zum Tode*, which we can merely mention at this point without going into detailed references. But two points in particular must be noted.

We have repeatedly insisted on one, namely, that the natural man cannot know himself to be a sinner by the light of his own reason, but needs revelation in order to realise this. "The idea by which Christianity most decisively and qualitatively differentiates itself from heathendom is precisely the idea and doctrine of sin; and accordingly Christianity quite consistently assumes that neither heathendom nor the natural man is aware of the nature of sin, it assumes in fact that the self-revelation of God is necessary in order to disclose what sin is. It is indeed

---

⁹ *Ibid.*      ¹⁰ XI, 128; VIII, 11.      ¹¹ XI, 194; VIII, 77.

not the case, as a superficial understanding assumes, that the doctrine of the Atonement constitutes the essential distinction between heathendom and Christianity. No, we must go far deeper, with sin and the doctrine of sin, as Christianity indeed does. What a dangerous objection it would be against Christianity if heathendom had a definition of sin which Christianity had to recognise as true."[12]

The other point is that whereas for Socrates sin is merely negative, Christianity declares it to be something positive. "That this is so, is a tenet for which orthodox dogmatics and orthodoxy in general has constantly contended, and every definition of sin which has made it out to be something merely negative, such as weakness, sensuality, finitude, ignorance, and so on, has been rejected as pantheistic. Orthodoxy very truly realised that the decisive struggle must be fought out here."[13] If, however, sin is not simply the imperfect, is not that which, in existential dialectic, has not yet ripened into being, the non-existent only in the sense of the not yet existent, if, on the contrary, sin is something positive, then the whole movement of existential dialectic is decisively changed: "the sphere of non-being is everywhere present as nothingness from which there arose deceptive appearance, sin, sensuality divorced from the spirit, time divorced from eternity; the point is now to clear this away and to call forth the sphere of true being and existence."[14]

Kierkegaard sees the solution to this problem in his idea of *renewal*. We consider that the future is not something completely new but something which restores the past. If the eternal lay only in the future without having any essential relation to the past, this would result, as Kierkegaard shows, in the spirit of Judaistic apocalyptic. And for the history of the individual life, the same misunderstanding would mean that by faith in revelation he could simply leave behind him his past history in order to become something entirely different. But the aim must not be that man should seek to escape from his temporality and finitude, but that he should seek to regain these in their plenitude of meaning. Finitude must not be left aside, but rather saved and redeemed, for "it is finitude and temporality

[12] XI, 200-1; VIII, 84.  [13] XI, 207; VIII, 91.  [14] IV, 352 n.; V, 80 n.

which are essentially at stake."[15] Here lies the task of renewal, the dialectic of which is accordingly: "What is renewed has already been, otherwise it could not be renewed, but renewal changes the very fact that it has once been into something quite new and other. When the Greeks said that all knowledge is remembrance, they were saying that the whole of life which now is has also been before; when we say that life is renewal we are saying that the life which once has been now enters anew into fullness of life."[16]

This renewal takes place in the moment of faith when revelation brings simultaneity, and for the Christian the passage into historical becoming is effected. This passage contains two acts: firstly, from a negative standpoint, the life of the body and temporality, which previously were not redeemed by the spirit and eternity, stand out as sinfulness. Thus sin is seen positively as non-being. In this it is not simply a question of the continuing consequences of particular sins, but of sin as a condition of life, of a "position which unfolds into an ever-increasing, positing continuum," and which therefore increases "with every moment in which the individual does not yet emerge from it."[17] This condition of sinfulness is the deepest essence of sin, and particular sins are not the continuation of sin but the expression of that continuation; in any particular sins the active presence of sin merely becomes clearly perceptible.[18] Thus what is negatively revealed in the moment of faith is sinfulness as a condition of life. At the same time, from a positive standpoint, the irruption of the eternal cancels the positive non-being of sin, not, however, by bringing to birth a new kind of being which did not previously exist, but by the fact that the temporality which previously was sinful now appears as the historical in which the presence of the eternal creates being and life—by the fact that the same life of the senses appears, but now as a synthesis held together by the operation of the spirit. It is clear that this event of renewal is concerned with the very problem which occupied Kierkegaard from the time of his first discussion of the Hegelian idea of mediation. The dual Socratic movement towards infinity, in

[15] III, 99; III, 45.    [16] III, 189; III, 137.    [17] XI, 216; VIII, 100.
[18] XI, 216; VIII, 100 (very freely translated).

which the ego resigned its finitude in order to win the eternal by the act of choosing its true life, could be accepted as a solution only if the ego already possessed the eternal in the depths of recollection. But this presupposition is destroyed by revelation and all the difficulties of any transformation of being recur to find their solution only in the act of renewal. From a purely logical problem there stems an ethical one which finds its solution in dogmatics. The question of this vital transformation thus extends to all spheres and hence Kierkegaard says: "Renewal is the *concern* of metaphysics and at the same time the concern in which metaphysics is wrecked; renewal is the solution in every ethical approach, renewal is the *conditio sine qua non* in every dogmatic problem."[19]

But everything depends on the point that renewal should not itself remain a merely metaphysical expression of an idea. Even in its dogmatic form it would be nothing other than this if it contained only an abstract statement about conditions of being in man without being defined by relation to some concretely existent "I." In this case the dialectical moment of the transformation would still remain a metaphysical or dogmatic abstraction. Hence it is essential to realise that this movement of transformation has to do with the existence of a concrete individual who finds himself on the way from sin to faith. And the dialectical moment in this transition lies in the experience of scandalisation.

Objectively, of course, the dialectical moment in this two-edged movement of renewal lies in the absolute paradox, working itself out both negatively and positively; but from the point of view of the concretely existing man it lies in the experience of scandalisation. The qualitative distinction between the divine and the human does not disappear for reason as a result of revelation. Rather it is for the first time truly brought out and man cannot remove it but only believe that God has removed it. But for this purpose he must first be able to realise his sin in order then to believe that his sins are forgiven. Every single step on the way towards the awareness of sin through the deepening of personal existence contains in itself the possibility of revolt against the paradox of the divinely

19 III, 189; III, 138.

human, i.e. the possibility of scandalisation. If man wishes to realise the fact of sinfulness and to believe in the forgiveness of sins, he must always do so in tension with the resistance called forth by the paradox itself, i.e. he must overcome through faith the possibility of scandal. If the ever-present possibility of scandal is set aside, then sin is no longer a positive and the qualitative distinction between the divine and the human is obliterated by man himself. Unless it is safeguarded by this possibility of scandal the doctrine of the divinely human merges into heathen pantheism and necessarily leads to blasphemy. "The fundamental misfortune of Christianity really lies in what the Churches have made of it: in the fact, namely, that the doctrine of the God-man (which, let it be noted, is to be understood in a Christian sense in the light of the paradox and safeguarded by the possibility of scandalisation) as it is continually preached is evacuated of its true meaning; with the consequence that the qualitative distinction between the divine and the human is pantheistically removed, first by the way of distinguished speculation, and then in the streets and lanes of the populace. Never has any religious doctrine on this earth brought God and man so closely together as Christianity has done; nor could any one do this but God himself; every human discovery of such a truth remains but a dream, an uncertain fancy. But never has any doctrine so cautiously guarded itself against the most horrible of all blasphemies, that of supposing that this step, after it has been taken by God, should come to mean no more than that the divine and the human in the last resort merge together—never has any doctrine been so protected against this as Christianity is by its insistence on the moment of scandal. Woe to feeble orators, woe to the frivolous thinkers who have explained away the moment of scandalisation! And woe to the whole tribe who have learned to think likewise and have praised these men!"[20]

In *Krankheit zum Tode* Kierkegaard has shown the progressive movement of man's self-understanding and the various stages in the growing awareness of sin with their corresponding forms of scandalisation. One of the ultimate and most intense expressions of sin is the sin of not believing in the forgiveness of

[20] XI, 227; VIII, III.

sins. "First it was weakness, in despair not to will to be oneself. Now this is an act of defiance, for it is defiance not to will to be the person whom one is, a sinner, and in consequence to wish to dispense with the idea of the forgiveness of sins. Formerly it was an act of defiance, in despair to will to be oneself. Now it is weakness that one wills to be oneself thus (a sinner). Formerly it was defiance to will to be oneself thus despairingly. Now it is weakness that in despair one wills to be a sinner for whom there is no forgiveness."[21] This despairing refusal to believe in the forgiveness of sins is accordingly sin as disobedience against God, because behind the offer of forgiveness stands the divine "Thou shalt": "Thou *shalt* believe in the forgiveness of sins."[22]

In this sin all earlier states of sin are raised to their maximum degree of potency. And likewise in the revolt against the possibility of the forgiveness of sins all other possibilities of resistance and revolt are summed up. If we wish to overcome this final scandal, then also all other possibilities of scandal must be dissolved in faith. But if we fail to deal with this final state of scandal then scandal itself becomes sin. But just here, where sin reaches its climax and thus has come closest to faith, it becomes especially clear that on the road from sin to faith there cannot be a simple dialectical complete change, but that scandal as the dialectical moment must form the last security of God against the intrusiveness of man. "In the life of the spirit all is dialectical. Thus scandal as a cancelled possibility is a moment in the life of faith; but scandal which moves away from faith is sin. We can accuse a man of not being able to be shocked by Christianity. Then we are speaking as though it were good to be capable of being scandalised. And on the other hand we must also say that to be scandalised and rebel is sin."[23]

Now, as regards this scandalisation which moves away from faith, there is still a final degree of intensification. This consists in neither believing nor taking offence, but in simply denying the right of Christianity to confront one with the decision between being scandalised and believing. "This is the

[21] XI, 223; VIII, 107.　　　　[22] XI, 226; VIII, 111.
[23] XI, 226 n.; VIII, 110 n.

sin against the Holy Ghost. Here the rebellion of the self
becomes most desperate. Not only does it repudiate Christianity as a whole, but makes it a lie and an untruth."[24] The
intention of revelation is to throw a ring around man in order
to bring him to the consciousness of his sin and so to faith. But
man can simply step outside the ring. Then sin becomes an
offensive war against God in His self-revelation. Since
Kierkegaard argues from the standpoint of the claim of God,
he must see in this too a scandalised revolt, and that in its
strongest possible form. "The sin against the Holy Ghost is
the positive expression of scandalisation."[25] Here man not
only turns against Christianity but gives it up completely
*modo ponendo*. The fact that Kierkegaard thus judges this
attitude, which is usually left out of the discussion, is extremely
significant for his whole dialectic, in which all existential
manifestations can appear only from the standpoint of the
opposition between sin and faith. Thus he says: "This type
of revolt forms the maximum intensification of sin and the one
which is most frequently overlooked, since people do not argue
in a Christian sense from the opposition between sin and
faith."[26]

If, on the other hand, at the parting of the ways man rejects
the possibility of scandal, and believes, then his faith will not
only have to contain the echo of this possibility as a phase which
has been overcome, but in every new act of faith as long as he is
an existing person, he will have to turn back again ever afresh
to that crux. This does not mean that life in faith is led only
by fits and starts and possesses no evenness and continuity.
He who grows in faith becomes ever more himself and remains
bound to that concrete personal identity. This confers upon
his existence its continuity. This continuity may be that of sin,
which, as we have seen, at every moment when it is not overcome by faith, develops as a mere condition into "an ever-
increasing, positing continuum."[27] But it may also be the
continuity conferred by faith—the continuous shattering of the
state of sinfulness—by the fact that man through the forgiveness

---

[24] XI, 234; VIII, 118.          [25] XI, 235; VIII, 119.
[26] XI, 241; lacking in *Ges. W.*, VIII, 124 (conclusion).
[27] XI, 216; VIII, 100.

of sins lives his life in creative renewal. This latter kind of existence Kierkegaard describes as a movement on the spot. "To become is to move away from the spot, but to become oneself is to move on the spot."[28] This means that the self in the free development of its possibilities is bound to the necessity of becoming what it is. Only under this condition is it true that "ideality breaks forth in a dialectical leap, accompanied by the positive note—'see, all things are made new'—and by the negative passionate awareness of the absurd, to which the idea of renewal corresponds."[29] Within the concrete context of his own existence the believer fights for the possibility of freely deciding within the bonds of his necessity. "This is the very struggle of faith—if you will, a mad struggle for the freedom of possibility. For possibility is the sole saving factor."[30] And he believes that with God all things are possible.

In spite of all the intermediate psychological stages of anxiety and repentance which Kierkegaard has shown to lie on the path from sin to faith, the emergence of faith itself cannot be tracked to its source and clearly established. In this matter we can only say what Kierkegaard in his *Taten der Liebe* has expounded with reference to the centurion of Capernaum: "If we imagine some one asking the Christian Church: 'Is it certain that I have faith?' the Christian Church would answer: 'Be it unto you according to your faith.' Or what would Christ have thought of the centurion if, instead of coming to Him full of faith, he had come in order privately to discover whether he had faith or not? 'Be it unto you according to your faith' —this means to say: it is eternally certain that things will happen to you according to the measure of your faith; Christianity guarantees you this; but whether you, just you, have faith, is a matter which is no part of the doctrine and message of Christianity, for it is not its function to tell you that you have faith."[31]

---

[28] XI, 149; VIII, 33 (very freely translated).
[29] IV, 289 n.; V, 11 n.        [30] XI, 151; VIII, 35.
[31] IV, 358; *Leben und Walten der Liebe* (cited below as *Walten der Liebe*), tr. A. Dorner and C. Schrempf, Jena 1924, 388.

## SECOND PROVISIONAL ACCOUNT OF THE DIALECTICAL
## METHOD

*(i) The dialectician derives the datum of revelation from the Christian tradition, and for this purpose makes use of the structure of Church doctrine, while realising that his own special task does not lie in dogmatic work.*

We have seen how Kierkegaard in the *Philosophische Brocken* has made the datum of revelation the central theme of his dialectic of existence. But he introduced this datum merely as "an experiment in thought," apart from its historical setting, which he added later in the *Unwissenschaftliche Nachschrift*. In this way he worked out the decisively Christian existential categories as distinct from existential understanding proper to philosophies of ethical and religious immanence.

But how does he arrive at this datum? Naturally he takes it from the Christian tradition, and in elucidating the problems to which it gives rise, he uses to a large extent the dogmatic definitions produced by Christian doctrine, partly in critical reaction to the theology of his time. Thus he by no means rejects dogmatic work, but himself makes use of the Church's elaboration of doctrine. In the introduction to his *Begriff der Angst* he even gives a short sketch of a Christian philosophy of knowledge in order to show how sin is to be treated from the point of view of the categories, and in that connexion defines the relation of dogmatics to metaphysics, ethics and psychology. But his primary concern in this is to insist on the correct preaching about sin, and he shows how such preaching is ruined if sin is expounded from a falsely scientific point of view, and adds that "dogmatics is seldom handled centrally and essentially."[1] However, he himself realises that his own special task does not consist in dogmatic work and can even say somewhat surprisingly: "Doctrine, as normally expounded, is on the whole correct. Hence I am not quarrelling about that."[2]

---

[1] *S. V.*, IV, 292; *Ges. W.*, V, 13.   [2] *S. K. P.*, x.3, 635.

*(ii) The direct communication of the datum of revelation must be worked into the oblique communication characteristic of the dialectic of existence.*

Thus Kierkegaard takes the datum of revelation from Church doctrine. But the question is how such a datum is to be communicated in order that it may impinge on the hearer's existence. Socratic dialectic, in which the interlocutors help each other towards a deeper personal self-understanding, does not suffice here, because the decisive truth about life is a fact that is external to man and that must be conveyed directly as a piece of information. Nevertheless, such direct communication must be worked into the oblique communication of truth characteristic of Socratic dialectic if it is to prove a challenge to existence. The dialectic of a discussion aimed at a deeper personal self-understanding remains also a task for Christian communication. Kierkegaard discussed the problems arising in this connexion in the sketch of a lecture dating from 1847, and entitled "Die Dialektik der ethischen und ethisch-religiösen Mitteilung."[3] There he says: "The difference between education in ethics and education in religiously based ethics is merely this, that ethics straightforwardly concerns the universally human, whereas religious or Christian education must first impart information. Man as such is moral through his awareness of the moral law, but man as such is not Christian through his religious sense; in the latter case a certain amount of communication of knowledge is first required and then the situation is the same as in regard to ethics. The ultimate aim of the instruction is not simply to convey knowledge but to educate and train as in the sphere of art. Here lies the merit of my use of the pseudonyms: within the sphere of Christianity I have discovered the usefulness of Socratic midwifery."[4] Hence the imparting of information is "merely something provisional."[5] Quite apart from the fact that this communication of information must take place directly, there is a further point: "The one who communicates has authority as regards the information communicated, an authority which is primary,[6]

---

[3] *Op. cit.*, VIII.2(B), 79-89.     [4] *Op. cit.*, 82₁₃.

[5] *Op. cit.*, 85₂₉.     [6] *Op. cit.*, 83, p. 160.

whereas in ethical communication the teacher and the pupil are on the same level.

### (iii) *For the direct communication of knowledge the teacher requires authority.*

The theme of the authority of the one who instructs—or his "competence," as we may translate the Danish "*myndighed*"— exercises quite a decisive influence in Kierkegaard's consideration of the method he should adopt. According to the above argument, it would appear that the difference between the communicator and the recipient of the information is merely that the one already knows what must still be learnt by the other. This in itself offers no special difficulty. The communicator needs only to state directly what is to be objectively known whether in the form of a hypothesis as in the experiment of the *Brocken*, whether as a dogmatic formula as in the case of original sin, discussed in the *Begriff der Angst*, so that he may then concern himself with the recipient's subjective appropriation of what is now for the first time known to the end that the provisional imparting of knowledge may become a communication of power. In thus far the matter offered no special difficulty for Kierkegaard, especially as he was speaking within the Christian sphere where the information was already known and therefore it could only be a question of turning mere knowledge into something which vitally impinged on the existence of the knower. This is the crux of the difficulty.

(*a*) *Authority lies in the power to make effective the demand which revelation makes on personal existence.* The difficulty therefore lies not in the mere objective communication of the datum of revelation and its dogmatic consequences and detailed description, but in making effective the claim which this datum raises as regards the subjective existence of the recipient. The authority of the communicator lies in his ability to make this claim felt. In the last analysis the claim inheres in the fact itself, since this is the truth and as such is itself *index et iudex sui et falsi*. But within what sphere of reference is it to prove itself the truth? Obviously reason, active in man's self-knowledge, cannot be the arbiter, since man, who by the light of this reason thinks himself to dwell in the truth, must now recognise by the light of revelation that he exists in untruth. Human reason cannot by its own unaided powers lead itself *ad absurdum*. At the most it can understand theoretically the implications that would follow if revelation consisted in the paradox of asserting that God becomes a particular man, and by arguing *e concessis* it can deal with the possible consequences for human existence of this hypothetical datum. Thus it can explicate the human situation on the basis of this presupposition, it can analyse its categories in contradistinction to those of Socratic existence and from a categorical point of view can establish the implications that would follow if this revelational datum exercised its effect and confronted the intellect inevitably as a paradox. It may even, from an anthropological and psychological point of view, investigate the modifications of human existence which would flow from the impact of this datum; it may equally well examine and categorically establish the subjective resistance which, in the form of scandalisation, would be offered to this paradoxical fact; and it may also do all this in regard to the condition of faith which triumphs over the scandal and brings man into happy acceptance of the paradox. All these matters can be communicated partly by direct and partly by indirect means. But any such communication would not convey the claim of the revelational fact on the total existence of the recipient, since the operative truth and reality of the fact remains *in suspenso* so long as the state of glad surrender is not attained in which the phase of scandal is overcome by the assured faith of the believer and therewith revelation has proved itself to be true.

(*b*) *As the author of the pseudonymous writings Kierkegaard speaks without authority and wishes only to draw attention to the fact of Christianity.* What we have been discussing in the previous section is the form of communication which Kierkegaard adopts as far as his pseudonymous writings are concerned. He lays the greatest stress on his repeated assertion that he speaks "without authority." At the close of his review "Über meine Wirksamkeit als Schriftsteller" dating from 1851 he says: "Without authority, to draw attention to the phenomenon of religion and of Christianity—that is the description which applies to the whole of my literary activity, considered in its entirety. From the start I stated with the utmost clarity and consistently repeated that I had no authority; I prefer to consider myself as the *reader* of my writings rather than as the *author* of them."[7] With this last sentence Kierkegaard, the author and teacher who communicates truth, plainly puts himself on a level with the pupil and recipient and renounces any use of authority.

Of course in this attitude he does not leave the truth of the revelational fact *in suspenso*, in so far as he leaves us in no doubt that he assumes its implied authority over human existence to be essentially right. In order to preclude the possibility of any such doubt he publishes concurrently with the pseudonymous writings the talks of a religious and, later, Christian nature which appear under his own name, and in which he addresses himself directly to "the individual," in order to urge upon him with all the force at his command the acceptance of Christian existence.

(*c*) *Kierkegaard presents the truth of revelation only dialectically and resigns any attempt to prove it.* That Kierkegaard in all this speaks "without authority" is a fact which has a twofold significance. Firstly, he gives up any attempt to prove the truth of revelation and of the dogmatic affirmations which flow from it. He unfolds this truth in a dialectical aspect only, i.e. in such a way as to discuss the pros and cons of it, and then to leave the reader to decide for himself. For example, as a criterion for the truth of the doctrine he can adduce the fact that two such different men as Pascal and Feuerbach, setting out from opposite presuppositions, the one a believer, the other a rebel, say the same thing: "That this is the true religious outlook on suffering I know from the fact that I can compare two writers who say the same thing. Feuerbach, who worships the principle of health, says that the religious life (especially the life of the Christian) is constantly a story of suffering; we need only look at the life of Pascal and we shall know enough about that. Pascal himself says precisely the same thing: suffering is the natural condition of the Christian (as health is that of the

---

[7] *S. V.*, xiii, 501; *Ges. W.*, x, 166. Except as stated, all further refs. in this section are to *S. V.* and *Ges. W.*

natural man), and he became a Christian and spoke out of the heart of his Christian experience."[8]

When Kierkegaard refers to and argues from dogmatic assertions, he does not use them as principles from which the truth is to be inferred, but as presuppositions in the dialectic process, which recur later as conclusions, as for example, in the *Begriff der Angst*, where he says: "Hence original sin is not to be explained on any dogmatic basis; its explanation can only be that we presuppose it as the Greeks presupposed that perpetual flux of which their nature speculation had much to say, and which lay beyond the grasp of all knowledge."[9]

Even in the *Reden* he claims no authority for himself; they are only a necessary part of his plan, which is to reduce the mass to its individual units: "In each of the pseudonymous writings this appears in one way or another in relation to the individual; but it is predominantly a question of the aesthetically inclined individual, the individual in a pre-eminent sense, the outstanding man, etc. In each of the edificatory writings this appears and as officially as possible, again in relation to the individual, but it is the individual who is or can be any man. The starting-point of the pseudonymous writings lies in fact in the differences between men as regards intellect, culture, and so on; the starting-point for the edificatory writings lies in what is edifying, i.e. the universally human. But in this dualism consists precisely the dialectic of the individual. 'The individual' can mean the unique and 'the individual' can mean each man. If, now, we wish to arouse attention dialectically, then we always use the category of the individual in this twofold sense. The pride in the one thought irritates some and the humility in the other thought frightens others away; but the confusingness in this dualism awakens attention dialectically, and, as we have said, this dualism is precisely what is implied in the idea of 'the individual.' "[10]

(*d*) *Kierkegaard also renounces any attempt to vouch for the truth of revelation on personal grounds.* We see therefore that Kierkegaard claims no authority, in the sense that he presupposes the truth of Christianity as a system of doctrine, or argues, for example, on the basis of the dogmas of the Church conceived as authori-

---

[8] vi, 428; iv, 426.     [9] iv, 292; v, 13.     [10] xiii, 601; x, 89.

tative. Secondly, however, he equally renounces the now more penetrating way of vouching for the truth of Christianity by the power of his own existence as a believer, and so acquiring authority as a teacher. On the contrary, he is constantly assuring us that while he knows indeed what Christianity is, he cannot consider himself a Christian and instead enquires of the reader whether he is one. In this connexion we should always be careful to note that Kierkegaard is speaking from within Christianity and aims at disintegrating the mass of Christians into individual units, because only as such have they any chance of truly becoming Christians. "The category of the individual has only once for the first time been used with decisive effect dialectically, and that was by Socrates for the purpose of breaking up the religion of paganism. Conversely, in Christianity it will be used for the second time for the purpose of making (Christian) men real Christians. It is not a question of a principle which the missionary has to use in preaching Christianity to the heathen, but of that principle which the missionary who has to introduce Christianity into Christendom must use within the framework of Christendom itself."[11]

Thus Kierkegaard is very well aware that there are other possible means of conveying the truth of Christianity, even if in consideration of his own special task he makes no use of them. The Christian preacher, for example, does not speak about suffering by simply confronting Pascal and Feuerbach dialectically, but says that Pascal is right and Feuerbach wrong. And he does not discuss dogmas as hypothetical assumptions in a dialectical argument, but appeals directly to their truth. Kierkegaard knows, too, of course, that Christianity was introduced into the world not by way of oblique dialectical communication but by direct proclamation claiming authority. This applies especially to the central fact of revelation, the God-man Himself, with which we must start in any enquiry into the correct use of authority.

(e) *The authoritative aspect of the self-attestation of Jesus.* As we have seen, revelation is not a simple historical fact, but contains a contradiction, inasmuch as it predicates of God historical becoming, although it is of the very essence of the divine to be

[11] xiii, 609; x, 97.

eternal. Thus it is manifested as absolute paradox, which repels by its very absurdity and can be believed only by a constant overcoming of its offensiveness. Since it cannot in its essence be directly apprehended, it has "no immediate contemporaries" but is equally near to all times. Here belief is only possible in a situation of contemporaneity and on the testimony of one who already believes, though the latter can never do more than arouse the attention of the other to the decision for faith which this revelation requires, he can never relieve the other of the necessity for that decision.

But in this account one point is still lacking: Christ did not merely arouse the attention of men to the need for a decision for or against Himself, He also said, "Blessed is he who shall not be offended in me." He did not thus relieve them of the need for decision, but without such a direct statement the *demand* for a decision between faith and scandalisation *would not have been clear*. Here is something more than an arousing of the attention of men. The self-attestation of Jesus as the Christ is thus not a mere communication of information, but rather the truth which Jesus incarnates makes by its very existence the claim to the obedience of faith which must assert itself to overcome all offence. To this extent, the self-attestation of Jesus in the first place draws the attention of mankind to the fact and presence of revelation; secondly, it imparts the necessary knowledge for the understanding of it; and, thirdly, at the same time, it claims to be able to demand authoritatively the decision against scandalisation. In the self-attestation of Jesus these three aspects of His self-communication are not separable, since He is the way, the truth and the life. Likewise for the recipient they merge together in the triumphant self-affirmation of faith.

(*f*) *The aspect of authority in the witness of posterity.* What is there in the witness of posterity which corresponds to the self-attestation of the revelation? Kierkegaard says in the *Brocken* with regard to the relation of the hearers at first and second hand: "Had the contemporary generation left behind them nothing but the words 'We have believed that in such and such a year God manifested Himself in humility as a servant of mankind, lived and taught among us, and then died,' it would have been more than enough. The contemporary generation did what was necessary; for its slight *avertissement*, its *"nota bene"* to world history, was sufficient to become, for posterity, a challenge to attention; and the most extensive and detailed report could not have done more." Or, to sum it up; "The belief of posterity is occasioned by the report of contemporaries but becomes effective in virtue of a condition which it receives directly from God."[12] This point about the "more than enough" is directed in the context of this passage against all attempts to attain a more direct access to the datum of revelation through a more exact knowledge of the historical facts. Furthermore, it should in this connexion be emphasised that the believer of a later day cannot believe in virtue of and for the sake of the belief of contemporaries, but that this testimony of contemporary belief can become for him only the occasion for the decision between faith and scandalisation. It is not even legitimate for him to enquire about the reliability of the faith of the first witnesses. Even the latter cannot guarantee for him the truth of what is to be believed. This can only be done by God Himself, whose action is manifested in the emergence of the believer's assured faith. "The historical fact that God has lived in human form is the main point."[13] But the problem is just this, namely how this historical fact in its *factuality* is attested for posterity.

*(iv) Revelation considered as an historical fact, and, through authoritative communication, the securing of its historicity against possible attempts to transform it philosophically into an eternal truth.*

After what has just been said, it might appear that the believer of later times, who must believe neither because of the faith of original witnesses nor on the strength of an historical report of facts, but must rather take both these only as an occasion for his own original decision to believe, comes to believe not only in the meaning and truth of the fact, but also in the factuality of the event itself, purely as a result of his own creative personal decision. But this would mean in effect that the believer simply postulates the fact of revelation as an

---

[12] IV, 266; VI, 94-5.    [13] IV, 265-6; VI, 94.

historical fact through his believing insight into its eternal truth. In the self-attestation of Jesus, however, the converse is the case, namely that the question of belief first arises through confrontation by the historical fact, and only then, as the believer by his personal assurance comes to appreciate the significance of the fact, does the transformation of his personal existence as believer take place. How is this reversal of the situation to be prevented, and how are we to avoid changing the Gospel proclamation which flows from the self-attestation of Jesus into the communication of a luminous, albeit paradoxical, truth of existential philosophy?

This question plays an important part in present-day theological discussion. It is a common criticism of the theology of Rudolf Bultmann, for example, who at decisive points refers to Kierkegaard, that as a result of the influence of the existential philosophy of Martin Heidegger he has succumbed to this very danger of reversing the order of fact and faith. In this work, naturally, we are not concerned with Bultmann and the correctness or otherwise of his understanding of Kierkegaard, but with Kierkegaard himself. For the latter the inferences which might be drawn from such a reversal were not so vividly urgent as they are for us today. But we must ask whether Kierkegaard himself was at all aware of this problem or secured himself against the danger of this reversal of meaning. In actual fact this means that we must ask whether, in the published work of Kierkegaard and in the dialectical method which it employs, there is to be found any attempt to see in the mode of communication by later witnesses any note corresponding to the fact of the incarnation of God in Jesus in its historical factuality.

What form then does the " 'nota bene' to world history" assume in the self-communication of later witnesses? "The absolute fact is an historical fact and is as such the object of faith. Hence the historical aspect of it must be duly emphasised. Of course the historical in itself may not become absolutely decisive for individuals (thus revelation confronts us as a plain fact of history, although this implies something self-contradictory; for an historical fact is not an absolute fact and does not possess the power to call forth an absolute decision);

but neither may the historical element be removed, for then we should have merely an eternal fact."[14] This seems to be a precise allusion to our problem.

If, then, we seriously take revelation as an historical fact, we must also reckon with its historical consequences. Kierkegaard would by no means dispute this, but would urge the following consideration: "If this fact appeared in the world as the absolute paradox, then this cannot be changed by anything which follows later; for to all eternity the later development remains a consequence of this paradox, and hence is, in the last resort, just as improbable as the paradox itself, unless we were to assume that the consequences had retrospective power to change the paradox itself, which would be about as easy as to suppose that a son had retrospective power to change the nature of his father. . . . Hence to be faced by the consequences is just as doubtful an advantage as that of having direct certainty; he who naïvely interprets the consequences is just as deceived as he who mistakes direct certainty for faith."[15]

(a) *The justification and the dubiety of the attempt to secure the revelational fact by means of the Bible.* In the historical setting given to this problem in the *Nachschrift*, this question is discussed with reference to the Bible. For posterity the testimony of Holy Scripture takes the place of the self-attestation of Jesus, and it finds in that testimony the historical fact whose purpose it is to challenge it to the decision between scandalisation and faith. Once again the difficulty is as follows: "Christianity is something historical (in relation to which the maximum degree of knowledge constitutes only a rough guide and the most masterly historical study yields only the most masterly approximate results), and yet as so much history it claims to have decisive significance for my eternal felicity."[16] If I attempt to prove the Bible to contain historical facts and hence on a historico-critical basis to establish that (1) Christ did in fact live on this earth, and (2) was such as He is reported to have been by the testimony of Scripture, I can still only arrive at approximative conclusions which cannot be decisive for or against the issue which is here in question. "What a piece of

---

[14] IV, 262-3; VI, 91.      [15] IV, 257-8; VI, 86-7.
[16] VII, 13 n.; VI, 120 n.

good fortune it is that this so desirable hypothesis, the supreme desire of critical theology, turns out to be an impossibility because even the fullest realisation of its aim can only yield approximate results! And again how fortunate for the scholars that the fault is in no sense theirs! If all the angels united their efforts, they could still only afford us approximative conclusions, because in this matter we have only historical knowledge, that is, an approximation as our sole certitude—but it is far too slender a basis on which to build eternal felicity."[17]

If, however, in this embarrassment we take refuge in a doctrine of inspiration as the dogmatic guarantee for the conclusions of historical science, the difficulty still remains. "The lack of agreement between inspiration and critical research is parallel to that between eternal salvation and critical considerations, because inspiration itself is only an object of faith. Or are people so eager to criticise because the books are inspired? Thus the earnest believer knows that the books are inspired, but he does not know which books it is of which he believes that they are inspired. Or does the doctrine of inspiration result from criticism, so that the latter in doing its work at the same time proves that the books are inspired? In this case we should never arrive at the hypothesis of inspiration, even in its highest form, for critical work is only approximative."[18]

Every attempt to guarantee the results of criticism by means of the doctrine of inspiration, or conversely to support this doctrine by critical conclusions, is an absurd self-contradiction. "When faith begins to cease to be faith, then proof becomes necessary in order that the unbeliever may still enjoy bourgeois esteem. The rhetorical stupidities which in this respect have been perpetrated by clerical speakers as a result of an interchange of categories does not bear speaking of."[19]

In its canonicity Holy Scripture, as a paradoxical-historical fact, may well *emphasise* the historical aspect of revelation, but in doing so it shows clearly that it is itself the outcome of a paradox and therefore is paradoxical. For neither can it change into immediate certitude the doubtfulness of faith called upon to decide against the moment of offensiveness.

[17] VII, 19; VI, 125.   [18] VII, 14 n.; VI, 120 n.
[19] VII, 19; VI, 126.

Just as the fact of revelation becomes dialectical as soon as I am personally to appropriate it,[20] so it is too with the witness which the Bible bears to this fact. And in this connexion it is impossible to bring in some authority in order to terminate dialectical questioning. If this were attempted and the credibility of the Bible were for instance based on the authority of the Church or of the preaching office, this again would not spell the end of dialectics. "For in that case dialectics would merely turn round and ask what then constitutes authority, and why this particular thing should be regarded as authoritative. Thus it would not question the faith which the interlocutor had on the basis of a certain authority but the faith which he had in that particular authority."[21]

(b) *Security through the ordination of the preacher.* Let us take a step further this dialectical questioning of the ecclesiastical preaching office in order to clarify the character of this type of authority. Here we must take into account what Kierkegaard says about the essence of a sermon in contradistinction to a religious discourse. He says with reference to his own discourses: "They are not sermons: the sermon implies the Christian and belongs to the office of a clergyman; and a clergyman is what he is essentially through ordination; and ordination implies a paradoxical change in a human teacher, whereby he becomes in time something other than he would be through the immanent unfolding of genius, talents, gifts, and so on. But no man is eternally ordained, or, as soon as he is born, able to remember himself as ordained. On the other hand, ordination confers a *character indelebilis.* What can this mean but that, here again, time is decisive for eternity, and consequently that an immanentist back-reference to eternal reality is precluded? In regard to ordination again we are confronted by the Christian *"nota bene."*[22] This paradoxical change in the clergyman as a result of ordination is something which flows from the fact of revelation and which accentuates the historical aspect of that fact thus attested. It imparts to the clergyman an authority over against the hearer. "Authority is a specific quality; conferred upon the Apostle through his

---

[20] Cp. above, p. 60, n. 2.      [21] VII, 14 n. 1; VI, 120 n. 2.

[22] VII, 232; VI, 345.

calling, conferred upon the clergyman through his ordination. By the mere fact that it is uttered with authority, the discourse becomes a sermon; and in our day it is wholly forgotten that preaching is of this character."[23] Thus the clergyman has this authority not as an objectively valid quality (in spite of the *character indelebilis*), but in virtue of his activity as preacher. His authority is seen in the fact that he does not depend for the validity of what he says on the insight and understanding of the hearer or on his own faith, but on the commission which he has received through ordination, in virtue of his office to challenge the hearer to decision exactly as Christ does. For this reason the preacher may not enter into a discussion with the hearer about the truth of his preaching. "To a certain extent it is legitimate for the Christian speaker to discuss doubts —but preaching operates solely through the authority of Scripture and of Christ's Apostles. It is therefore absolutely heretical to argue with doubt in a sermon, however well one might be able to do so."[24] "A preacher, if he is to preach in the right spirit, after announcing a word of Christ, should go on to speak as follows: 'This word is the voice of Him to whom according to His own statement all authority is given in heaven and on earth. You have now, my friend, to consider in your own mind, whether you are willing to bow to this authority or not, whether you will to believe and accept this word or not. But if you are unwilling to do so, do not, for God's sake, accept the message merely because it is deeply thought-out or clever or finely expressed; in that case you would be presuming to criticise God and mocking divine things.' Thus as soon as the authority, the specific paradoxical authority of the Christian preacher supervenes, then the situation becomes fundamentally different; then that kind of affectionate adjustment to the hearer which otherwise is both desirable and permissible becomes guilty presumption."[25] And how can the preacher prove that he has this authority? In this respect, what Kierkegaard says of the Apostle applies to him also: "If he could *materially* demonstrate his Apostleship, he would in fact not be an Apostle at all. He has no other proof than his own state-

[23] XI, 101 n.; x, 148 n.    [24] *S. K. P.*, VIII.1(A), 6.
[25] XI, 106; x, 153.

ment. And it must be thus, otherwise the believer would enter into a direct relationship with him, rather than into a para-doxical one." Thus he proves his authority only by the fact that he employs it, in that he preaches and in so doing under no circumstances appeals for confirmation to any worldly power or recognition.

Does then the authority which the clergyman wields spell an end to dialectics? In no sense. It merely directs the dialectical questioning to the essential point. Inasmuch as preaching with authority draws attention to the fact of revelation and requires its appropriation, it plainly invites a dialectical approach. In so doing the preacher refers the hearer back from his own authority *via* the authority of Scripture and the Apostles to the authority of Christ Himself, and thus, both in virtue of his own ordination and by means of these other references, em-phasises the historicity of revelation. The authority of the ordained clergyman, of Scripture, and of the Apostles constitutes that "*nota bene*" to world history which suffices, for men of later times, as an occasion of faith—no more but also no less. This makes clear the distinction between a faith which the believer has through confidence in those authorities and a faith which he has in them. In no event must he believe in them.

(*c*) *Security through the historical fact of the Church.* These paradoxical-historical facts—the canon of Holy Scripture, and the ordination of the clergyman as well as the authority which they exercise—would not exist apart from the *Church* which confers on them this authority. The matter might also be expressed by saying that in the authority claimed by them the authority of the Church finds expression. But this may not be taken to mean that the Church (which of course is itself only a paradoxical-historical fact) could by its peculiar authority guarantee these other authorities. Kierkegaard explains this in the *Nachschrift* in reference to the attempt, which in the main goes back to Grundtvig, to replace the collapsing authority of Scripture by that of the Church. In this connexion he does not go into the most undialectical conception of the Church which Roman Catholicism represents, since he considers it altogether too misguided: "The armour of the Catholic Church against the intrusion of dialectics, which it believes it

has in the visible presence of the Pope, we will here leave out
of account."[26]

"As formerly the Bible was supposed to decide objectively
what is Christian and what is not, so now the Church is meant
to constitute the secure objective criterion. To describe it in
more detail, this means the living Word in the Church, the
credal confessions, and the Word operative in the sacraments."[27]
Let us take first of all the credal confessions. If these are taken
to be the guarantee of objective truth, then the problem
immediately arises as to how the subject is to be related to
them. "If the truth is the spirit, then the truth is interiority,
and not the naïve and, as it were, unembarrassed attitude of
direct mental assent to a sum of doctrines, even though this
attitude, to introduce new confusion, is described by the most
decisively subjective term 'faith.' "[27] Thus here again we would
have only a new form of that attitude of "believing in something"—this time in the objective truth of doctrine—an attitude
which the dialectic of interiorisation prevents. But, in any
case, what can be the meaning of "objective truth" in this
connexion? The difficulty which, with regard to Scripture, it is
desired to avoid consisted in the fact that Scripture was something past, a series of historical documents, and thus permitted
no relationship to itself based on direct certainty. In the reality
of the Church, as seen in its credal confessions, I am, on the
contrary, confronted by something alive and present. It needs
to adduce no other proof of itself than just the very fact that it
is there. But it goes on to assert, of course, that the Apostolic
Church is present in it, and that therefore it is identical with the
Church of the Apostles commissioned by Jesus Christ. This
implies that it is an historical factor, and it must consequently
produce the proof of its identity. If it is attempted to prove
this identity by demonstrating its historically continuous life,
and the Apostolic origin of the credal confessions, then we are
landed in exactly the same situation as we were in when the
Bible theory was in question. For now a certain amount of
introductory scientific instruction is necessary, and this can
only lead to approximative results. Hence with regard to the
credal confessions no other attitude is possible but that of

[26] VII, 23-4; VI, 129-30.            [27] VII, 27; VI, 132.

renouncing a false authority claiming to be objective, and such
as would exclude dialectics, and contenting oneself with that
authority which, as being itself a paradoxical-historical fact,
calls attention to the decisive significance of the paradoxical-
historical fact of revelation in order to overcome the gulf of
history through the contemporaneity which marks the assured
faith of the believer.

(*d*) *Security through the Sacrament.* If we wish to base objective
certainty on the sacrament of baptism, the question again
arises whether faith can legitimately cling to baptism as an
empirical fact such as would preclude dialectics. Quite apart
from the almost inevitable demand for a repeatability of
baptism in order that the baptised might be more strongly
assured of the actual performance of the sacrament, everything
again depends on personal appropriation. "If it is said that
the security of baptism against all doubt lies in the fact that
thereby God does something for us, that is of course merely an
illusion intended to exclude the dialectical approach; for at
once dialectics demands the inner personal appropriation of
this idea. Every genius, even the greatest that has ever lived,
must use exclusively all his strength for the purpose of such
inner personal appropriation. But people want to be free
from doubt once for all, and when doubt assails them, their
faith turns not to God but to the external fact of having been
once truly baptised. If there were not concealed here much
sham and pretence, long since there would have been seen
psychologically remarkable cases of distressed souls yearning
for this certainty of knowing that they had been truly baptised.
If only it were a question of ten thousand dollars, people would
hardly leave undecided the question of the certainty attaching
to '*our*' baptism."[28] In this connexion we have to think not only
of the relatively easily producible certification of our baptism as
having actually been performed, but of the whole problematics
of its rightfulness and effectiveness both as regards the baptiser
and the one who is baptised. But even if we were to cut the
Gordian knot with a purely magical theory of baptism as
effective *ex opere operato*, we should still be getting no further
than the forbidden attitude of believing "in something"—"in

[28] VII, 33 n.; VI, 139 n. 2.

this case, believing that one has been truly baptised"—hence "relieving our uncertainties by the support of a purely superstitious point of view; for, as has been said above, every fixed limit intended to exclude the dialectical approach is *eo ipso* superstitious."[29]

*(v) The relation of Kierkegaard's dialectic of existence to the exercise of authority by the being, the pronouncements, and the action of the Church.*

We have now seen what significance attaches to the exercise of authority by the being, the pronouncements, and the action of the Church, namely, the significance not of excluding the dialectics of subjective appropriation, but of emphasising the historical factuality of revelation in order thereby to set in motion the dialectics of inner personal appropriation. We now proceed to ask why Kierkegaard for his part speaks without authority and lays such decisive stress on the fact that it is his special task to arouse attention to the fact of Christianity in a non-authoritative way, whereas the Church does the same thing with authority.

*(a) The dialectic of Kierkegaard does not stand in opposition to the authoritative proclamation of the Church, but is dialectically related to the latter.* In the light of our discussion so far there can be no question that Kierkegaard would consider the authoritative action of the Church through Scripture, doctrine, preaching, and the sacraments, as false and unjustified only in so far as the intention of such authority might be to facilitate for the believer a direct, externalised certainty such as would exclude dialectics. To this extent, the work of Kierkegaard is even a contribution of fundamental importance to the philosophical clarification of the true basis and right use of such authority. None of the theological insights which Kierkegaard expressed through his pseudonymous writings could basically have prevented him from accepting an office in the church and exercising the authority it gave. Everything which he does without authority depends even on the presupposition that others do the same thing at the same time with authority. This is true

[29] VII, 32; VI, 138.

not only in the sense that his activity as a writer presupposes the background of organised Christianity—in order to be able to come forward as a corrective to it—and hence presupposes also the authoritative action of the Church which is necessary to its continuance. Besides this, he must desire the use of authority by the Church, because otherwise he could not fulfil his own mission rightly and dialectically. The fulfilment of that mission is only possible through a dialectical relation to the activity of the Church, and would have no meaning otherwise.

Let us recall the question as to whether Kierkegaard's dialectic of existence is secure against the possibility that the fact of revelation might become a mere philosophical, albeit paradoxical, truth, and that belief in its actuality might become dependent on insight into its true meaning. As a result, the fact of revelation might degenerate into a postulate of existential dialectics, and finally, in consequence, might altogether be lost.[30]  In answering this question we found that Kierkegaard was very well aware of the danger of this reversal of meaning and in order to combat it repeatedly emphasised that the absolute fact of revelation is not an eternal fact but an historical fact.  But the whole question is how this historical element can be effectively conveyed in the dialectics of communication.  This happens by means of those paradoxical facts in which the authority of Church proclamation inheres: the Apostolate, Scripture, the credal confessions, and the sacraments.  These constitute the " *'nota bene'* to world history"

---

[30] On this question cp. my work *Kritischer Idealismus in theologischer Sicht,* Munich 1934, note 12, pp. 104 ff.  There I brought forward this point in a discussion with Heinrich Barth and said: "It might be shown that with Kierkegaard, in spite of his more correct ideas, the subordination of reality to truth is just as little excluded as it is in the work of H. Barth, and for the same reason: because he too argues without taking into account the fact of proclamation."  Put in this way, this is not tenable.  It would only be correct if we considered Kierkegaard's existential dialectic in itself apart from the contemporaneous event of proclamation, as philosophers and theologians have constantly attempted to do.  But that is just what we must not do.  Kierkegaard does not himself argue with open reference to the fact of proclamation but assumes that the latter is at the same time taking place through the ministry of the church.

in the testimony of posterity, by means of which the historicity of revelation is emphasised.

Since Kierkegaard in the exercise of his own dialectic in its twofold aspect—that of subjective interior appropriation and that of communication of truth—does not himself make use of this kind of authority, but nevertheless needs it if familiarity with the fact of revelation is not to degenerate into an existential dialectic of human self-understanding, therefore the dialectics which he practises stands in an indissoluble dialectical relation to the authoritative proclamation of the Church.

(b) *For the purpose of his own dialectics Kierkegaard makes no use of Church authority because only so can he make clear the misuse of that authority by organised Christianity.* We are now in a position to consider the question why Kierkegaard made no use of Church authority in the fulfilment of his own special task. That he did not become a clergyman was based on personal grounds which do not concern us here. Essentially, at all events, he might have become one. But if the oblique form of communication practised by Kierkegaard stands in a dialectically integral relation to the direct authoritative communication proper to Church proclamation, then the question arises whether the converse is not also true, namely that such proclamation dialectically requires for its completion an oblique mode of communication as its counterpart.

This converse is not so easily to be inferred, for the two sides are not faced with the same exigency. The direct communication of proclamation is a *conditio sine qua non* for Christianity. But the same necessity cannot be postulated for the oblique communication of existential dialectics, which serves the purpose of inner personal appropriation. The extent to which this mode of communication is necessary depends on the spiritual situation in which proclamation takes place; and here it is a question of judgment. In any event, Kierkegaard was of the opinion that in his time it was scarcely possible any longer to receive a direct impression of what Christianity was. The reason for this, he considered, was that the epoch was so deeply involved in sophisticated thought that one must compel it to think things through to the end in order that it might once more reach the starting-point of the simple believer. On the other hand, it appeared to him ever more doubtful whether Christianity was sure enough of itself to enter into the necessary discussion with its intellectual environment. It had already made far too many concessions to the latter, with the consequence that its own authority had become discredited and could no longer make itself felt in the right way. This was true not only of its relation to secular knowledge, particularly philosophy and historical science. It was equally and perhaps even more true of the Church as a sociological factor within society. Just as the proclamation of the Church had been over-adjusted to secular knowledge, so the Church as a community and its ideas of Christian living had been levelled down to the state and secular society and their characteristic ideals of life.

(c) *Whether Kierkegaard's work signifies an attack on the Church or a defence of the Church is for the Church itself to decide.* The dialectical inward personal appropriation of Christianity with which Kierkegaard's work was concerned had inevitably to reveal the condition of existing Christianity, i.e. especially the state of the Church, with whose life and proclamation his own task was indissolubly bound up. The Church might conceive this as an attack on itself. But just because of this integral dialectical relation to the Church, there could be no question, for Kierkegaard, of making such an attack directly and undialectically. His intention was rather to defend the Church by putting into its hand points of view which were calculated to make it unassailable in controversy. But whether the Church looked at the matter from the one or the other standpoint was its own business, which it must decide for itself, "for from a dialectical point of view defence and attack are within a hair's breadth the same thing."[31]

Thus matters stood when the pseudonymous writings had reached a certain conclusion with the *Nachschrift*. In the light of the categories which Kierkegaard employed in this work it was of no consequence whether the Church saw in his work an attack or a defence. His dialectic remained the same in significance whichever way it was regarded. But he had now completed other writings in which he exposed the state of

[31] *S. K. P.*, x.2, 163.

organised Christianity still more aggressively and sharply than heretofore and thus pressed upon the Church the urgency of deciding whether it was prepared to see in his work an attack or a defence. His realisation of the possible consequences caused him, before the publication of these writings, carefully to review once more his whole position and the method he was adopting. We must now enquire what fresh points of view as regards his dialectical method result from this new survey, though we shall take account of Kierkegaard's own purely personal motives in this final phase of his work only as far as seems necessary for the clarification of the essential problem.

## 14. ATTACK OR DEFENCE?

It is mainly a question of the two writings *Die Krankheit zum Tode* and *Einübung im Christentum*. The attacks on the present state of Christianity which they contain is nowhere made an independent theme. Just as in the earlier writings the criticism is implied in this, namely that the interiorisation of Christianity through the dialectic of existence which is always its necessary counterpart must question direct forms of communication in the doctrine and preaching of the Church as to the categories employed, and must show where these fail of their purpose. This Kierkegaard does continually and with much severity, constantly reproaching the clergy for their confused use of the categories. But at the same time there is no attempt to call in question the authorities of the Church as such. When, for example, in *Krankheit zum Tode* Kierkegaard brings forward as the decisive point that sin is something positive, he stresses his agreement with orthodox dogmatics: "Orthodoxy has correctly understood that Christianity as a whole loses its firmness and consistency if sin is described in negative terms. For this reason orthodoxy makes it quite clear that a divine revelation must teach fallen man what sin is. And it goes without saying that the paradox, faith, and dogma, these three points, form an alliance which is the surest stay and the firmest bulwark against all heathen wisdom."[1] Hence it is not *dogma* as such, but the misuse of it made by speculative dogmatics which is the object of attack.

It is just the same with regard to the *clergyman*. Kierkegaard does not attack ordination in itself, but will not admit it as valid that a means of livelihood should be made out of the calling of the clergyman as out of all other callings. If the clergy are lacking in the inspiration of faith, then it is no wonder that they suppose it is their job to justify or defend

---

[1] *S. V.*, xi, 207; *Ges. W.* viii, 91. Except as stated, all further refs. in this section are to *S. V.* and *Ges. W.*

Christianity. "But just the same attitude is adopted by 'believing' parsons; either they defend Christianity or they make themselves important by 'understanding' it speculatively. This is called preaching; and it is generally considered a fine thing that the clergy should preach in this way and that such lectures should be listened to. And this is the very reason—and the proof—that Christianity is so far from being what it claims to be that the life of the majority of men, from the Christian point of view, is even too mindless and unspiritual to be described in the stricter sense as sinful."[2]

The point at which the preaching of the clergy is most at fault is that they do not confront men with the scandal of the Gospel because they do not proceed from the Christian imperative "Thou shalt believe," and they are no longer aware of the decisive idea that the opposite of sin is not virtue but faith. If from a Christian point of view it must be right to say that the very indifference to Christ is a form of revolt against the Gospel, yet "in times when Christianity is so badly and scantily proclaimed, that must be understood in a limited sense. Certainly many thousands are living who have heard Christianity preached but have never heard anything of this 'Thou shalt.'[3] Hence the fault of the clergy is not that they use too much authority in their preaching, but that they use too little. "Hence they preach Christianity. But they never speak of authority, and are unable to exercise it; the 'Thou shalt' is never used by them for fear that they should make themselves ridiculous."[4] Instead they entrench themselves falsely behind the authority of their office, when they are being questioned about their own existence.

When the consequences of such preaching are that Christian truth becomes an object of intellectual understanding, instead of the attempt being made to embody it in existence, it is hardly possible to ask the parson any more if his life expresses what he talks about. But "it is his task to be himself. And in the house of God! In an environment, therefore, which requires of him (in the eyes and ears of all) this alone—that he should be himself, true and sincere. That he should be true

---

[2] XI, 214; VIII, 98 (shortened).        [3] XI, 239; VIII, 123.
[4] XII, 211; IX, 202.

means that he himself should be what he preaches; or else should strive to be that; or else should be honest enough to admit that his own life does not accord with his preaching. Ah, of those who ascend into the holy place to preach Christianity, how many there are only perceptive enough to discover the indignation and mockery which they arouse in the sanctuary because they proclaim in an inspired and moving fashion, and with tears, that of which their life is the direct opposite."[5] This criticism of Kierkegaard's concerning the clergyman's personal existence, or rather lack of existence, has nothing to do with the usual requirement of exemplary morals or sincere faith in the pietistic sense. The point is rather that the parson is no longer an integral human being and so does not notice that no real man can exist integrally through the nonsense which he preaches. Of course, in so far as this is not merely comic, it falls under moral categories, for the apparent laziness and thoughtlessness which prevent the preacher from realising that the total personality of the preacher must make itself felt in his preaching spell sheer dishonesty.

But neither does Kierkegaard suggest that the preacher is required to prove the authority of his preaching through his personal existence. But he does attack the opposite case in which "the speaker to a certain extent ceased to be an 'I' and (if this is possible) became a thing."[6] For if the parson has to expound something which has nothing to do with his personal existence, then he can no longer address his hearer as an existent personality either. "Thus the personality of the speaker has faded: he is no longer 'I,' but is identified with the theme of his consideration. And since the 'I' of the speaker faded, of course the hearer's 'thou' similarly disappeared, the 'thou' of him who sits in the congregation, and to whom the discourse is addressed. Yes, matters have now come to such a pass that it is considered being personal to address the congregation thus directly. . . . I, the speaker, am not the man about whom I am speaking (hardly am I the one who am speaking)—it is just a series of reflexions. Whether I do what I preach is no business of yours—as long as my reflexions are true; hardly is it any business of mine, for I owe to myself the same respect as I owe

<hr />

[5] XII, 215; IX, 205-6.     [6] XII, 215; IX, 206.

to any one else, and this forbids me to be personal even with regard to myself. Whether you do what I am exhorting, is no concern of mine, hardly is it your own concern, this is simply a series of reflexions; and at most the point is whether they have given you satisfaction."[7]

In sermons of this kind, which are no sermons at all, Kierkegaard sees the root evil of modern organised Christianity, where all without further question are assumed to be Christians. One's concern is no longer with Christ Himself, but people are content to accept the net result of his life as it lies before us in the 1800 years of Christian history. "In the most illegitimate way people have become those who *know about* Christ, whereas the only legitimate relation to Him is to believe in Him. People have helped each other to know by the net result of his life and the 1800 years of Christian history and the consequences of the original facts, those facts themselves. And as this attitude has gradually come to be considered as the part of wisdom, all the vitality and power have been distilled out of Christianity; the tension of the paradox has been slackened; people become Christians without noticing that they no longer know not the slightest thing about the possibility of scandalisation. . . . People do not know what it means to be shocked and offended by Christianity, still less do they know what it means to worship. And they extol in Christ the very thing in particular about which they would have been most incensed had they lived through the events as contemporaries. . . . Christendom has, without being aware of it, got rid of Christianity. If anything is to be done about this situation, it can only be one thing: that we should attempt to reintroduce Christianity into Christendom."[8] But how can this happen?

This 1800 years of Christian history must be swept aside! But we must carefully consider in what sense Kierkegaard means this. He does not wish to put the clock back in Christian history, and hence his demand has nothing to do with all those attempts to go back to an earlier stage of Christian development, primitive Christianity for example, in order to set over against modern Christianity as an ideal or critical criterion a type of

[7] XII, 216; IX, 206-7.    [8] XII, 33-4; IX, 29-30.

Christianity which has not yet become involved in the complications of history and has developed no dogmatic positions. Kierkegaard is by no means such an unhistorical thinker. His concern is not to replace a later stage of history by an earlier one, but to insist on the presuppositions underlying the situation of contemporaneity with Christ, in which these historical differences—that cannot and ought not be to removed—lose their relevance for faith.

Hence Kierkegaard's intention—and this is important for our question—is not to set aside Church authorities, but to enable them effectively to exercise their true authority. He wishes to prevent them from basing their claim on the "proof of centuries," such as would exclude the shock and scandal inseparable from true Christianity, but rather wishes so to confront individuals with the Christian witness that they cannot avoid the recurring necessity to decide for faith against the moment of scandal, and cannot be in a position simply "to inherit" Christ. "Realising my responsibility before the highest seat of judgment, I therefore am so bold as to say that the words 'Blessed is he who shall not be offended in me' belong essentially to the message of Christ; if not in the same way as the words of the Last Supper, yet in the same way as the words 'Let every one examine himself.' They are Christ's own words; and, especially in the sphere of the Christian Church, they must be repeatedly emphasised and declared explicitly to all. Wherever these words do not sound their note along with other themes, wherever the account given of the Christian Gospel is not at every point penetrated by this thought, there so-called Christianity is blasphemy."[9]

Christian doctrine, too, dogmatics, must not come to mean that, instead of confronting us with the shock of the Gospel and with the offensive event which demands of us a decision, it gives us an understanding of the meaning of that event and its offensiveness. "Christianity is not a matter of doctrines; all talk of its scandal from the doctrinal point of view rests on a misunderstanding. When people talk of the offensive aspect of the doctrine of the God-man, the doctrine of the Atonement,

---

[9] XI, 237-8; VIII, 121-2.

it means that they are weakening the shock of the offensiveness. No, the moment of scandalisation is connected either with Christ or with the fact that one is oneself a Christian."[10]

To become a Christian, to be offended or to believe, is only possible to the individual. "Yet organised Christianity refuses to realise that it consists of anything so loose as a collection of millions of individuals. It wishes to be a totality, subject to no higher authority, but subjecting every individual to itself, and with the power to judge every individual who has been incorporated into this collective whole."[11]

But what significance has the Church for the individual Christian? We have already seen that the preaching of the Gospel must in various ways be clothed with an authority in which the authority of the Church is expressed. To this extent, even for Kierkegaard, there can be no individual faith apart from the Church. But we have noted at the same time that the Church cannot guarantee these authorities or remove them from dialectics, but that it is itself still only an object of faith. Thus the Church is not simply the organisational form of current Christianity, for as such it would no longer be the object of faith, but in its essential character immediately and undialectically knowable. It would be what Kierkegaard, in view of modern Christianity calls the "Church Triumphant," that is, the net result of an 1800-years process of historical development; for "what to a large extent has occasioned the fancy of a Church Triumphant is just this: that Christianity has been regarded as the truth in the sense of achieved result, whereas it is the truth in the sense of 'the way of life.' "[12] No one is delivered from the necessity of travelling this way because of a historical predecessor, nor can he be relieved of this obligation by his incorporation into a community or society. Each one can travel the way of discipleship to Christ only as an individual. Christ did not bequeath His victory to the Church as a *depositum* in such wise that the individual merely through his incorporation into the Church can without more ado share in this victory. He says, in criticism of this misunderstanding, quite sharply and emphatically: "An idea such as

[10] XII, 101-2; IX, 93.  [11] XII, 87; IX, 77.
[12] XII, 191; IX, 179.

that of the Christian community (with which people have been so largely concerned in these days) is really, in its application to this life, an impatient attempt to forestall the eternal. If we view the struggle of the Christian life in a spiritual sense, then it is always individuals who struggle in this way; for the spiritual is just the individual as an individual before God, and implies also that the idea of the community is of lesser value than the idea of the individual which each can and must be. And even if there were thousands of such individuals uniting their efforts in the fight, still from a Christian point of view each individual strives within himself as well as in union with others, and it is as an individual that he must render account of himself on the Day of Judgment, when his life as an individual will be tested. For this reason the idea of community is proper only to eternity; the community is at rest, whereas the individual is engaged in struggle. But the truth is that this earthly life is the time of struggle and trial; hence the community has no home in time but only in eternity, where in peace it is the congregation of all those individuals who have stood the test in earthly strife.''[13]

"The illusion of a Church Triumphant has a second cause in addition to the error that truth is an achieved result. This second cause lies in the illusory supposition which has arisen in the course of time that we are all Christians . . . . For then a Militant Church would be an impossibility. Wherever it

---

[13] XII, 204; IX, 194. On this passage Kierkegaard notes in his diary of 1849: "It is a shock which arouses attention to note that in the Church Militant there are only individuals and that thus one cannot recognise Church community" (*S. K. P.*, x.2, 366). In a notice of the same diary, under the heading: "The Difference between the 'Crowd' or the 'Public' and a 'Community',," we find: ". . . Each individual in the community guarantees that community; but the public is a chimera. The individual in the community is a microcosm reflecting qualitatively the macrocosm; in this respect it is very true, '*unum noris omnes.*' In regard to the public, there is no individual, the whole is nothing; here it is impossible to say, '*unum noris omnes,*' for here there is no 'one.' The community is no doubt more than a sum of individuals but it is in truth a sum of individuals: the idea of the public is nonsense: it is a sum of negative individuals, of individuals who are not such, they become so only through the collective whole, whereas the community is a community through the individuals which compose it" (*op. cit.*, 390).

appears that Christianity already exists as a visible entity we see the attempt to form a Triumphant Church (although this expression may not be used); for the Militant Church is in the process of becoming, and an *existing visible* Church does not become but *already is*."[14]

The purpose of the *Einübung im Christentum* is to enable this compact, organised, current Christianity to enter once again into the process of becoming. Our question was whether in this work, which criticises the present condition of Christianity more aggressively than previous works, Kierkegaard has introduced new categories which must inevitably have produced a change in his dialectical method. Our considered conclusion is that this is not the case. Here, too, he remains faithful to his method of oblique dialectical communication, which itself claims no authority, but stands in a dialectical relationship to the Church and the authority it exercises in proclamation. His method, even in the *Krankheit zum Tode*, remains as described in the *Einübung* the art of oblique communication: "To bring defence and attack so closely together that no one can directly assert whether one is attacking or defending, and so that the most zealous champion of the matter in hand and its most bitter opponent both think that they have found an ally—and thus to be oneself nobody, absent from the work, an objective something rather than a personality. When at any given time faith has disappeared from the world and has to be declared missing, then this method may perhaps be useful to arouse faith once more (but I am not deciding that this is so, I am simply giving this as an example of oblique or two-edged communication), then one should expound and present faith in its unique essence and in such a way that the orthodox sees in this exposition a defence of faith and the freethinker an attack on faith, while the communicator himself remains neutral, not a man, but an objective something—yet after all he may be a clever spy, who by his methods of address gets to know how matters stand and who is the believer, who the freethinker; for this becomes plain when the result, which is neither an attack nor a defence, is judged."[15]

[14] XII, 194; IX, 183.
[15] XII, 124-5; IX, 118.

## 15. AN ADMISSION

Nevertheless, Kierkegaard did not once more simply publish these two works pseudonymously in order "himself to be nobody, to be absent, an objective something rather than a personality." They appear indeed under a new pseudonym, "Anticlimacus"—but Kierkegaard publishes his own name as editor. "So, the *Krankheit zum Tode* is now published, but pseudonymously with my name as that of the editor. It is described as being 'for edification' which is more than my own category, the poetic category: edifying."[1] The emphasis lies on the phrase "for edification," which later is expanded on the title page to "For edification and awakening."[2] "As the River Guadalquivir once plunges under the earth, so the edifying part which bears my name covers a certain distance. There is something that is lower (the aesthetic), which is pseudonymous, and something which is higher, which is also pseudonymous, because my personality does not correspond to it. This pseudonym is 'Johannes Anticlimacus,' by contrast with 'Climacus,' who declared that he was no Christian; Anticlimacus is the exact opposite; he is a Christian in quite an extraordinary degree—but what I myself profess to be is just a simple Christian . . . . In this way the *Einübung im Christentum* can be published."[1] Kierkegaard inserts in it a "Publisher's Foreword," solemnly repeated before each of the three main sections, and in this he says: "In this writing, which dates from the year 1848, the pseudonymous writer's demand for Christian existence has been screwed up to the highest degree of idealism. But such a demand must be stated, urged, and listened to; from the Christian point of view one must not cheapen it at all, nor pass over it; one must not attempt to make concessions and special terms for oneself. The demand must be heard: and I understand what is said as though it were said to me alone— I understand that I must not only take refuge in grace, but take refuge in grace in such a way that I use grace."

---

[1] *S. K. P.*, x.1(A), 510.

[2] *Op. cit.*, x.1, 529. "This phrase 'for awakening' is really the additional point, and it is also an addition which so far surpasses my own personality that I need a new pseudonym for it. I use merely the poetic predicate 'edifying,' not even 'for edification.' "

What Kierkegaard did in this respect was the fruit of long and deep reflexion. Not only would it have seemed to him personally dishonest to publish such aggressive writings under a pseudonym and thus to evade the responsibility for them, but he feared that as a result the categories might have been muddled. The publication of these works might have led to a conflict with the organised Church, in which case it would have had to be made clear what attitude he himself adopted with regard to the claim which the discourses make. For this reason he wondered whether he should not undertake some ecclesiastical office before publication. There was some question of his taking an appointment as teacher in a theological seminary. If this had happened, his own involvement in the Church would have shown that he could not personally identify himself with the claim of his writings. No one could then have supposed that he was a prophet, and hence the effect of the whole of his previous work would have been ruined. "The effect of this whole *monumentum aere perennius* is to be a purely ideal one! It is as if a judgment were passed, but I am not the judge, I submit myself to the judgment."[3] This was one possibility which was complicated by the difficulty that such an appointment in his economic circumstances must appear desirable for financial reasons, and this caused him serious scruples with regard to the purity of his motives. The opposite possibility was "to speak directly in the character of the extraordinary Christian"[4] and to accept personally all the consequences. There was still a third possibility—"to withdraw with all my poetry into an ivory tower and seek the aloofness of the poet in order to avoid all occasion of being misconceived, as though I were expressing poetically my own existence."[4]

In the event, Kierkegaard decided for none of these three possibilities, but chose the way we have mentioned above, indicating that he was himself responsible for the publication, and stating directly in the foreword in what way alone he could personally vouch for what was said: as one who in consequence of the idealism expounded here must take refuge in grace.

What does Kierkegaard mean by this? The expression "idealism" might easily be misleading here, because it is

[3] *Op. cit.*, x.1, 56.            [4] *Op. cit.*, x.1, 94.

associated with Christian perfectionism of a pietistic nature, from which Kierkegaard was far removed. In his review of 1850 he says: "Never have I thought for one moment of introducing the note of pietistic severity which is quite alien to my whole being and would dull my mind."[5] What Kierkegaard means by this demand for Christian living in its maximum degree of ideality can be seen by considering the relation of Christ as pattern to His requirement of discipleship. "Christ is in truth our example, and also is externally exacting to man, because he merely said that He was a man like other men. He makes the divine commensurable to the living of human life in its universality."[6] Thus Kierkegaard quite simply equates Christ as example with the ideal of the universally human: "As far as the history of Christ is concerned, what is always true is this, that He *is* the ideal, not like the historical in other connexions which is not the ideal, for which reason the interpreter must add the ideal element. Here the ideal is the historical—the greatest contradiction that can be conceived, and again implying that Christianity in its pure ideality bursts the framework of existence as a whole."[7]

But this shattering does not mean a playing-off of the absolute *telos* against the relative ends of actual human existence. Man must not be lifted out of his actual circumstances, but must, on the contrary, be held to them, so that as such a concretely existing individual he may at the same time express the universally human. This shattering means simply the act of renewal in the moment of the "fullness of time," where man breaks the confinement of his natural being in order to win back his life through faith in forgiveness—it is a question of that movement on the spot which Kierkegaard can dialectically describe as follows: "By becoming contemporaneous with Christ your pattern, you discover that you never equal Him, not even in what you term your best moment; for in such a moment you are not in the tensions of actuality, but reflective. Hence it follows that you learn to flee with profit to faith and grace. The pattern is that which requires that it should be mirrored in you, and you feel with fear the gulf between you and it; then

[5] *S. V.*, xiii, 506; *Ges. W.*, x, 168.   [6] *S. K. P.*, ix(a), 101.
[7] *Op. cit.*, x.4, 208.

you flee to the pattern and it will have mercy on you. Thus Christ as our example is He who most severely and endlessly judges—and at the same time is the One who has pity on you."[8]

The journals of Kierkegaard dating from these years are full of reflexions about the right relation between example and discipleship, effort and grace. Kierkegaard is concerned about the two points equally, namely, that on the one hand the exigency of discipleship should not make the atoning work of Christ illusory and empty, and, on the other hand, that grace should not be misused in such a way that effort is neglected. "But in spite of the fact that it is wise to stress the need for discipleship, even though—instructed by the error of the Middle Ages—in a new and different sense, yet above all the matter must not be so viewed that Christ appears merely as our example and not as our saviour, as though the spiritually mature, at any rate, did not need the atonement. No, no, no— and for this reason: the more mature one is, so much the more will one discover that one needs the divine atonement and grace. No, atonement and grace is and remains the decisive thing. Every effort towards discipleship, at the moment of death which terminates it, will be wretched in the sight of God: therefore grace and atonement are necessary. Further, during every second of the struggle, the atonement is needed so that this struggle does not become a torturing anxiety which as it were brings man near to collapse and makes him less than ever able to strive. Finally, during the phase of struggle we fall short, we fail, we sin, every other moment: *ergo*, the atonement is unconditionally necessary. Discipleship should—although accompanied by every effort—be only an amusement, something childish, lest it should be taken to mean something ultimately serious, in the eyes of God and to signify our merits— it is atonement which is the serious thing. But it is terrible to think that some one, 'because there is the fact of grace,' should desire to use the latter in order to neglect all effort."[9]

Hence this ideal demand can no longer be understood as the

---

[8] *Op. cit.*, IX(A), 153.

[9] *Op. cit.*, X.4, 491; cp. the passages from the diaries translated under the title "Discipleship and Grace," in *Z. D. Z.*, 1931, pp. 4 ff.

maximum requirement of a characteristic Christian ethic. This
is impossible, if only because the Christian life in faith has to
fulfil nothing special but only the universally human, which
every man has to express, and so the Christian is not distinguished
from other men by the observable results of his struggle. Hence
Kierkegaard cannot make clear the condition of Christianity
by a heightened preaching of the law although he has been
persistently misunderstood in this way not only by his contemporaries but up to the present. The power and pathos of
one who preaches the law might easily be counteracted. In
answer one could point to the success of one's efforts in the
moral struggle, or parry his attack by a counter-question
concerning the preacher's own existence. But if the attacker
not only makes no sort of claim for himself, but from the outset
credibly confesses that he himself lives by "grace," then the
ground is withdrawn from any false self-assertion. By this
we do not of course imply that Kierkegaard made a concession
of this kind in the foreword to the *Einübung* for tactical reasons
only—just as in 1855 he will retract it for tactical reasons—but
rather such a concession is the sincere expression of his personal
faith. It is true, in point of fact, that he lives by drawing on
the resources of grace, and because in this respect he expresses
himself also in the correct dialectical categories, the strategy
he must adopt is implied: "And, further, the whole account,
although the points bear the sting of truth, is conceived as
kindly as possible, for the talk is only of concessions and admissions and indeed concessions and admissions which each one
has to make to God only on his own account. Yet this very
gentleness is perhaps inconvenient to some people; the whole
thing could more easily be got rid of with a clear conscience, if
the author were a confused thinker who exaggerated every
item of the indictment and demand. And since this is in fact
not the case, some one or other might no doubt be tempted to
spread the report that it is so. But with the help of God this
attempt will, for sure, come to nought."[10]

By the publication of the *Einübung* together with this foreword
Kierkegaard did not dialectically go beyond the point that it
is for the reader himself to decide whether he proposes to see

[10] *S. V.*, xiii, 507; *Ges. W.*, x, 168.

here an attack or defence, but, in—from a categorical point of view—the only possible way, he was emphasising through a personal testimony the urgency of making such a distinction. Now organised Christianity is asked whether it is prepared to make the same concession. Now Kierkegaard has done everything possible. Contemporary Christianity has the word.

But Kierkegaard is not merely concerned whether this or that reader of his work is going to make such an admission for himself: he expects an answer to his question from the official Church as the responsible representative of "current Christianity," in other words from its leader, Bishop Mynster of Seeland.

That Kierkegaard makes Mynster rather than any one else his opponent has not only personal grounds. He needs a representative of existing Christianity who shows the slightest possible symptoms of decline and decay, in order to challenge the Church at its strongest point. Above all, he was concerned to avoid the misconception that he had at heart certain reforms of the Church as regards its external organisation, and such as were sought after at that time by, on the one hand, the followers of Grundtvig and, on the other, by the alliance, in the aftermath of 1848, of theological and political liberalism. In face of all such attempts Kierkegaard's attitude was as conservative as possible, and in resisting them he was constantly on the side of Mynster, and even reproached the latter for his too great indulgence in the matter. With regard to the significance of Mynster for his own work, he himself says: "My task has been to supply a corrective to what exists rather than to bring forward anything new, intended to revolutionise or replace what is established. Had I had from the start a clear view of my whole purpose, and had Mynster not existed, I must first have created some figure or other to represent established Christianity, and for this purpose must have touched it up well. But as I did not so clearly understand my task from the start, I would probably have failed in this and the whole thing would have been something different and perhaps ruined. But Mynster was there as my symbol of the established order. This I had *gratis*; it was quite a matter of course for me, since I greatly respected Mynster and did everything to express my respect. Thus I got a right appreciation. See, here is again my good

fortune! For purely personal reasons my veneration for Mynster was a matter of necessity, and it was thus only gradually
that I realised how important this was for me and that in
consequence I might be correctly viewed."[11]

Now Kierkegaard expected Mynster in the name of the
Church to make such an admission in the name of established
Christianity and his fear simply is that the Bishop might confuse
the attack implied in the *Einübung* with a popular revolt against
the Church: "It is pathetic that organised Christianity (at least
for the most part) so little understands how to rule that without more ado the *Einübung im Christentum* is confused with an
opposition movement from which it is as different as possible
and of which in fact it is the exact opposite. The opposition
party wants to do away with the Church *hierarchy*—what does
Anticlimacus want? He is a solitary individual (by no means
the representative of any party, indeed he is a hater of every
party, an opponent of the crowd, the populace, etc., and is
aware of the sort of danger of which every true leader ought
nowadays to be aware). On the contrary, he criticises the
leaders in these terms: 'For heaven's sake, how is it that you
sit there and rule and do not know what real government is,
and yet you are the governors?' Is that opposition against the
government? But those who govern have lost sight of the high
notion of what government means and so cling to the shreds
of power and suppose Anticlimacus to be their opponent. The
matter is quite simple. The leaders of the Church have lost
authority, have bargained and enslaved themselves to the fear
of men, in proportion as they have lost the reins of government.
In order to regain the power of government concessions must
be made. 'Another concession,' I can hear them say—and so
they think that it is the opposition to which they must make a
new concession because they have not even yet made enough
concessions. Oh no, no, you rulers are called upon to make a
concession to God and Christianity, to do a kind of penance—
and see, if you do so, the reins of government will once more be
firmly within your grasp. In this way you could well steer
existing Christianity once more. Yet at the same time the
matter had to be handled with such God-fearing artifice as to

[11] *S. K. P.*, x.3, 565.

challenge the Church to consider whether it was going to classify Anticlimacus officially as an opponent and so compel me to express myself still more severely. God knows, with fear and trembling I considered, even for my own sake, whether the task would not be too hard for me. But, *eh bien*, I have dared it."[12]

In order to anticipate: it is well known that Mynster never made the admission for which Kierkegaard had waited with unbearable tension year after year; and in the polemic against Martensen after Mynster's death Kierkegaard said that for him the essential point was that the Church, through Mynster, "should concede as solemnly as possible that it did not represent New Testament Christianity."[13] In the context of our work we have neither to consider whether Kierkegaard's requirement was one which Mynster could regard as reasonable, nor whether Kierkegaard might have hoped, and did hope, his procedure to be successful. We are merely concerned with the question what such an admission, had it taken place, would have signified from Kierkegaard's own point of view.

This question has very much occupied the attention of Kierkegaard researchers, and the judgment of Eduard Geismar has been very largely accepted. He says: "It has always seemed to me that in this sequence of thought there is something dishonest. And after the clarification of Kierkegaard's thoughts about the relation between discipleship and grace it appears to me as if Kierkegaard was offering Mynster a proposal on conditions whose impossibility he himself realised, the conditions of a spiritual moratorium, allowing the admission to take the place of action. One cannot be strict with oneself and indulgent towards others in such a way as to accept in others something whose dishonesty one has perceived as regards oneself. In the causes of the storm which shook the Church there is something here which has not been cleared up."[14]

Our next concern is to ask to what extent Kierkegaard, as far as he personally was concerned, can be said "to have per-

[12] *Op. cit.*, x.3, 599.
[13] "Faedrelandet," No. 304 (30 Dec. 1854); *Angriff auf die Christenheit*, cited below as *Angriff*, tr. A. Dorner and C. Schrempf, Stuttgart 1896, p. 112.
       Geismar, *Sören Kierkegaard*, Göttingen 1927, 449.

ceived the dishonesty" of such an admission. Geismar says that as regards the relation of discipleship and grace Kierkegaard hesitated between two conceptions of the Godward relationship, and that they stand side by side in the diary of 1851. In the one, the Godward relationship implies rather the fact of suffering in the world. Those who live thus "do not experience grace primarily; their life expresses an intensity of spiritual effort; and while they recognise that they are saved by grace, we must deeply respect their position. Then there is the second relationship; man recognises how terrible a thing it is to approach God (which however is God's requirement) but confesses the weakness in consequence of which he does not dare to do so, at any rate not yet—and so he puts grace first, and grace permits him to spare himself the maximum of spiritual effort." Before going into the inferences that Geismar draws, let us note at once that Kierkegaard continues in this passage thus: "In His infinite love God can and will tolerate even this attitude— but He wills that it should be adopted in all honesty and truth and that man should confess it sincerely. Man must quite humbly recognise that the fault is in him, that he is afraid to be spiritual in the strictest sense and thus is evading something. The mistake in the usual kind of preaching is the drivelling talk about 'I would so much like to.' Twaddle! The fact of the matter is that I am the kind of person who would *not* so much like to—and yet God in His grace wills to forgive me. Since He is infinite love, He is willing, in spite of everything, to enter into relation with a person even under this condition."[15]

Geismar thinks that, at the time when he still expected an admission from Mynster, Kierkegaard was already clear in his own mind that he at all events must adopt the first of these two attitudes. In practice this meant that he must not accept any office in the Church, in order to escape the suffering of poverty, after his means were almost completely used up, but must dare all in order to experience spirituality in the strictest sense. It must be noted that for Kierkegaard the question whether grace permitted one to spare oneself the maximum of spiritual effort was complicated by the fact that it was difficult for him to decide whether he wanted to accept an ecclesiastical office as

[15] *S. K. P.*, x.4, 446.

a sign that the grace of God offered a time for repentance even to current Christianity, or whether he wanted to do so merely out of fear of the poverty which threatened. And that when once involved in such thoughts, this dejected, scrupulous thinker spared himself nothing, and that nothing escaped him that might have been said against him, is sufficiently clear from the journals. But there can be no question that it would not be right to affirm he had already found a decided answer to the question at the time we are thinking of. It constantly engages his attention, as also we find that he continues to exert himself with regard to an ecclesiastical appointment, however hesitantly, until he notices in a conversation with Mynster on August 9th 1851 that the latter is no longer willing to give him the post in the theological seminary which he had originally proposed.[16] And in recollecting this, Kierkegaard later expressly makes Mynster responsible for the consequences.[17]

The question of the right relationship of discipleship and grace was further complicated for Kierkegaard by the fact that he was personally concerned about whether he ought not himself to achieve an unusual degree of spirituality as a corrective to Christianity as currently practised, and such as could not be expected of any other. How could he escape the danger either of shirking his own special obligations through his alleged kindness towards the man in the street or of doing violence to the latter by demanding an exceptional degree of spirituality from all? Nor was he able to convince himself of the plain solution that from him with his special call to spirituality more was expected than from any one else.

For all these reasons we consider it wrong of Geismar to say that Kierkegaard was demanding of Mynster something "the dishonesty of which he had perceived as regards himself," or that "he was offering the Church and Mynster a proposal on conditions beyond which he personally had progressed."[18] No, he had by no means advanced beyond them, but was unceasingly pondering the problems involved, which for him were still open questions. We should be extremely cautious about

---

16 *Op. cit.*, x.4, 373.
17 *Op. cit.*, x.4, 604, p. 422.
18 Geismar, *Sören Kierkegaard*, 444.

making such judgments on Kierkegaard's character, and, above all, in so complicated a question as that of the relation of discipleship and grace, where the emphasis in the tenseness of the dialectical situation is being constantly shifted.

In addition, the question arises whether Geismar does *in fact* do justice to what Kierkegaard means by the "admission" when he regards it as something "taking the place of action" and calls it a "spiritual moratorium."[19] Here there can be no question either of a "moratorium" or of a substitute for action. It may have been fantastic of Kierkegaard to have expected such an admission at all. But if it had been made it would have constituted action in a quite pre-eminent sense, though not, of course, in the sense of an outward change in the life of the Church. In the most positive way Kierkegaard had issued a warning precisely against such a thing as a mere subterfuge.

But just let us suppose that the Church had made such an admission and that every one who had understood it to have been made for himself personally had asked himself what difference it must have made to have regarded his life as a time given for repentance. In the Danish State Church as such, with all its organisations, perhaps nothing at all would have been changed from an external point of view, and this in fact would have been quite as Kierkegaard intended. Perhaps also many or even most of its members, perhaps even its pastors, would have regarded the whole thing merely as a piece of rhetoric by which they did not feel that they incurred any special obligations. In that case the matter would have amounted for them to a specially refined misuse of grace as remission. But if we do not deny that in spite of everything this Church was still the Church of Jesus Christ—and of course Kierkegaard did not deny this—and hence if we still believe that the third article applied to it, then we cannot consider it impossible that the resurrection of the dead would have happened to it also—in such wise that here and there some one and even a theologian or a pastor would have concerned himself about Christian existence as moving between the law of discipleship and the gospel of grace.

[19] Geismar, *op. cit.*, 449.

I

To begin with the theologians, this would have meant that they would have effaced from their dogmatics the misuse of the 1800 years of history as an achieved result, with the consequence that their dogmatic work might have worn an essentially different appearance from that of the publication of Martensen in 1849 for example, which disregarded the dialectical corrective to Church doctrine effected by the pseudonymous writings. And then Kierkegaard would not have felt compelled to say, with regard to such dogmatics: "In the whole dogmatic work of Martensen, at least in the part which I have read, there is not a single sentence which is an honest 'yes' or 'no.' It is the old sophistry of being able to talk but of not being able to talk *to* some one. For conversation at once presupposes the 'I' and 'thou' and poses questions which demand an answer—'yes' or 'no.' But a mere talker develops his theme thus: 'On the one hand and on the other hand,' and in the meantime both teacher and listener become so involved as not to notice that they are getting to know nothing whatsoever."[20]    What a conspicuous difference it would mean for Christianity if such books on dogma could no longer be written, or, if they were, would be seen through and rejected! Or let us think of the whole anxious business of apologetics. Let us suppose that this discipline could no longer use as proof the 1800 years of Christian history and its achievements, and therefore had to speak of Feuerbach, for instance, as Kierkegaard did: "In truth the revolution is nearer than one thought. The last development of free thought (Feuerbach and his school) has made its attack and come to grips with the matter far more centrally than has been done hitherto; if you look at the thing more closely you will see that they have really undertaken the task of defending Christianity against those Christians who are now living. The point is that Christianity as at present practised is demoralised; people have lost all regard in the deepest sense (for the regard which they say they have means nothing) for the existential obligations of Christian living. Now Feuerbach says, 'No, stop! if I am to be permitted to live as I do, then I must also grant that I am not a Christian.' Feuerbach has well understood the challenge, but he cannot bring himself to accept it—

[20] *S. K. P.*, x.1, 566.

*ergo*, he prefers to give up the idea of being a Christian. And he is not incorrect in his grasp of the essential position, however great a responsibility he incurs. It is in point of fact untrue for modern Christianity to say that Feuerbach is attacking it; that is not true; he is attacking Christian people in order to show that their lives do not correspond to the doctrines of Christianity. (And so in relation to Feuerbach one may say '*Et ab hoste consilium.*') This is a fundamental distinction. That he is an evil spirit may very well be true, but tactically he can be of use to us."[21] What a pre-eminent change it would signify if the leaders of Christianity in speech and writing—think only of the authors of the Christian Sunday papers—by this sort of frank admission of the truth became free to express such insights, and drew the consequences!

Or think again of the preachers. Let us suppose that by such a concession they were to admit the question how their preaching stands as regards their own existence poised between sin and grace. Then they could no longer engage in considerations on the subject of Christianity, which had nothing to do with their own existence or with that of their hearers, but they would themselves be an existing "I"—no matter how this measures up in fact to the idealism of the Christian demand—and as such would be confronted by a concretely existing "thou," and so would be in a position to address themselves to the existent "thou" and to be questioned by the latter. What an undreamed-of revolution in Christian preaching this would entail! It should not be forgotten that Kierkegaard did not just summarily require such a concession but also criticised *in extenso* false preaching and furnished the necessary categories for its rectification. What a vital action would be implied by such a change in preaching, and that quite apart from any external changes!

And then it could not but happen that a twilight of the idols would fall over that whole superstition of existing Christianity which assumes without further question that all are Christians. It would not come about as a result of any separation of those who were more awake in order that they might make special demands about Christian living on the rest of the Church, but

[21] *Op. cit.*, x.2, 163.

simply as a result of the fact that by this concession it would be impossible to preach in such a way as to confirm men in their petulance and to nourish this superstition.

A concession of this kind would thus accomplish what Kierkegaard tried to effect through his *Einübung*: it would once more plunge contemporary Christianity into the process of becoming. What Kierkegaard means by this must be examined in more detail, especially as regards the relation of Church and State, which in any case decisively determines the character of Christianity as established.

## 16. CHURCH AND STATE

In an article in *Faedrelandet* of 31 Jan. 1851[1] Kierkegaard protests emphatically against the expressions of Dr A. C. Rudelbach in his book *Über die bürgerliche Eheschliessung* (1851), where, in order to support his fight against the State Church, Rudelbach makes the following reference to our author: "This agrees closely with what Søren Kierkegaard, one of our distinguished modern writers, tries to make clear in the strongest possible terms, and, as Luther says, to drive home to all those who are willing to listen." Kierkegaard says on the contrary: "I am supposed to have made an attack on State Christianity, yes, this Søren Kierkegaard is supposed to have the wholesale significance of criticising the State Church, or more precisely of striving for the emancipation of the Church from the State, or at least 'of making clear his opposition in the strongest possible terms and driving it home'! In Ursin's arithmetic book, which in my day was in use in the schools, there is promised a reward to any one who can find a mistake in the exercises of the book. I too promise a reward to any one who can point out to me in the whole series of my books a single proposal for a change in the outward form of the Church, or even any trace of such a thing, or anything that even for the most shortsighted was remotely suggestive of such a proposal, or might lead to the opinion that I thought the defect might lie in externals, as though I considered external changes necessary, or hoped from them any help" (p. 378). "Nothing makes me

[1] *Angriff*, pp. 376 ff.

so doubtful as anything which even smacks of this unfortunate confusion of politics and Christianity, which can so easily bring about and make fashionable a new sort of Church reformation, a reformation in reverse, which by way of reform would put something new and worse in the place of the old and better, and which however would without a doubt be celebrated by the whole town with fireworks" (p. 379). He is especially scornful of the possibility that the cause which he has at heart might be brought under the heading of "emancipation," and says: "Neither have I ever fought for the emancipation of the Church—just as little as for the emancipation of Greenland's trade, of women, of the Jews, or of anything else. But as an individual addressing myself to individuals and aiming at the interior Christian life in individuals, I have consistently and solely fought with weapons of the spirit the fight against the 'illusion of the senses,' I have drawn attention to it and warned against it. And as in my opinion it is a matter of sensuous delusion if any one imagines that the outer forms hinder him from becoming a Christian, so also it is equally a delusion and the same delusion, if any one imagines that the outer forms can help him to become a Christian" (pp. 379-80).

Kierkegaard also says on the same occasion: "Also I have never occupied my attention with affairs of Church and State, since such matters are too high for me, and to deal adequately with them a man of different vision from myself is required, and moreover the matter can quite simply be left to those who are properly called and appointed to deal with it" (p. 379). This, of course, is true, only of Kierkegaard's published speeches. In the diaries of these years, he has, on the contrary, gone quite deeply into these questions.

He was not, however, interested in theories of the State and philosophical foundations for the power of the State, and he considers: "Instead of all these hypotheses about the origin of the State and so on, we ought to be more concerned about the question: 'In face of the given situation of official Christianity, how shall we create new and inspiring points of view?' "[2] For

---

[2] *S. K. P.*, x.4, 72. K. E. Lögstrup, "Die Kategorie und das Amt der Verkündigung im Hinblick auf Luther und Kierkegaard," in *Evangelische Theologie*, cited below as *Ev. Th.*, 1949, pp. 249 ff., has either overlooked

this purpose there is needed especially a strengthening of official Christianity through the effective exercise of its implied authority. It is just here that the work of the State lies by contrast with the work of the Church: "The 'Church' should really stand for vitality, the 'State,' on the other hand, for what is officially recognised. That is why it is so dangerous if State and Church grow together and become identified. Even if some institution is not so successful, provided it is official, the State must see that it is not hastily done away with, just because the State stands for what is official; and it is perhaps better to

---

the fact that K. declares himself uninterested in any philosophical justification for worldly authority, or, in the light of his Lutheran prejudices, has misinterpreted this lack of interest when he says that K. "denies any sort of divine basis for the authority with which secular civil offices are exercised" (p. 263). Things are not so simple as that with a dialectician. Lögstrup himself says that with K. authority "is in relation to all other qualifications, τὸ ἕτερον, whether it is a question of an Apostle or of a man on whom authority is conferred by his civil office" (p. 264). But, he goes on to say, "the positive characteristic that man has authority from some other source applies on the contrary to subordinate officers whose authority is derivative, e.g. the ambassador's, or the police officer's, it does not apply to those who wield intrinsic authority, such as magistrates and superior officials and parents. Here we are left completely in the lurch" (p. 266). We must dispute the last point. Why should not this justification of authority apply to superior authorities also, namely its derivative character? In these conversations which he reports in detail in his diaries, K. says to his King, not of course that he has his office from God and that therefore it cannot be called in question, but he tells him to use his authority and promises to support him in his use of it. K. is not at all concerned about the metaphysics of authority, but he is concerned that authority should be used, and that in responsibility before God. What concern could K. have in directly establishing the divine authority of the King, and so forth, such as would remove it from all criticism, after he insists as strongly as possible on its actual use? But that he does not deny, on the other hand, a divine basis to this authority is shown in the fact that he requires of those individuals who decide to act against this authority that they should do so with a sense of utmost responsibility before God. He certainly does not recognise an undialectical, absolute authority which, in virtue of its office, even when it is misused, cannot be called in question, and against which there would be no justifiable struggle of the individual acting with a sense of responsibility before God. And incidentally it is to be questioned whether Luther himself recognised this sort of authority. We refer the reader to the distinction which we draw in what follows between K.'s conservatism and that of conservative politicians.

conserve a weaker institution than to reform it prematurely. The exact opposite is true of the Church, since it is based on the idea of vitality and development. To be engaged in the process of becoming is more spiritual than to exist officially; therefore the servants of the Church ought not to be officials, hardly should they be married, but *expediti* apt to further the process of becoming."[3]

If this is the essential relationship of Church and State, then the danger of their identification lies in the possibility of their corrupting each other, with the result that the fulfilment of their specific tasks is hindered. This may happen on the side of the State in that it becomes a Christian State, in the sense that it guarantees the institution of the Church, by legally authorising the arrangements and offices of the Church and financing it by taxation and thus fostering the illusion that all its citizens are Christians. In that case the Church no longer needs to justify itself intrinsically by caring for its inner life and progress, for the State by its external provisions on behalf of the Church would discourage the latter from examining the question of the actual spiritual state of the citizens and the actual condition of the Church. "The whole idea of a Christian State is really a self-contradiction, a piece of jugglery. . . . No doubt it is permissible for me to be paid for my work as a Christian teacher (for the labourer is worthy of his hire); but then there ought to be real Christians whom I can guarantee to be such in return for my accepting payment, and whose existence makes my taking of payment a reasonable Christian action. But I ought not to receive my recompense through a third party which, if necessary, will use secular power in order to procure for me my dues, a third party which . . . merely maintains the fiction that all are Christians. Thus we have the parson, appointed by the State Church to a parish with a certain stipulated salary, and so it does not matter whether or not there is a single Christian in the whole parish, whether any one goes to church or not, and so on. The parson preaches as arranged and the State sees to it that he receives his income. The State essentially belongs to the category of race and community, Christianity to the category of the individual.

[3] *S. K. P.*, x.1, 552.

For this reason alone it is clear that they are incompatible. One can see, therefore, how grievously mistaken is the desire of spiritual servants to be paid directly by the State. If one cannot persuade men of the high significance of Christianity so that they willingly pay, then one ought not to take their money. The origins of Christianity are too lofty for it to become a *protegé* of the State. If the individual members of a State sink so low that they have no sense of art and culture, and the State tells them, 'I can't help that, you must nevertheless pay for these things'—good, that is in order and praiseworthy. But Christianity is infinitely higher than the State; if men despise Christianity, then the punishment must be that they no longer have a chance of hearing its message."[4]

A Church whose whole life is corrupted in this way by the help of a State guarantee can no longer fulfil its duty over against the State, i.e., the duty of caring for vitality in opposition to the officialdom of the State. This vital becoming, which is historical as distinct from natural becoming, can only take place through individuals, who, realising their supreme responsibility before God, take the universal moral law so seriously as to embody it in their individual concrete circumstances and the specific situation of their time. If, in doing this, the individual feels compelled to go beyond those ethical standards which the State as the guardian of officialdom expresses in law and custom, he can justify himself only by pointing out that he is ready to make sacrifices for this end. Thus only through the life of the individual acting in responsibility before God and men can there be genuine vitality and progress in society. But a Church which is upheld by the State has neither the outer nor the inner freedom to serve the end of this spiritual transformation. Since by its alliance with the State it is involved in the interests of the latter, and with worldly shrewdness must care for the maintenance of what is officially recognised, so it can no longer demand from its servants and individual members that in the life of faith they should take risks and make sacrifices. In fact it cannot even desire this, for then the condition of the official Church would be exposed. And hence nothing remains to it but to become

[4] *Op. cit.*, x.2, 240.

"conservative" in a false and undialectical sense, i.e., to be politically conservative by lending an absolute divine authority to the ordinances and offices of this Christian State which guarantees officially a state of things so profitable to the Church. Hence it is not conservative, as Kierkegaard was, in order firmly to uphold the validity of the moral law and to make the unjustified evasion of the individual as difficult as possible, so that a genuine transformation might be effected, but it is conservative in order to preclude any challenge to official Christianity and to make impossible this vital movement of change.

But when it is attempted to hinder genuine spiritual change, then you necessarily invite false changes such as those aimed at in movements of political progress. In this case the movement no longer takes place through the personal responsibility of individuals, but individuals group themselves together in order to take part, as a collective, in the progress of the race. Kierkegaard clearly makes the Church responsible for the uprising of such movements which are so deeply repugnant to him. He constantly reminds us how shameful it is for a Christian society that the common man should play the part he does in the Christian State, and he describes it as the great merit of Rudelbach's book *Die Kirchenverfassung* to "have shown that the State Church is responsible for or has contributed to, the rise of the proletariat. How important this is Rudelbach himself does not seem to have realised. In official Christianity people certainly do not live in a Christian way, even as regards their life with and their responsibilities for the common man. In this respect my life has been something like a revelation—and alas, in a certain sense, I can say a very sad revelation. The un-Christian and unethical thing is to base the State on a substratum of men who are completely ignored and with whom one repudiates any relationship—even though on Sundays you hear moving sermons about the love of your neighbour."[5] Even the experiences of the year 1848 did not change his attitude in this matter. "The uprising in the world is calling for visible action,"[6] but the Church withdraws itself into the sanctuary of the house of God, as Kierkegaard shows

[5] *Op. cit.*, x.1, 669.  [6] *Op. cit.*, x.3, 346.

in a sermon of Mynster, who says: " ' To suggest preaching this out there in the streets would not help at all; but here in Your holy place, in this solemn sanctuary, I will proclaim it to any one who is willing to hear,' and so on. What impudence, thus by worldly wisdom to contradict, without more ado, Christ, the Apostles, and all the witnesses to the truth, who were unwise or fantastic enough to proclaim it in the streets and to take the prcolamation seriously. . . . Now, in modern Christianity, when we are all supposed to be Christians, they do not dare to proclaim the Gospel in the streets, yet when all were either Jews or heathen, they did this. . . . It would have been right if Mynster had said, 'I lack faith and courage and power to proclaim this gospel in the streets.' "[7] This subterfuge of taking refuge in the stillness of the house of God for the preaching of the Gospel, arises from that other subterfuge, of cleaving only to an elect circle instead of to the people who of course are assumed to be mere Christians: "Let us form a small circle which will stick together. [This occurs in one of his last published sermons, where on the occasion of '48 he wishes to offer the comfort that there are still circles in which in some degree matters can be safely arranged]. I do not propose here to linger long over the point that the circles or the circle which sticks together is hardly the best assembly of Christians, but consists of those who are distinguished from a worldly point of view. No, even if such a circle were composed of the best Christians, what an untruth it expresses! It derives profit from the fantasy that a Christian State is there (. . . the profit of being a bishop or high official, etc.), and existentially it declares that the mass of men are anything but Christians, are merely a rude and ignorant rabble."[8]

Kierkegaard is quite clear about the fact that the two delusions: a Christian State and official Christianity are mutually conditioned and support each other and therefore must fall together. But in spite of this he wrote the article against Rudelbach, and up to the outbreak of the struggle after Mynster's death, he did everything to defend the State Church and its government against the demands of the Free Church movement, whether that of Grundtvig or of the orthodox, as

---

[7] *Op. cit.*, x.1, 359.                    [8] *Op. cit.*, x.1, 611.

also against the liberal party. To this end he also supported the authority of the Church, just as on political ground he was more conservative than the most conservative of his contemporaries, and issued warnings against the slightest concessions to the demands of the time. This might seem the more remarkable as even in the sphere of secular politics he had long realised the untenableness of existing conditions.

On the occasion of a discussion of the short novel *To Tidsaldre* he gives as early as the year 1846 a criticism of the contemporary political and social situation[9] and foresees with astonishing clarity not merely the events of the year 1848, but the whole political and social development up to the present time. He realises that the levelling-down of all authority and the general process of disintegration can no longer be held up. "If authority and power have formerly been abused in the world and so have brought the nemesis of revolution upon themselves, it was in truth powerlessness and weakness which insisted on standing on their own feet and so have brought this nemesis on themselves."[10] Hence there is no possibility of going back to a former stage of political development. But likewise the way by which the socialistic or communistic movement wishes to progress offers no solution by which man might come into his own as an individual existing in responsibility before God. "It must not be supposed that the idea of socialism and community life will prove the salvation of our time; it is on the contrary the fruit of scepticism which belongs to it so that the process of individualistic liberation can go straight ahead, each individual either getting lost and perishing, or, reared in abstractions, conquering his rights."[11] This will happen in the following way: "The principle of association (which at the most can be justified in regard to material interests) is not, in our time, affirmative but negative, it is a subterfuge, a distraction from the main issue, a snare, the dialectic of which is that in strengthening the individual, it enervates him, for it strengthens by numerical collectivisation, which is, from the ethical

---

[9] *S. V.*, VIII, 1-105; *Kritik der Gegenwart*, cited below as *K. G.*, tr. T. Häcker, Innsbruck 1922. Except as stated, all further refs. in this section are to *S. V.* and *K. G.*

[10] VIII, 100-1; 65.                    [11] VIII, 99; 61-2.

point of view, a weakness. Not until the individual has won an ethical bearing in face of the whole world, not until then can there be any talk of truly uniting, otherwise the union will be a union of the weak, who are each for themselves, and will prove as ugly and corrupt as the marriage of children."[12] Thus the development towards socialism cannot be stopped by any attempt to put the clock back, but one must ask what will follow it when individuals begin to work themselves free from the levelling-down process. "And when the human race, which aimed at egalitarianism, emancipation, at the destruction of all authority and themselves, has thus started the ruinous forest-fires of abstraction through the scepticism of socialism, when it has thus crushed out all individuality and removed all organic concretions, and has set up in their place 'humanity' and the numerical equality of man and man; when the race has rejoiced for one moment at the far stretching prospect of this dreary abstract monotony, which is limited and disturbed by nothing at all pre-eminent, not the slightest thing, but is merely so much empty 'air and water,' then begins the work by which individuals must help themselves, each for himself."[13] Thus alone can the levelling-down process be overcome in a progressive way by such individuals as have worked to win their way through it, and without claiming any authority for themselves have introduced a new measure of greatness and order of merit. Only so can the failure of the authorities now collapsing be repaired—a failure due to the fact that "men have lost sight of the religious isolation of the individual in the presence of God and of his responsibility in eternity."[14]

This is the line of development which Kierkegaard foresees. As he thinks of its inevitable consequences, the huge losses in the concrete forms of civilisation, with their priceless value for the ethical and cultural development of mankind, will he strive to stem the tide? Or will he hasten to support the inevitable future, thinking of his idea that in the last resort the levelling-down process can only be halted inasmuch as "the individual in his isolation wins strength and courage to attain religious awareness"?[15] Kierkegaard can do neither of these two things,

---

[12] VIII, 99; 62.       [13] VIII, 100; 64.
[14] VIII, 80; 31.       [15] VIII, 81; 32.

for "the levelling-down process must remain," yet "it is as unavoidable as the fact that offences must come into the world, but woe to him through whom they come!"[16]

Kierkegaard's dialectical position with regard to the official connexion of State and Church is defined in the following terms: "Hardly anyone is more knowledgeable than I am about the objections which, from a Christian point of view, are to be made to a State Church, a democratic Church, and Christianity as it at present exists, etc.; *item*, that in the strictly Christian sense the demand is separation—that is, the demand of supreme idealism. But I say that to undertake to effect this separation is a religious concern in so lofty a sense, that only a qualitatively distinguished religious character could carry it out, strictly speaking an Apostle, and at the least a witness to the truth would be required. And it must be done properly and in keeping; we must not chatter about it in an idle and character-less way. To get a characterless muddle-head to dare a thing of this kind would be infinitely madder than to set a stay-at-home pork-butcher to command a brigade or to set a barber to do a difficult surgical operation. Now I have not discovered a single individual on the scene who might even be taken to resemble such a distinguished religious character. On the other hand, there are some who attempt this operation, botching and bungling it in a characterless and inadmissible way. That is absolutely ruinous (as they say, *corruptio optimi pessima*). The mess of existing official Christianity is by no means praiseworthy, but it is infinitely preferable to a characterless reformation. Here lies my own relevance to the situation. If I were to give myself out to be a witness to the truth or something of that kind, I should be without significance. For this very reason I am true enough to hold in check characterless unethical attempts at reformation. But in order to be able to do so, I again demand what I demand from myself—concessions. As when a regiment has failed in its duty, and as a whole is degraded, it is my opinion that if we may not and will not dare by a long way to make an end of this popular Church, then we must unite in realising that we are degraded, and in confessing that in the strict sense we are not Christians. And how do I

[16] VIII, 82; 35.

personally proceed in this issue? Do I come forward as one who so to speak has a command from God to degrade present official Christianity? Oh no, I have no such competence. Myself moved by the ideal, I find a joy in feeling myself degraded and without competence in striving to move others to the same feeling."[17]

Everything now depends on whether Mynster will make this concession.

## 17. THE CONCEPTION OF A WITNESS TO TRUTH

Kierkegaard was forced very soon to realise that Mynster would never make the expected concession. But he did not on that account become untrue to himself. Not he, but Mynster, must decide what was the next move. But in consequence of the long expectation of this decision and in view of eventual future possibilities, Kierkegaard thought further about the problem of the conditions under which it might be possible to take the next step and "to come forward in character." In this connexion the conception of the witness to the truth had to be clarified dialectically from every angle.

Kierkegaard had already been working in this direction through his intense preoccupation with the case of the Danish pastor Adler. In 1843 the latter had appealed to a revelation made especially to him, had been relieved of his office, and in 1846 published papers relating to his situation which Kierkegaard at once studied with great eagerness. The book which Kierkegaard wrote on the subject in 1846-47 was never published.[1] But in 1847 he did publish, under the pseudonym H. H., two essays bearing closely on this and partially taken from his *Buch über Adler*. They were: "Has a man the right to allow himself to be put to death for the truth's sake?"[2] and "Concerning the difference between a genius and an Apostle."[3]

Adler appeals to a revelational event, and, as far as official

---

[17] *S. K. P.*, x.4(A), 296.
[1] *S. K. P.*, VII.2, 6-230; *Der Begriff des Auserwählten*, cited below as *B. A.*, tr. T. Häcker, Innsbruck 1926.
[2] *Op. cit.*, 273-313; *S. V.*, XI, 47-91; *Ges. W.*, X, 103-37.
[3] *Op. cit.*, 313-33; *S. V.*, XI, 93-109; *Ges. W.*, X, 139-56.

Christianity is concerned, he thus has, as an "extraordinary individual," a different starting-point from the "ordinary individual," and must relate himself to the common life differently from the latter. This latter reproduces and "develops the life of organised Christianity in his personal existence; the institution is for him the basic thing, which in its affinity with him penetrates and moulds his personal gifts; he is an individual whose life follows the pattern of the official."[4] It is otherwise with the extraordinary individual who "deviates so far that as an individual he does not renew and reproduce the common life within himself, by subjecting himself to it with a sense of eternal responsibility, but he wishes to renew the common life by providing it with a new starting-point, i.e., new in relation to the presupposition basic to the official institution, and by his sense of *immediate* dependence on God he wishes to remodel the institution: in this way he is extraordinary, which is to say that he is to be recognised as such whether he is personally justified or not; it is in this sphere proper to him that he must win his victory and submit to judgment, the institution must exclude him completely."[5] "Hence the new point of view was the difference between the sincere ordinary man and the sincere extraordinary man; the essential human criterion, the ethical, they have both in common. If the individual is really a genuine extraordinary person and really has a new creative point of view, if he sees the crushing difficulty of his life in the light of that *discrimen* between the universal and the particular *extra ordinem*, then he must be immediately discernible by the fact that he is prepared to *make sacrifices*. And he must be prepared to do so both for his own sake and for the sake of the majority."[6]

The question whether he will succeed is his smallest concern, and in this he differs from the spuriously extraordinary men, the men who initiate movements. The latter have "no place and no time to dare to do something especially noble. Their business is co-ordinated with the affairs of time, the question of success is therefore not merely the *telos* of their efforts. But for them it is basically *success* which must prove that they are

---

[4] *S. K. P.*, vii2.40; *B. A.*, 47. All refs. in nn. 5-12 below are to *S. K. P.*, vii.2, and *B. A.*

[5] 41; 47-8.        [6] 45; 52.

right and their ideas just. Thus he has not merely to use once more the majority, he *needs* them, if only in order to dress them in a new uniform in accordance with his plan."[7]    Hence he cannot stand alone; "on the contrary, he himself desires to carry the majority with him, in order to convince himself that what he wishes is true and useful."[8]    It is just the opposite with the sincerely extraordinary man: "he has triumphed already, for his relationship to God is his triumph; in fact, even if what he has to proclaim never triumphed in the world, his answer would be, 'So much the worse for the world.' "[9]    The man of movements "has not the courage to become the *discernible* outstanding person who wills something and is prepared to take every risk for what he wills."[9]    Not until after his victory does he cause himself to be celebrated, whereas the sincerely distinguished man "was recognised through his suffering and martyrdom: it goes without saying that he cannot later go around and receive congratulations—but neither can he be mistaken for what he is."[10]

"The conditions of the time in which he lives must always be of service to a truly extraordinary man; thus, as regards our own day, he would have to have supremely at his command what constitutes our special characteristic: the power of reflexion and understanding.    The essential phenomenal difference between a man of our time who has received a revelation and such a one of earlier times will be that the former appropriates the revelation with a more highly developed power of reflexion.    Our time is an epoch of reflexion; it can hardly be supposed that the divine providence is not aware of this.    The reflexion of the chosen one must not destroy for him the extraordinary character of the revelation, no, but he must avail himself of the whole power of reflexion when he fits himself and his revelation into the context of the times.    He must be dialectically aware of dangers and difficulties of which the prophet of former days had no suspicion.    In a period of advanced thought the chosen one must be both inspired by a revelation (and he must be unshakably convinced that it was and is a revelation) and also the greatest interpreter of the day. His gifts and level of moral development do not make him at all

---

[7] 48; 36.        [8] 51; 59.        [9] 52; 61.        [10] 53; 62.

*worthy* to be chosen of God—there is no question of merit in face of God's election—but the fact that he has these gifts and is highly developed ethically is his phenomenological mark."[11]

He needs these gifts in order that he may succeed in relating himself to the official institution, for "the extraordinary must be imparted, must be fitted into the context of the common life; and the chosen one, the unique one, must receive the terrible jolt of *being* a paradox if he is to communicate it. Dialectically there are two points here; that the shock should qualitatively and decisively be the shock of truth; and, on the other hand, that the common life should as far as possible be spared. Just as little as God is a God of confusion, so little is the elect man called to confuse minds and then to run away. He must love the common life and be willing to sacrifice himself. Just as one uses the caustic stone with extreme precaution (not for fear of using it but in order to use it correctly), just as a man wraps it up so that no one can directly touch it, so the elect man must take heed to consecrate himself as the inspired individual so that none may suffer harm by direct contact. The one who is called is at the same time the one who consecrates himself. For what in him, if he is sincere, is eternal truth, the gift of divine grace, is in any other by mere contact with the extraordinary, dallying, falseness, lostness."[12]

How far may his self-sacrifice go? Is it legitimate for him to allow himself to be slain for the truth which he represents? Here the question is not whether he has the courage and power for this, but whether he has the right thus to make others guilty of his murder, hence whether his responsibility for the truth which he expresses goes so far. Christ did so. But Christ may not be brought into the consideration, firstly because by His death of which He allows His murderers to become guilty He brings about the forgiveness of their sins. In regard to every other man who comes forward in a similar way, the question must, however, be posed: "Has the death of the witness to the truth any *vicarious* power? No, only the death of Christ had such, for He was more than man and died for the whole human race. Even if the death of the witness to the

[11] 55; 64-5.        [12] 64-5; 75-6.

K

truth makes the guilty aware of the truth, their guilt remains none the less, and then even shows itself for the first time in all its enormity.  Hence have I the right to use such a violent and terrible means of warning?"[13]

The question may be put (1) in regard to the relation between heathen and heathen.  Here the answer is "no," because in their case we cannot assume that any one of them may raise the claim to be in possession of absolute truth, and thus the distinction between them is only relative.  "Hence Socrates would certainly not affirm that he was in the strictest sense put to death for the sake of the truth."[14]  (2) In the relation between Christian and heathen, the Christian, through his communion with Christ, is rooted absolutely in the truth.  "Thus the difference between him and the other is an absolute one and finds absolute expression just in the fact that the Christian is put to death by the heathen."[15]  Hence here the answer is "yes."  (3) "In the relation between Christian and Christian it can only be a matter of a relative distinction as in the case of heathen and heathen.  Hence a Christian might well allow his fellow Christians to become guilty of mocking and jeering at him.  No doubt this, too, would involve the responsibility of his making them guilty by this means: but this much relatively to them he may owe to the truth: so far he may be above them in his knowledge of the truth.  This may also serve to arouse their awareness.  But in this situation there is no crime which cannot be atoned for.  If, on the other hand, it was said to be permissible in Christianity to let oneself be slain for the truth, then it would first have to be established that so-called Christianity is not Christian, but as 'unspirituality' is more heathen than heathendom.  But if we feel that we cannot altogether deny that professing Christians are Christian (and may any man go so far as that?  If anyone dared do so, would he not have to know the human heart as only omniscience knows it?), then we may not allow ourselves to be put to death for the truth's sake nor allow others to become guilty of such a death."[16]  Hence the question is to be answered negatively.

[13] S. V., XI, 74-5; Ges. W., X, 122-3.  Except as stated, all further refs. in this section are to S. V. and Ges. W.
[14] XI, 88; X, 131.          [15] XI, 88; X, 134.          [16] XI, 89; X, 135.

But this still does not answer the question which is for Kierkegaard the central issue of his life's mission in its bearing on Christianity as established.  The case is rather that one must reckon with the possibility that so-called Christianity is in reality heathendom, and in fact far worse than the latter, and that therefore he who is certain of this has the right to allow himself to be put to death for the truth's sake just because this is his conviction.  What categorical qualifications must such a one have?  He would need to have not only the authority which the Apostle claimed with regard to the heathen world, but as a prophet within Christianity he would need to have the competence to challenge the latter to resist him and to martyr him, in order that he might make clear the condition of existing Christianity.  Kierkegaard concerned himself with this figure of the "martyr prophet" ever since the "Adler case" had come forward, and long before he demanded the admission from Mynster.  Such a figure has first to be characterised in relation to the figure of the *Apostle*, whose authority must be the starting-point for its own effectiveness.

We have already met the question as to the definition of an Apostle in connexion with our consideration of the way in which the communication of the later Christian corresponds to the self-attestation of Jesus, or more exactly the authority with which Jesus demands that faith, in obedience, should decide against scandalisation (pp. 88, 89).  The point here is how the relation of the Christian teacher to the hearer of his message goes further than the Socratic relation between man and man.  Such communication must contain an "historical '*not abene*' " forestalling the possibility that revelation through history might be made into revelation as eternal truth.  This emphasis on the historical ensues when the communication takes place through an Apostle or through an ordained clergyman as the continuator of the Apostolic witness, for both these, in consequence of their commission, have been so paradoxically transformed in time as to have become endowed with the specific quality of authority in relation to their hearers.  As regards this authority Kierkegaard makes no difference between the Apostle and the clergyman: "Authority is a specific quality given to the Apostle through his calling and to the pastor through his

ordination.''[17]    Kierkegaard does not take into account the
difference between these two orders, which springs from the
fact that the authority of the clergyman is derived from that of
the Apostle and in practice is rendered effective by invocation
of the authority of the Apostle in the preaching of Scripture.
Equally, he does not consider how the Apostle is related to the
Christ from whom his authority flows, i.e., how his calling comes
about.    Kierkegaard simply says:    "It goes without saying
that an infinite and qualitative distinction exists between Christ
and every elect soul.    Christ Himself embodies the sphere of
the paradoxical, whereas the elect person is derivative, marked
out to belong to this sphere.''[18]    The centre of interest here lies
clearly in the fact of being thus marked out, in consequence of
which the historical aspect of revelation is accentuated.    In this
respect, at all events, there can be no difference between the
pastor and the Apostle, however great the difference between
them would be if we asked how the derivation of their authority
originated.    The latter question, however, from the point of
view of the right assertion of this authority in modern preaching,
can have only, for Kierkegaard, a historical or speculative
interest.

Of course it would become an acute issue in face of the
possibility that someone in the present arose claiming direct
revelation and in consequence claiming to belong to the order
of the Apostle as contrasted with the only mediately-appointed
pastor.    Then quite a different set of questions would have to
be broached.    The question seems to be implied in the Adler
case.    As the latter, however, soon showed himself to be a
crazy fellow, he served Kierkegaard only as an instance in the
light of which to work out dialectically the problems involved
in such cases.    To do so was an obvious step for Kierkegaard to
take, since he reckoned with the possibility of a personal call to
the "extraordinary" in his own case, although he was not able
to entertain firmly the conviction of a special vocation.

Alongside the equation of Apostle and pastor as regards the
paradoxical-dialectical basis of their authority, are also to be

[17] XI, 101 n.; X, 148 n.
[18] S. K. P., V.112, B.S. 66 n.; B. A., 78 n.  See also Appendix I (below,
208 ff.).

found in Kierkegaard statements which seem to distinguish the Apostle from the pastor in specific ways. Once in the *Stadien* the question is directly put "whether the pastor is, then, an Apostle; and, if not, in what way he is distinct from the Apostle, and wherein he resembles the latter."[19] No answer is given, and in this direct form the question is not again asked by Kierkegaard or his pseudonyms. In various passages of the *Nachschrift* where it is a question of the Apostle, various points of view are apparent. On one occasion it is a question of the historically peculiar situation of the Apostle, who has to introduce Christianity as an unknown truth, and the implied demands on dialectical communication are discussed.[20] At another time, the question arises of the difference between an Apostle and "one who is awakened." The latter is immediately certain of his faith and can make his relation to God outwardly manifest without any concealed inwardness. The Apostle, on the contrary, is described as follows: "One should remember that the life of an Apostle is paradoxical and dialectical, therefore he turns his attention outwards. Any one who is not an Apostle, if he does this, becomes a misguided aesthetic."[21] In this sense it is true of the Apostle that "his existence is right if it is as nobody else's may be."[22]

This paradoxical-dialectical form of the Apostle's existence rests on the revelation which has come to him. As a result of this the commission and the competence for his message is granted him—in other words, what the clergyman receives through ordination. But with the revelation the Apostle's existence is transformed and rooted in a communion with God which is qualitatively different from that of all other men because it has originated in a different way. According to what was said about the difference between the Apostle and the one aroused to attention, this Godward relation would seem to be capable of being imparted directly in a unique way. How is this to be understood?

In any case it cannot mean that the Apostle, by a special

[19] VI, 319; IV, 309.
[20] VII, 204, 376; VI, 315; VII, 124.
[21] VII, 440 n.; VII, 192 n.
[22] VII, 394; VII, 143. Cp. also VII, 337, 494; VII, 82, 948.

mode of existence capable of outward manifestation, can and must make the authority of his message sensibly felt and its truth guaranteed. If he did so, he would do more than what Christ Himself was able to do. Here, too, there cannot be in question anything more than arousing attention. "An Apostle has no other proof than that of his message itself; to which at most may be added that he is ready to suffer willingly and joyfully everything that his message entails in the way of suffering. Briefly then his manner of address is: 'I am called of God; do with me as you please; scourge me, kill me—my last word is still the same as my first: I am called of God and make you responsible for your conduct towards me'."[23] But this would not fundamentally differentiate him as a witness to the truth from the pastor, but only to the extent that the latter in general does not invite such opposition and perhaps also would not be ready to endure it (if need be) in terms of suffering. But this outward suffering does not even necessarily belong to the vocation of Apostle as such. He is simply "the official representative". "And as the messenger has only to convey the message faithfully, the ambassador his instructions: so in the main it is the sole business of the Apostle to be faithful in his service, and to fulfil his office truly. If he does this, he is essentially sacrificing himself, even though he is never persecuted: 'namely by the fact that he, himself poor, has only to make others rich,' that he may never permit himself to enjoy in carefree quiet and leisure the wealth which he brings to others. In the sphere of divine things he is like the busy housekeeping mother who, in her anxiety to provide food for others, hardly manages to get any food herself."[24] All this can again apply equally well to the pastor, especially when one sees his task as Kierkegaard once described it: "Pastors who, having at their disposal a very desirable culture, are expert not so much in arid scholastic exercises but rather in the struggle where the decisive factor is presence of mind, in the struggle not so much against the attacks and questionings of the learned but rather against human passions; pastors who know how to divide up the mass of humanity into real individual persons; pastors who do not make great claims to study and learning and desire

[23] XI, 106; X, 154.        [24] XI, 107; X, 154-5.

nothing less than to rule; pastors who, eloquent when need
arises, are no less skilled in the art of silence and patient
endurance; pastors who, knowing the human heart as far as
possible, have learnt no less how to restrain themselves from
judgment and condemnation; pastors who have understood
how to exercise authority through their readiness for self-
sacrifice; pastors who have been trained and educated in the
school of obedience and suffering so that they might soothe,
exhort, edify, and stir the heart, and if need be, coerce—not
indeed by might (in fact nothing less!), but by the influence of
their own obedience, and, above all, so that they might bear
all the rudeness of their 'patient' without allowing themselves
to be disturbed any more than a doctor is disturbed by the
cursing and kicking of his patient during an operation."[25] In
this respect, at any rate, we do not find any categorical discrimination between the witnessing of the Apostle and that of
the pastor.

But by introducing the contrast to the person who is awakened Kierkegaard seems to have considered that the distinctive-
ness of the Apostle does not lie merely in the different way in
which his relation with God *arose*, but also in the different way in
which it is *communicable*, for the Apostle communicates his
message in such a way as to make an aesthetic reaction impossible. But can this mean anything other than that the apostle
effectively communicates his paradoxical-dialectical situation
by referring as his authority to the call that was mediated to
him through revelation and thus by pointing to the absolute
paradox, setting in motion the process of interior dialectical
assimilation? For "it must happen just so; otherwise the
believer would make direct rather than paradoxical contact
with the Gospel."[26] But does not this apply just as essentially
to the pastor?

The examination of the distinctive dialectical qualifications
of the Apostle in his communication of truth does not go further
than this point. But this is not Kierkegaard's special *concern*.
After he has established that the Apostle enjoys an immediate
revelation and an immediate relation with God, his interest is

[25] *Eftirladtfe Papirer*, III, 484, quoted in Geismar, *S. K.*, 390-1.
[26] XI, 106; X, 153.

not in deciding how the Apostle's own existence, in its stricter form, is distinguished from that of all others—certain as this is— but, on the contrary, in the question what this implies for all others in regard to discipleship to Christ. This is especially clear in *An exhortation to self-examination at the present time* (1851), and especially in *Judge for Yourselves* (1876), the second part, which did not appear until after Kierkegaard's death.

The pastor of course is not an Apostle. But this can hardly mean that he is not to be a witness to the truth. The Apostolate is a specific form of witnessing to the truth. Kierkegaard distinguishes from the Apostle the witness in the broader sense, e.g., the teacher of Christianity in the early pre-Constantine centuries.[27] The latter is not a witness to the truth in consequence of some immediate revelation, but he enjoys this dignity as a result of the fact that he obtained no profit from the declaration of Christian truth, on the contrary he lived for it and if necessary also died for it.

Witnessing to the truth is the appropriate form of the communication of Christianity because only so can the opposition of Christianity to the world be made clear, only so can the transformation of life wrought by the Gospel be thrown into relief and a vital impulsion towards it be given.[28] But again this must not be taken to imply that the paradoxical-dialectical change in the status and being of the Christian teacher flowing from the Apostolic call or from ordination is thereby made superfluous. This "historical '*nota bene*'" can neither be replaced by the existential character of the witness to the truth nor can the authoritative commission it implies first be made good in this way. But neither is the converse true, namely that ordination releases the clergyman from the obligation to be a witness to the truth. Nor can it confer upon him a dignity similar to that of the witness. "But look, the clergy are constantly hankering after this sort of dignity, though their lives are totally different from the lives of these splendid men and the preaching of Christianity has become the same thing as any other secular calling or source of income, an utterly worldly thing. And this sort of spiritual dignity does not belong to it. A pastor of our time can really make claim to no other dignity

[27] XII, 404; XI, 106.        [28] *S. K. P.*, x.3, 59; 62.

but such as any other man can acquire through his exertions in his profession. Ordination can give him no sort of personal consequence. For if the life of the ordained person is thoroughly worldly, he cannot plead his ordination as a source of dignity."[29]

The same is true with regard to the relation of the teacher and his doctrine to the witness to the truth. If the Christian teacher is such a witness, then the witness of his life cannot take the place of the doctrine he proclaims or alone validate its truth. Its truth rests rather solely on the fact of revelation, by which his personal existence was changed. But, conversely, the testimony of the life of the witness cannot be replaced by the objective truth of the doctrine he teaches and by such a communication of it as would be without effect on the personal existence of the teacher and his hearers. "For it is not true that doctrine remains the same whoever the teacher. For in one case the proclamation of doctrine is truth and certifies itself as such through its proclamation; in another case the manner of the proclamation turns the doctrine into untruth; so that the doctrine does not really remain the same."[30]

But what is to be done when, in the present situation of official Christianity, the latter has "conquered," the world has become "Christian," with the result that there is really no need and no room for the witness to the truth? This is the old question from the *Einübung*: "How can the 1800 years be revoked in their consequences?" In *Judge for yourselves*, again, the "concession" is required as the first essential prerequisite for a change in this false situation, "so that there may arise not something different, something external, a revolution in outward conditions."[31] "Every competent clergyman will certainly see that for himself and every younger man will find it a reasonable demand and will be concerned about it. If some are so rooted in this false scale of values that they cannot decide to make such

---

[29] XII, 404; XI, 106. Cp. *S. K. P.*, x.3, 325.

[30] XII, 406; XI, 108. Cp. *S. K. P.*, x.2, 431: "My thesis is not that what is thus proclaimed in official Christianity ought not to be regarded as Christian. No, my thesis is that proclamation in itself is not Christianity. What I am concerned about is the 'how,' the personal enforcement of the proclamation: without that, Christianity is not Christianity."

[31] XII, 408; XI, 111.

admissions, that rather in spite of the possibly dangerous consequences (in a time like this which is so critical for Christianity) they prefer to leave things as they are, then that is their business."[32] Here, also, it is particularly plain that this admission is not conceived as contrasting with action, but is only the first necessary step in the achievement of true Christian discipleship.

In official Christianity the situation requisite to witnessing to the truth has been lost, and so the imitation of Christ has also faded from our minds. Hence this situation must be restored. This does not necessarily require any change in outward circumstances. But when people have realised that we can no longer be content with the mere proclamation of Christianity, but that understanding must develop at once into action, then they will no longer aim (for example) at meeting doubt in the sphere of doctrine with reasons *pro et contra*: "No, a situation is required—dare to take the first decisive step! Proof does not precede but follows, it lies in and comes with true discipleship to Christ. If you have taken the first decisive step in consequence of which you have separated your life from the life of this world, and can no longer have your life in the life of this world, but must bring your life into opposition to the life of the world: then gradually you will come to such a tension that you can perceive the truth of which the Gospel is speaking."[33] Then there will spontaneously arise a situation in which one must again and again stake one's existence on faith and the imitation of Christ.

Kierkegaard shows this with reference to Luther. The superiority of the Middle Ages as contrasted with modern Christianity is that its attention was orientated towards the transformation of existence. But the unspirituality which characterised it as a result of its erroneous preoccupation with works, and with the question of merit, led either to presumption or despair, and hence Luther broke with "the whole set of apish tricks which passed under the name of Christian discipleship."[34] But he did not do away with the idea of discipleship, on the contrary it consisted for him "in witnessing to the truth and in the many dangers which he voluntarily took upon himself,

[32] XII, 407; XI, 109.    [33] XII, 459; XI, 168.    [34] XII, 461; XI, 169.

without making a merit out of it."[35]   In the next generation, however, the situation required for decisive action was again lost.   They were no longer capable of attaining faith for their fear of over-valuing works but began with the assumption that all had faith "of course," and made Christianity an object of thought.   Thus truth was held *in suspenso* by considerations *pro et contra*, and no decisive step was taken towards true discipleship.

Even in this work, although the tone of his comments has become sharper, Kierkegaard does not go beyond the *Einübung* either as regards his own attitude towards official Christianity or as regards the categories he employs, and he already introduces quite a number of those destructive satires on established Christianity which will appear later in the pages of the *Augenblick*.   He concludes with the words: "In this way must we bring out the inspiration of Christ as our example;  yet not in order to create anxiety, though perhaps today it is quite needless to worry about the possibility of frightening people by means of Christianity;  but, in any case, we must not wish to frighten people, we should have learnt that lesson from the experience of former ages.   No, we must make effective the authority and inspiration of our example and pattern, in order to awaken at least a certain amount of respect for the religion of Christianity;  in order to make it clear, to some extent, what it means to be a Christian, in order to transfer Christianity from the objective plane (the approach of learning, doubt, and chatter) to the subjective.   That it truly belongs to the latter sphere is just as certain as that the Saviour of the world, our Lord Jesus Christ, did not bring a system of doctrine into the world, neither did He teach, but rather as a pattern demanded discipleship—and, at the same time, through the power of His atonement, drove, as far as possible, all fear out of the human soul."[36]

The essay, however, has a postscript, headed by the word "Moral" and above it stands in the smallest print: "In case this should be needed."[37]   In this passage he again discusses the possibility which we found discussed in the *Buch über Adler*

[35] XII, 461; XI, 170.          [36] XII, 474-5; XI, 185-6.
[37] XII, 478 ff.; XI, 187 f.

that some person might unmask the existing condition of contemporary Christianity and would claim the right to do so (with all its inevitable consequences) by referring to the authority of an immediate revelation vouchsafed to him as an individual, and as the "extraordinary" man "would dare to undertake the position and task of a reformer." Kierkegaard is prepared to admire and respect such a one, but also "if he should fail to be consistent with that character" to challenge and attack him with deadly certainty. But if no one dare undertake this task, "then the official Christian religion must remain as such and be maintained in its authority—so long as it is prepared to make the concession, which truth demands, that from a strictly Christian point of view it is only a mild approximation to the religion of Christ; instead of insisting that it is an exact representation of true Christianity in the New Testament sense and thus by implication judging and destroying itself." "And then it should be declared as loudly as possible and heard wherever possible and (may God grant!) wherever heard, earnestly pondered: that the evil of our time is not official Christianity with its many faults; no, the evil of our time lies precisely in that evil desire to foster velleities of reform: that false hankering after reformation without willingness to make the necessary sacrifices; that frivolous fancy that you can reform without having any idea, still less a noble idea, how unusually lofty the whole conception of reformation is; that hypocritical failure to appreciate one's own uselessness which officiously indulges in the distracting fancy of wishing to reform the Church without realising that our epoch is the least suited to and least capable of any such thing."

Up to the time of Mynster's death, Kierkegaard did not develop beyond this attitude. Nor in the many reflections of the diaries of those years did he evolve any categories going beyond what he had hitherto worked out, but sought merely to give increasing clarity to his own position within this framework of thought.

Official Christianity still has the last word, and Kierkegaard writes in his diary for 1851: "If I clash with the official Church, then that is solely possible through Mynster's mishandling of the situation. My whole idea is to defend existing Christianity and to make the only defence of it that is possible. Everything has been done to spare Mynster as much as possible. But if finally he hardens himself in the attitude that his whole misguided preaching of Christianity which has made the Church like a theatrical show is the part of wisdom, is Christianity, then it is his fault if I begin to behave differently."[38]

## 18. THE ATTACK

The situation developed precisely as Kierkegaard had foreseen, except that it was not Mynster himself who made the blunder which compelled Kierkegaard to take further steps, but Mynster's successor, namely Martensen. Mynster died on 30 January 1854 without having made the expected concession. Martensen said in his memorial sermon: "Follow the footsteps of those who in faith have borne witness to the truth! The man whose beloved memory now fills our hearts will take our thoughts to that chain of witnesses to the truth which extends from the days of the Apostles to our own time. . . . In this sacred line of witnesses our departed brother was a member who faithfully served his God, our Father in Heaven. How he exercised the witness of faith among us with every manifestation of the spirit and of power!"

Thereupon Kierkegaard immediately wrote an article entitled "Was Bishop Mynster a Witness to the Truth, one of the genuine Witnesses to the Truth: Is this *true*?"[1] In this article he raised the strongest objections to the assertion and based his reasoning on the New Testament. After its publication, Kierkegaard waited ten months until Martensen had been appointed Mynster's successor, and until certain other attacks on Mynster, in which Kierkegaard did not wish to co-operate, had died down. Then on 18 December the article in the *Faedrelandet* appeared and gave the impetus to that direct attack on official Christianity which Kierkegaard conducted with ever-increasing severity, at first in newspaper articles, and later in the pages of the *Augenblick*.

[38] *S. K. P.*, x.4, 228.
[1] *S. V.*, xiv, 5 ff.; *Angriff*, 91 ff. Except as stated all further refs. in this section are to *S. V.* and *Angriff*.

We are here concerned with this attack only from the point of view of the categories which Kierkegaard used and the question how it is related to his previous thinking and behaviour. It is remarkable that, contrary to Kierkegaard's custom of writing down far-reaching thoughts concerning every point of tactical procedure, the diaries of this last period contain hardly anything of the kind and, in general, but few entries directly relevant to the struggle which now claims his whole attention. This again shows that the decisive step he was now taking was not the consequence of philosophical reflexions and decisions as to the path he should now follow, but rather a spontaneous reaction to the blunder of Martensen, who at this moment of extreme tension could hardly have done anything better calculated to put the match to the powder barrel. "How this incomparable epigram will flash forth in the night of time, as a comment on official Christianity: that Bishop Mynster was to be buried as a witness to the truth, as one of the right genuine witnesses!"[2] The simple spontaneity of Kierkegaard's reaction in the matter does not mean that he acted over-hastily and thoughtlessly. Such an idea is contradicted by the mere consideration that Kierkegaard felt he could wait seven long months in the consciousness that he was now absolutely sure of his point and had time to spare.

Hence for us the question is whether Kierkegaard was right in feeling that he had remained true to himself by this spontaneous action, and, indeed, to his previous line of conduct. Only once—probably soon after the appearance of the article—did he himself discuss the question in the diaries. What he is concerned about is that his clash with official Christianity should not be allowed to fade out without any concrete result, but should lead to a catastrophe in which he would be ready to sacrifice himself. How can such a catastrophe be consciously contrived? "For such deliberateness alone is the truly Christian thing, the truly Christian idea of self-sacrifice, i.e., a voluntary sacrifice." But he immediately adds: "But here I stand again and am tempted to ask: Has a man permission to do such a thing? Does it not imply hardness towards others?"[3] It is the old question of the privilege of the one who is called to do

[2] *S. K. P.*, xi.2, 265.                    [3] *Op. cit.*, 263.

and be extraordinary things, the question whether a man has the right to allow himself to be put to death for the truth's sake. "How anxious men would become on my behalf if they knew this; how strange it would seem to them if they realised that this problem has occupied my mind in the whole of this last period of my life, the problem whether God does not require of me that I should stake everything on this issue, bring about a catastrophe, be arrested, condemned, and, if possible, executed. And my soul is overshadowed by the worry that if I fail to do this, I might repent it eternally; a worry which I can counter by no other means than the thought with which I constantly commend myself to God: the thought that He will watch over me to ensure that I do not neglect to do anything which I would eternally repent of neglecting. If matters were to be brought to a climax, I had thought of unexpectedly raising the alarm, after deepest silence, and shouting that the public worship of God is blasphemous and that it is criminal to take part in it. But before I was really clear in my own mind about this, I had already decided to do something else, namely to publish the article against Martensen and Mynster. For that very reason the catastrophic bearing of it was toned down." But Kierkegaard then realises himself: "Official Christianity is so demoralised that if you make a row, face to face, it prefers secretly to withdraw and to take good care not to start proceedings with you."[2]

Thus before launching the attack Kierkegaard is not clear in his own mind whether he can and should adopt and carry through the attitude of the "martyr-prophet who has even the right to allow himself to be slain for the truth's sake, in order thus to make clear the position of existing Christianity. What, according to his own categories, he feels seriously lacking for this, is authorisation by a special revelation. But, on the other hand, he must now by all means go farther than heretofore, because official Christianity has compelled him to do so. So he takes up the struggle and terminates all reflexion by action.

In this connexion he is clear about two things. First, he must make every sacrifice that is required of him; that he does

2 *S. K. P.*, xi.2, 265.

so will be the sole justification for his procedure. Secondly, even now, he must need no follower nor place himself at the head of a movement, but must carry through the struggle as a lone individual. According to his own ideas he is justified only by the fulfilment of these two conditions in acting as the extraordinary individual without having the authorisation of any special revelation.

Kierkegaard fulfilled both these conditions. He strictly refused the help of any association or fellowship in his fight. And as he personally carried it on quite consciously and relentlessly against his adversaries, so, above all, he spared himself in no way and paid no heed to the fact that the outraged public considered that he was acting not only without Christian seriousness and sense of responsibility, but even without human propriety. Further, he has now made that sacrifice which was especially costly to him, and thus occasioned the utmost heartsearching: the renunciation of a secure economic basis for his life. He used up the remainder of his income in financing his strife. On 2 Oct. 1855 he collapsed in the street and was taken to hospital. The illness of which he died on 11 Nov. remained a mystery to the doctors. When the costs of his funeral were paid, his means were entirely exhausted.

What was at issue for Kierkegaard in this struggle he expresses most plainly in the article of 31 Mar. 1855, "What do I want?"[4]

"Quite simply, I want honesty! I pay no attention at all to what angry, mad, weak, gossiping enemies think of me. Neither do I represent—as some well-wishers would like to think—the severity of Christian discipline as opposed to the usual Christian mildness of disposition."

"Certainly not, I represent neither laxity nor discipline—I represent human honesty."

"What I have intended is to bring out the contrast between official Christianity as it is organised in our country, and the Christianity of the New Testament, so that people can see them side by side."

"If it can be shown, if I or anyone else can show, that our official Christianity can stand its ground in face of New Testa-

[4] xiv, 52 ff.; 146 ff.

ment Christianity, then I will go into the matter with the greatest pleasure."

"But one thing I will not do at any cost: I will not, by concealment of evidence or any touching-up process, try to make it appear that the Christianity which prevails in our country and the Christianity of the New Testament resemble each other."

"If the official Christianity of the country feels compelled, as a result of what I have said, to use violence against me, I am ready; for what I want is honesty."

"For this honesty I am prepared to risk all. But I do not say that I am risking anything for Christianity itself. Let us suppose that I wished to sacrifice myself, yet it is not for Christianity that I want to sacrifice myself but purely for honesty."

"While I do not venture to say that I am daring all for the sake of Christianity, yet I am fully and blessedly convinced of this, that my venture is well-pleasing to God and has His approval. Yes, I know very well that He is well pleased with this fact, that in the midst of a world of Christians where millions and millions call themselves Christians, there is a man who expresses himself thus: 'I may not call myself a Christian, but I am determined to have honesty, and to that end I will dare all'."

In the programmatic pamphlet, "This should be said; let it then be said,"[5] published on 24 May 1855, the following consequences of this demand for honesty are drawn:

"Whoever you may be, and whatever else your life may be, my friend, by the fact that you no longer (if up to now you have done otherwise) take part in the public worship of God as it is now performed (with the claim to be New Testament Christianity); by that fact you are continually incurring a lesser degree of guilt, and of heavy guilt; for you do not take part in it to hold God a fool that people should declare to be New Testament Christianity what is clearly not so."

Since the "concession" was never made, there remains for Kierkegaard no other recourse than to expose the contradiction between the spirit of the New Testament and official Christianity as currently organised; and all his articles and pamphlets

[5] XIV, 83 ff.; 186 ff.

attempt nothing else but to do this as sharply and inexorably as possible by every means at his command.  In the ruthlessness of the attack with which he now pillories official Christianity and especially the clergy, he doubtless exceeds his former manner of presentation, though he does not intrinsically surpass the substance of his previous contention.  All possibilities of defending and justifying official Christianity, which there might still have been had the concession been made, are now no more.  For this reason, therefore, everything must now be said with a certain *one-sidedness* such as Kierkegaard in his diary of 1849 applies to himself in his role of *corrective* to the official version of Christianity:

"The description 'corrective' implies something relative, as when we say 'here' or 'there,' 'right' or 'left.'  Any one who wishes to supply the corrective, must carefully and deeply study the weakness of the official version, putting forward the opposite view as one-sidedly as possible, and as correctly as possible.  It is just in so doing that correction lies, and in this, too, that the resignation of the corrector consists.  For correction is thus in a sense freely bestowed.  When this work has been correctly done, there may come along a man of supposedly acute mind and object that the corrective is one-sided—and then bring the public to believe that there is something in what he says.  Good heavens!  Nothing is easier than for the one who supplies the correction to set down also the other side of the matter; in so doing, however, he would cease to be the critic and would identify himself with what he criticises."[6]

When in May 1855, at the height of his struggle, Kierkegaard brings out a second edition of the *Einübung im Christentum*, he says with reference to it in an article in a newspaper dated 16 May 1855:[7]

"I have allowed this work to be reprinted in a quite *unchanged* edition because I regard it as a document of historical significance."

"Were it being brought out now for the first time, now when pious respect for the dead Bishop has faded, and I, too, in consequence of its first edition have reached the conviction that established Christianity, from a Christian point of view,

<hr />

[6] *S. K. P.*, x.1, 640.                    [7] xiv, 80 ff.;  184 ff.

is untenable, then I would have arranged some things differently: I would not have used a pseudonym, but named myself
as the author, I would have omitted the thrice-repeated
Foreword, as also the 'Moral' of Part I, where the pseudonym
expresses the point of view which I personally supported in the
Foreword. . . ."

"My earlier thought was that if official Christianity is
capable of any defence at all, then it can only be in this way,
that judgment was passed upon it figuratively (hence through
a pseudonym), and then, secondly, grace was brought to bear
on it so that Christianity found in grace not merely forgiveness
for the past, but also was afforded by grace some degree of
remission in the imitation of Christ and in the tension of effort
to fulfil Christian existence in itself. In this way some sincerity
and truth could be restored to the official Church. It justifies
itself by condemning itself; it recognises the Christian demand
and confesses its own failure to fulfil that demand, while also
renouncing any claim to be making any real effort to come
nearer to any such fulfilment of the demand: rather it seeks
refuge in grace, 'even for the sake of the use which is made of
grace'. . . ."

"Now, on the contrary, two points are quite clear to me:
first, that the official Church, in any Christian sense, is indefen-
sible, and that every day of its continued existence, from a
Christian standpoint, is a crime; and, secondly, that one has
no right to call upon grace in this way."

"So remove the pseudonymity, remove the thrice-repeated
Foreword, and the 'Moral' to Part I: then the *Einübung im
Christentum* is, from a Christian standpoint, an attack on the
official Church. But out of pious consideration for the old
Bishop and cautiousness and patience, its true purport was
concealed behind the mask of a final defence of what passes
for Christianity."

Clearly this does not mean that the Foreword has now to be
omitted because the relationship of discipleship and grace
which it implied was false, or that Kierkegaard himself was
now no longer living by grace in the way there suggested.
No, but the presupposition for the Foreword which must now
be considered no longer to apply was that at that earlier time

it was still thought possible to count on the Church making the "concession" awaited of it. After the Church has declined to do so, its condition has become untenable, and Kierkegaard must remove the Foreword in which his own concession was intended to draw from the Church a similar concession. The Church has repudiated the grace offered for its salvation and so has itself turned into an attack what was intended as its defence.

But even now Kierkegaard does not claim any *authority* for himself and here, too, does not go beyond his former attitude. In "This should be said . . .," the pamphlet already mentioned, we read:

"This should be said. I am not obliging any one to do as I suggest, and I have no competence to do so. But if you have heard and paid heed, then you have become responsible and must now act on your own responsibility, as you think you will be able to answer before God. Perhaps one person considers that he is already acting as I indicate, another thinks it to be well-pleasing to God, and a service to God, to join in the hue and cry against me: neither of these two attitudes is my concern: my sole concern is that this should be said."[8]

[8] xiv, 85; 186.

*(i) Kierkegaard as corrective to official Christianity*

We have been told: "The description 'corrective' implies something relative as when we say: here or there, right or left" (see above p. 154, n. 6). This means that the one thing can be defined only by its relation to the other and cannot have the character of independent significance. We might also express the matter by saying that the two things must be dialectically related to each other.

Kierkegaard also compares the corrective with the bit of cinnamon added to one's food: "Just a bit of cinnamon! Which is to say that in this connexion a man must be sacrificed, his role must be to give to the rest a certain flavour. That is the meaning of the corrective. The unfortunate mistake occurs when he who is to be used for the purposes of correction becomes impatient and wants to make the corrective a norm for others: that is attempting to bring everything into confusion."[1]

Hence during his attack on the Church Kierkegaard did not succumb to the "unfortunate mistake" of wishing to make of the corrective a norm. To misunderstand him in this way must be impossible, if only for the reason that he refused to have any adherents and made no sort of proposals for the improvement of the Church. From all that he said and did, no norm could be deduced such as might be of general validity. Even the one practical demand which he made of Christians, to stay away from the services of the Church—but let it be noted, not to leave the Church—was no solution, nor an attitude ultimately compatible with his own understanding of the Christian religion, but simply a demonstration, for he did not attempt to gather into a different kind of church worship those who followed his advice, and desired to be nothing less than the founder of a sect. Moreover in his challenge to the Church he gradually found that he had nothing more to say and could

[1] *S. K. P.*, x.4, 598. Except as stated, all further refs. in this Final Account are to *S. K. P.*

only continue to compose variations on the one theme. And if anyone were foolish enough to ask what would have become of Kierkegaard and his work if he had had to live longer, the answer would have to be that his desire had been to solve all his problems by being allowed to die at the right time. And the fact that this desire was granted could only confirm him in the view that "Providence" had thus willed to accept his sacrifice. In fact there is no other explanation of the dialectic underlying Kierkegaard's attitude in this challenge, except that he understood himself to be the bit of cinnamon which in the interests of official Christianity had to be sacrificed.

In contrast to the widespread view which sees in Kierkegaard's attack a going-off the rails and a revocation of his earlier insights, we feel that we must say, on the contrary, that at this juncture, above all, he maintained himself clearly and unambiguously within the categories which his dialectic of existence had developed. An indirect confirmation of this can also be seen in the fact that, in spite of all the admiration that he has won, he has up to the present found no successor at this particular point.

### (ii) Kierkegaard and Luther

It is interesting to see, however, that Kierkegaard, who in his role as corrective wished to have no successor and in the very nature of the case could not have one, nevertheless insists on having a predecessor, namely Luther. It is not in Luther the Reformer that Kierkegaard finds his predecessor—we know of course that Kierkegaard had no intention whatever of being a reformer—but he criticises him precisely on the grounds that he became a reformer and did not remain like himself a mere corrective. "Lutheranism is a corrective—but a corrective which has been made into a norm, generally valid, becomes *eo ipso* confusing to the second generation (where that which it was originally desired to correct no longer obtains). And with each generation that adopts it, things get worse and worse until it is seen that the corrective which has established itself on an independent footing produces precisely the opposite of its original description. And this is just what happened with the Lutheran corrective which, aspiring to be independently

Christianity as a whole, engendered the most refined type of worldliness and paganism."[2] And in an article of March 1855 he writes: "Protestantism is quite simply, from a Christian point of view, false and dishonest. It falsifies the doctrine and the whole world and life view of Christianity, as soon as it is taken to be the constitutive principle of Christianity, and not merely a necessary rectification (a pure corrective) adapted to the specific circumstances of time and place."[3] This harmonises with the fact that in the diaries Kierkegaard directs his criticism not merely against the misuse of Luther by Lutheranism but also against Luther himself. In his published writings, on the contrary, Kierkegaard speaks of Luther always only with the greatest respect. The significance of this difference must not be overlooked.

In his diary of 1847 Kierkegaard writes: "Fine. The category 'for thy sake' (subjectivity, interiority) with which *Entweder-Oder* closed (only truth which edifies is truth for you personally) is precisely that of Luther. As a matter of fact, I have never read anything of Luther's. But now when I open his book of homilies—straightaway on the Gospel for the first Sunday in Advent he says 'for thy sake,' which is the decisive point."[4] Subsequently Kierkegaard concerned himself unceasingly with Luther but confined his reading almost entirely to Luther's sermons. Thus in his debate with Luther there can be no question of his confronting the whole of Luther's works, the discussion centres on points which are of special importance for Kierkegaard himself, and which of course take one to the heart of Luther's work. Hence, in our account of this debate, we have not to give a comprehensive survey of the points of contrast between Luther and Kierkegaard, and from the outset we must say that we have no intention of defending Luther's position against Kierkegaard's criticism. In the whole context of our work, this criticism concerns us only in so far as, in this discussion, Kierkegaard himself takes up a position which deviates in certain essential ways from the existential dialectic as we have found it to be developed and applied in his published writings.[5]

---

[2] XI.1(A), 28.  [3] *S. V.*, XII, 47; *Angriff*, 142.
[4] VIII.1(A), 465.  [5] See Appendix II (below, 212 ff).

(a) *Kierkegaard's criticism of Lutheranism.* In so far as Kierke-gaard's criticism is directed not against Luther himself but against Lutheranism—naturally not as distinct from the Reformation as a whole but against Protestantism as such—the central point which is constantly recurring is: "It has clearly been the misfortune of Christendom that the dialectical aspect of Luther's doctrine of faith has been disregarded; hence the latter has become a covering for mere heathenism and Epicure-anism. It has simply been forgotten that Luther emphasised faith in opposition to fantastically exaggerated asceticism."[6] The dialectical moment, which must not be forgotten, would therefore mean that every communication about the attitude and life of faith and every action springing from faith is only true when dialectically related to its opposite, but taken by itself alone is false. When for example Luther marries a nun by way of protesting against celibacy and the life of the cloister and in order to demonstrate the wrongness of an ascetic refusal to marry, and then someone else who is not personally implicated by those demands takes it into his head to make of bourgeois married life a work that is intrinsically well-pleasing to God, the latter's attitude is false. If in reaction to the type of *imitatio Christi* which is made apparent through the externality of meritorious works, the true *imitatio* is referred to the "incog-nito" of hidden interior spirituality behind which is concealed the genuine passion of faith, and someone, without concealing anything at all behind the "incognito," invokes such hidden spirituality as a merit, then his attitude is false.[7]

In this connexion, Kierkegaard is of course aware that his very anxiety lest the dialectical moment should be lacking implies for him personally a certain danger: "I must take good care, or rather God will take good care for me, that I am not led astray by concentrating too one-sidedly on Christ as our pattern. The related term through which it becomes dialectical is Christ as gift, as He who bestows Himself on us (to call to mind Luther's regular classification). But dialectical as my nature is, in the passion for the dialectical it always looks as if the opposite thought were not there at all—and then it emerges

---

[6] x.1, 213.

[7] Cp. viii.1 (A), 369; ix(A), 243, 362; x.3, 219; x.4, 45, 324; xi.1 (A), 106.

principally and most strongly."[8]   Kierkegaard sees just the opposite danger in the world around him: "The great danger in regard to everything dialectical, where the thing must be turned into its opposite, is that this is done too easily (e.g., severity into mildness), inasmuch as the dialectical is transformed into something of which one at most understands that it is implied in the inner life, etc.   In the sphere of the spirit the greatest deception and cunning will be practised in respect of that dangerous type of dialectic where the antithesis is brought about all too easily, with the consequence that the second proposition (in this instance, mildness) becomes an untruth."[9] And this is the essence of Kierkegaard's doubt with regard to Luther, namely whether he has not promoted the possibility of just this danger.

(b) *Kierkegaard's agreement with Luther*.   This doubt, however, does not in the first instance imply any criticism of Luther personally.   Only "the harmonisation of the world and religion was achieved somewhat too rapidly.   Luther was perhaps right as far as he personally was concerned, in his case it was certainly inner truth, for which he was permitted to risk all:  to do the opposite and yet to remain unfettered by that opposite, to be married and yet to be as though unmarried, to be in the world and yet a stranger to the world, although taking part in everything, etc.   But what a dangerous thing it was to try to teach this without more ado to others, for it meant making religion all too easy for worldly people, who were satisfied with a mere verbal assurance and then gave way to downright worldliness. . . ."[10]   More precisely, one should rather say that Luther made things both too easy and too difficult for men:  "Never was Christianity really more popular than when the Pope said plainly: 'If you wish to be sure of eternal felicity, it will cost you 4 marks 8 shillings and a tip for the priest, if you wish to attain the summit of heavenly beatitude, then it will be 5 marks: but it is quite certain that you will be thus saved, we will give you a receipt.'   At bottom it is this kind of thing which is and remains popular."

"The idea that Luther was popular is based on a pure misunderstanding.   No, no!   How did Luther apparently

[8] x.1, 246.          [9] x.3, 165.          [10] x.3, 153.

become so popular? Now, look at the matter more closely and you will see the connexion. People were finding that the Pope had become too dear—and they took Luther in such a frivolous sense that they supposed that by means of the new turn which he gave to things you could obtain salvation still more cheaply, in fact for nothing. If people are going to go into Luther's ideas seriously then he will never be popular. No, the root of the popular movement was that people were finding the Pope too dear, especially when they heard there was even talk of getting the same thing *gratis* and without the slightest personal cost."

"The Pope was essentially a man who understood just how to be popular . . . but Lutheranism in its deep truth and insights is far too lofty and far too much exclusively concerned with spiritual values for it ever to be able to become popular."[11]

What Luther symbolises is the religion of mature manhood, by contrast with the religion of youth, symbolised by the Middle Ages, which with extreme energy holds the attainment of the ideal possible.

"But the religion of mature life is on a much higher plane and is recognisable by the fact that it feels itself to be a stage further removed from the ideal."

"In proportion as the religious awareness of the individual develops, his vision of God expands infinitely and he feels himself to be further and further away from God. In consequence the doctrine of Christ as pattern can no longer directly assume first place in our thoughts. Thus faith now comes first— Christ as self-bestowed upon us. The ideal is so infinitely high that all my striving now appears to me as delusive and vain if it is supposed to reach that height, or a sort of God-fearing joke, however manfully and earnestly I strive."

"The matter can be expressed thus, that I am at peace solely through faith. The youth does not notice how enormous the task is, he starts out with freshness and enthusiasm, and with the pious illusion that he is sure to succeed. The older man understands that the gulf between himself and the ideal is endless—and so faith must intervene to fill the gap, faith through which he truly attains peace, faith that satisfaction has

[11] x.4, 371.

been wrought, faith that through faith alone I shall be saved."

"Thus Luther is completely right and his work signifies a crucial stage and turning point in the development of the religious consciousness."

"But the fault in the religion of our times is that faith is made a matter of private conviction in such wise that it is in effect completely lost, and that life feels permitted in consequence to fashion itself quite coolly on purely secular lines, and for faith itself is substituted a doctrine about faith."[12]

In this connexion Kierkegaard emphasises that he too had first to learn to be humbled in the deepest sense by the ideal of Christianity, so that he could get a true realisation of the meaning of "grace":

"The earnestness of the youth is seen in his beginning hastily and *bona fide* to aspire to achieve the ideal; the earnestness of the older man is seen in his putting faith in the gap as a token that he understands and respects the qualitative difference that lies between all this striving and the absolute ideal. The characteristic of modern times is its jugglery and its transformation of faith into a fictitious private religion."[12]

But how has this jugglery of modern times come about? Despite Luther or because of Luther? "Luther is, next to the New Testament, the truest form of the Christian consciousness. What does Luther express? Luther expresses a pause in which takes place an act of reflexion and recollection. In him humanity or Christianity pauses to recollect that between the God-man and us other men, in fact between the Apostles and the rest of us, there lies a qualitative distinction, and, therefore, that grace must be our one resource. The early Christians and the Church fathers did not understand the matter thus, but went straight ahead in their imitation of Christ. Luther reacted against this. What I blame is that he did not make more effectively known the nature of his reaction, that he referred to it at most *en passant*, e.g., among the articles concerning abuses, II. *De conjugio sacerdotum*," XIV. *Et cum senescente mundo paulatim natura humana fiat imbecillior.*"[13]

Would everything have been in order had Luther himself made clearer the nature of his reaction, in consequence of which,

[12] x.2, 207.        [13] x.5(A), 96.

too, the admission which Kierkegaard wanted would have followed spontaneously? On the whole it would seem so, especially as Kierkegaard's own experience of faith confirms the supposition:

"Alas, what I have suffered in this matter because I have sadly thought it was my desire to make the New Testament the straightforward model and guide of my life, I who yet have no immediate sense of communion with God. . . . Those existences which the New Testament brings before us move on an utterly different plane from that of normal humanity. . . . At this point we see the relevance of the doctrine of grace . . . *grace is primary* . . . grace in relation to the future. This means that I am only an ordinary mortal and have no sense of immediate communion with God, but on my own responsibility must try to find out what (*in concreto*) my task is and what it is my duty to do in life; thus as far as in me lies I must use my reason and am responsible for so doing; but, on the other hand, even though I use it to the best of my ability, alas, it is but folly!— *ergo*, I must have the resource of divine grace primarily; if not, I must either quite literally lose my reason or sink into despair."[13]

Here Kierkegaard seems to be completely at one with Luther and also to be moving in precisely those categories to which he has adhered in his published work.

(*c*) *Kierkegaard's criticism of Luther.* Alongside this we find in the diaries a far more penetrating criticism of Luther; and, moreover, it is not subsequent to the previous estimate and cannot be regarded as Kierkegaard's summing-up, on the contrary it develops at the same time as his other views. Here it is made a matter of direct reproach to Luther that he fell away from the height of his insight and thus demoralised Christianity:

"Besides, the more I study Luther, the more I am convinced that he was confused in his thought and ideas. Men are always grateful for a reformation which amounts to casting off burdens and making life easier—in this way you can easily get friends to help you. But true reforming always means making life difficult and imposing burdens; and for this reason the true

[13] x.5(A), 96.

reformer is always put to death as though reformation meant hostility to the human race."

"But Luther's dictum, 'Hear me, O Pope,' and so on, is almost repulsively worldly, to my way of thinking. Is this the holy zeal of a reformer who realises his responsibility in fear and trembling and realises that all truest reformation lies in the deepening and interiorisation of religion? This saying of Luther's is so much like a journalistic challenge or something of that sort. And this unholy political element, all this about the overthrow of the Papacy is and remains Luther's madness."

"But now in our time it is clear that what should be brought out is Christ as our living example. Only, the point is to learn how to avoid medieval errors in this respect. But that is the aspect of religion which should be emphasised, for Lutheranism and all its talk about faith is now become just a sort of fig-leaf to cover up the most un-Christian shirking of the issue."[14]

Hence it would appear that Luther himself did not stick to his real task, which was to be an individual and as such to be sacrificed:

". . . This is the meaning of 'the individual.' It means a sacrifice or the sacrifices which from time to time are necessary in order to deepen and interiorise given doctrine. . . ."

"Oh, but it is so difficult to stick it out and to stand alone. Yet that is the essential task. Think of Luther, that splendid man, and yet what chaos and confusion has been wrought through him because he did not refuse to form a party. He was an individual, an extraordinary man. His true task lay in the work of interiorisation, he did not have to bring any new doctrine into the world, for Christianity already existed, but it was interiorisation that was necessary—and instead of becoming a martyr himself, he founded a party and in a very short time Lutheranism degenerated into externalities and was the same old story as Catholicism."[15]

Even so, Kierkegaard still refuses to say anything against Luther as a personality, he sees the fault in his preaching and doctrine: "Luther acted rightly, but his preaching is not always clear or in conformity with his life; in this case we must say

[14] X.1, 154.                    [15] X.3(A), 121.

the rarer thing: his life is better than his preaching."[16]  And
in what lies the defect of Luther's doctrine?

(d) *Luther's lack of Dialectics.*  "Luther was no dialectician,
and constantly saw only one side of the issue."[17]  Kierkegaard
means by this that in his teaching and preaching Luther did not
do justice to the 'dialectical moment.'

"In his sermon on the Epistle for the second Sunday after
Trinity, his text is 'Marvel not if the world hate you.'  On the
following Sunday he preaches about humility ('God resisteth
the proud') saying that without humility one is loved neither by
God nor by men.  But he forgets that the Christian approach is
rather 'Do good, and suffer for it'—hence 'Be humble, and in
one way or another you will be hated by men.'  Then in
another passage of the same sermon, dealing with the theme—
'Cast all your cares on God'—Luther begins to speak of the
necessity that the Christian should suffer."

"The totally undialectical attitude in this way of speaking is
quite clear.  When you preach encouragingly about humility,
you leave out of account the hardships and difficulties, and so
you give an un-Christian slant to the matter; next Sunday you
comfort the congregation."

Kierkegaard knows, however, from his own experience that
in demanding that you should also and at the same time express
the dialectical opposite, he is requiring something extremely
difficult, and so he continues: "I have expressed my thoughts
on this matter at the end of Part I of *Leben und Walten der Liebe*;
but I cannot stress it sufficiently.  For it is no easy matter.
For many years now I have unremittingly practised the technique, and yet even now I can often catch myself out deserting
the true Christian approach."[18]

We propose to consider in more detail the passage alluded
to in *Leben und Walten der Liebe*, because Kierkegaard there
makes a very interesting attempt to distinguish the purpose of
his *talks* from that of *sermons* in the ordinary sense, and to
clarify their method by comparison with the latter.  In the
passage in question[19] Kierkegaard is speaking on the text "Owe
no man anything but to love one another," and he points out

---

[16] x.2, 263.    [17] x.4, 394.    [18] x.1, 651.
[19] *S. V.*, ix, 183 ff.; *Walten der Liebe*, 200 ff.

to his hearer that it will fare ill with him in the world if he does this. The whole discourse is full of observations concerning the true Christian technique of speaking. The talk must "not cast a spell on the listener so that he gets a false impression," it must not in this way forget to define in detail how the ideal should be carried out in practice, and "omit all mention of how the Christian will fare in the world." It must not "now and then extol the Christian attitude while leaving out of account some of its essential difficulties, and then at another time (perhaps on the occasion of another text) hunt out some comforting considerations for him who is tempted and tried in life. No, it is precisely at the moment when the Christian attitude is being recommended most strongly that in the very same breath the difficulty should be stressed." Thus the idea must be excluded that "the opposition of the world is only an incidental phenomenon rather than its essential reaction to the Christian consciousness." Christian address must be as though "one were handing to another an enormously sharp-cut two-edged sword." "Every discourse about the Christian attitude must constantly suggest the possibility of offence, of a clash; thus it can never *directly* recommend Christianity." It is important to notice the difference resulting from the fact that we now are speaking from within a Christian context and are no longer in the situation when Christianity was first introduced into the world and the offensiveness of its message could at once be realised. "If Christianity is to be preached out of the delusive charm and distortion to which it has been subjected, then the first thing to be done is to reawaken from its deathly sleep the aspect of offensiveness in its message. Only the possibility of being offended (as an antidote to the drunken sleep of the apologetic line) will be able to arouse those who are sunk in slumberous insensibility and to shock those whose senses have been charmed, with the consequence that Christianity will once more be itself." The possibility of scandalisation must, then, not only be implicit in the form of the exposition and its discovery left to the listener, but it must be directly stated as a constant warning against immediate acceptance of what is said, so that the hearer may not suppose that he can seize upon grace without being led into the path of discipleship, and so misuse grace. "Take away from Christianity its aspect of offensiveness or detach the forgiveness of sins from the struggles of the tormented conscience (to which, according to Luther's excellent account, this whole doctrine must be referred) then close the churches, the sooner the better, or use them as amusement parks which will stand open all day long."

So far we have simply pointed out that Kierkegaard refuses to have his talks described as sermons because only an ordained clergyman may preach sermons and he can and must do so with authority. We now see how this difference makes itself felt in practice. The ideal technique of Christian speaking, which Kierkegaard himself says that despite many years of practice he has not mastered, consists then in directly and immediately stating the difficulties consequent upon the appropriation of the message and so arousing the possibility of offence. Thus it does not confine itself to speaking about the situation of the hearer poised between grace and repulsion, but intends through the event of the speaking and listening to bring about this very situation itself. Thus it is a dialectical echo of the reality actualised in the moment of balance between grace and repulsion and its intention is to awaken the reality of this experience.

This has far-reaching consequences. Of course every preacher of any experience will find noted here many faults which he repeatedly makes and which he should avoid. We are thinking, for example, of the comforting sermon which can so easily be misused to impart an immediately accessible comfort, and as a result of which the preacher has already anticipated the hearer's decision as to whether he proposes to emerge from his sorrows strengthened and comforted or to become paralysed by them. But even with the better type of sermon what produces the necessity of decision is the hearer's own situation, and what brings about that decision is his attitude in that situation. And the preacher himself has no control either over the situation or over the reaction to it and therefore cannot prevent any evasion or the taking up of a false attitude. But it is just this which the discourse of Kierkegaard claims to be able to do and to have to do. Hence it is not merely a correlative to preaching but a substitute for it, intended dialectically to overcome the inevitable shortcomings which characterise *all* preaching.

We must however conversely point out certain dialectical difficulties in this Christian type of address which persist even when the necessary high degree of dialectical competency is there. We ask first: what is it, properly speaking, which in this form of communication, confronts the individual with the necessity to decide between scandalisation and faith? It is *not* the truth of what is said as objectively valid doctrinal truth, since, on the one hand, its truth lies only in the dialectically correct existential form of communication, and, on the other, it can prove itself to be true only in so far as what is said is existentially appropriated by the hearer. But this again implies that the recipient might be confronted only by a theoretical truth, even if it were a truth about existence and recognisable as such only by existential fulfilment. But what has become of the factual aspect which, following from the historical fact of revelation, attests the truth to be believed as an event? Without that the recipient cannot be confronted by the living event, and the religious speaker who neglects this factuality attesting the event has turned the reaction of offence into a theory about offence.

Nor can ordination, with its paradoxical transformation of the teacher, be of any help in this matter, since the ordained clergyman could not deliver such an address but would have to preach a sermon in which he not only explains dialectically the offensive aspect of the revelation, but with the authority of his charge, refers to the event of revelation and so confronts the hearer with the scandal—of course with the risk that the hearer might not be willing to face up to it and might wish to accept the proffered grace without realising its challenge to discipleship, and thus would misuse grace. Kierkegaard wishes to prevent this misuse of grace by his "correct" type of Christian address and thinks that such misuse arises only from false preaching, though it is quite clear from the New Testament that not even the Apostles could prevent it.

Hence if the Christian preacher wishes not to "preach," then the only possible way in which he can attest the actuality

M

of revelation as a fact is to add to the living power of truth which flows from its existential communication the further enhancement springing from the personality of the communicator. The speaker must therefore be able to compel a facing up to the decision between repulsion and faith by expressing the communicated truth existentially through the power of his personality. But this will have still further consequences: between the communicator and the recipient the truth is no longer to be found as something valid independently of their existence. Truth, for the communicator, is a mode of existence which supposedly has its origin in the effects of the revelational event, but which is not recognisable in that connexion. On the part of the recipient, in so far as he receives the communication in faith, truth lies in his own existence, which corresponds to that of the communicator. The consequence is that doctrine loses its significance, not merely in the sense of truth that is objectively valid regardless of subjective existence (against this conception we have understood so far Kierkegaard's polemic against doctrine to be addressed), but, further, in the sense of a transmissible tradition claiming truth and validity. But with doctrine the Church, too, as the bearer of this doctrinal tradition, must lose its significance, since the conveyance of truth can be effected only from existing individual to existing individual, hence by immediate communication from the communicator as a believer who has actualised his faith both through an existential form of communication and through the power of his own existence, to the recipient who appropriates that truth by a faith which overcomes the moment of offence. Apart from this specific type of communication there is no other real communication of Christian truth, or what there is is not only irrelevant but positively harmful and misleading.

This means that the historical fact of revelation can have no historical consequences of real significance. But, just as between the communicator and recipient there are now no intermediate historical forms, so it is also with regard to the relation between the communicator and Christ Himself. The insistence on the contemporaneity of the believer with Christ must now mean that all historical intermediaries, such as the Church, doctrine, the preaching office, and even the Apostolate, lose their significance. All that is derivative can now only mean what is diluted, the whole history of Christianity can now only signify a history of the continuing falling-away from Christ and be considered only as a process of the continual depravation of true Christianity. True Christianity can only exist where the recipient, with the help of a communicator whose existence is moulded and penetrated by the power of his communication, enters into direct contemporaneous relation with Christ and so in the most radical fashion sweeps aside the 1800 years of Christian history; it is not only that the latter cannot help him to find Christian faith; they are not only simply irrelevant for faith, but must be abolished as an obstacle which constantly threatens and endangers his faith.

None of these consequences can be checked when we bring into action the Christian address in the Kierkegaardian sense as a counter-move to Luther's sermon. But we have not merely constructed these consequences *a priori*, in point of fact we find them inferred by Kierkegaard in the sequence of his Luther criticism. And were this not so he would not be the passionately consistent thinker that he is. After this excursus, then, let us continue our examination of Kierkegaard's criticism of Luther.

(*e*) *The relation of teacher and doctrine.* "To be sure, Luther was no dialectician. In his sermon on the Epistle for the sixth Sunday after Easter, he develops the point, which he develops elsewhere, too, that in regard to faith one ought not to be concerned about persons, but only about the Word: even were it an Apostle who taught something different from Holy Scripture, then he should not be followed."

"That is all very well; but Luther ought to be a little more cautious. It is clear, on the contrary, that Christianity spread in the world because the person was valued more highly than the doctrine. How am I to know whether something is the Word of God or mere doctrine? Luther's answer is, by testing doctrine—in that case all is lost, and Christianity is a human discovery. On the contrary, faith comes about by the opposite process, by my accepting someone's authority; hence the person is more important than the doctrine." "Luther ought to have thought of this at the same time; though, for the rest, what he says about the presumption of man in the face of the Word of God may well be right."[20]

Thus the problem of authority emerges once more, though with a certain simplification. The question is now put simply in the following way: does the believer attain faith through the acceptance of some doctrine which he considers as true, and by which his personal existence does not need to be changed, or not rather by submission to the authority of a person who by his personal authority guarantees the truth of what he declares and thus challenges the hearer to express that truth similarly in his own existence? Since in any case the possibility of objectively true doctrine, regardless of subjective existence, is not in question, the only other possibility that remains lies in seeking authority in the subjective bearing of the communicator: "Since Christianity is not a set of doctrines it is consequently not a matter of indifference (as it would be if it were merely a question of doctrine) who expounds it as long as he says what is objectively correct. No, Christ did not institute lecturers— but disciples. If Christianity (just because it is not a matter of doctrine) is not embodied in the existence of the teacher, then he is not teaching Christianity; for Christianity is an existential communication and can only be expounded by the fact of human existence. Generally speaking, to exist in a Christian way, to express it existentially, etc., is the most powerful way of propagating it."[21]

Properly speaking, it is no longer here a question of the relation between teacher and doctrine, for doctrine has been dissolved in existential communication, and hence there can no longer be a "teacher" in any legitimate sense, but only the caricatural figure of the "lecturer." "Christianity is not a body of doctrines (this is how the irrelevancy of orthodoxy arose, with quarrels about this and that, so that there is contention as to what the true Christian doctrine is and so on), but it is an existential communication. For this reason, each generation makes a completely fresh start, all learning about the teaching of previous generations is essentially superfluous—though not to be despised if it understands itself and its limitations, but extremely dangerous, if it does not." The limitations within

---

[20] X.2, 448.    [21] IX(A), 207.

which doctrinal erudition must move can only mean that
doctrine loses whatever validity it supposed itself to possess
apart from and prior to the event of existential communication.
The same applies to the teacher. The discipline of thinking
about doctrine, quite apart from its existential communication,
in order, for example, to formulate it in terms of the correct
categories and to give it critical support outside its existential
fulfilment (as previously Kierkegaard himself referred to the
task of dogmatics) is now quite given up. The teacher can
now play only the same miserable part within Christendom as
is played by the philosophical thinker who in his search for
objective truth leaves his personal existence out of the reckoning
and does not even notice that he is doing so. But in the case of
the Christian thinker matters are even worse, because the
object of his teaching is the fact of revelation, which of all that
exists in the world is the truth that can be least indifferent
to the personal existence of the thinker. It is in this context
of thought that we should situate Kierkegaard's notorious
words about the professor—"Here Christ was crucified and the
Apostles stoned again."[22]

Since both the teacher and his doctrine have ceased to exist
as legitimate factors, the question of authority, which arose
from a consideration of the proper relation between these two,
can now only be how that personal existential enforcement of
truth comes about, in which alone now can lie the authority
of the communication. To put it more exactly: in what
precisely does such authority consist? Such personal authority
has nothing more to do with that "paradoxical transformation
of the teacher within history" such as followed from the
Apostolic calling or ordination, for there it is the fact of
commission which lends authority. The fact of commission
cannot really play a part any longer. Even if it were said that
the existential confirmation in the life of the teacher must be
added to the commission, it would of course be right. But still
the decisive question remains the same, whether the source of
authority is the commission or the personal existential factor,
in other words, to what authority can the teacher legitimately
appeal when he demands faith of his pupil. And if it were the

[22] X.3, 121.

case that both the commission and the personal factor together conferred authority, then we should have to ask whether the personal factor alone can legitimate the commission or whether, on the contrary, the commission remains valid independently of its personal enforcement and the latter's weakness. But this second possibility is now really excluded by the whole tenor of Kierkegaard's argument.

How in reference to his Luther criticism does Kierkegaard follow up the first possibility? For him to be consistent, all previous authorities if not done away with, must now be questioned in their authoritative significance.

( f ) *The Authority of the Bible.* With the authority of the ordained preacher, who invokes his orders to preach Scripture, the authority of the Bible itself is challenged.

"Luther's teaching is not, after all, a simple return to primitive Christianity, but a modification of the essence of Christianity. He one-sidedly prefers Paul and makes less use of the Gospels."

"He himself best overthrows his own theory about the Bible, he who rejects the Epistle of James—and why? because it does not belong to the canon? No, he does not deny that; but for a dogmatic reason, so that he has a personal set of views which he places above the authority of the Bible. Of course, he himself realised this since he postulated the authority of Scripture only for the polemical purpose of his struggle with the Papacy and in order to have some firm standing ground. In so doing he conceded that he would let himself be convinced if they could convince him from Scripture. And this was certainly right; for what he wanted to do away with was just the rubbish of tradition, for which they would never be able to find support in the Bible."[23]

Thus Kierkegaard allows the validity of the Bible only in the sense that it offers a more original source of Christianity than does tradition, but he repudiates its dogmatic significance. His criticism of the allegorical, philological and eruditely doctrinal exegesis of the Bible is based on the consideration that this approach conceals the original significance of Biblical events in their actuality.

"In particular, the purely natural historical truth of things

[23] X.2, 244.

is overlooked. Thus it is forgotten that the Apostle is a person engaged in existence, who with flashes of insight flings out a few words of comfort in order to keep a Christian community going."

"At first people transformed the Apostle's hastily-written letters into something fantastic, God knows what. Now they are distorted in a doctrinal sense. In reality they are impulsive. When everything is at stake, and when each day it is a question of winning new converts or of maintaining the faith of those who are already won, there is no time for fantastic speculations or doctrinal applications. People forget Paul the man over the shreds of manuscript which he dashed off and which are now treated in the most un-Pauline way."[24]

Because on account of this mass of traditional exegesis it is no longer possible to read the Bible in a *human* way, it would, after all, be best if it were not read at all: "A reformation which aimed at abolishing the Bible would have the same value as Luther's abolition of the Papacy. The use of the Bible has developed a religiosity of learning and legalism which is a distraction from the main issue. A knowledge and approach of this kind has gradually percolated to the simplest and most uneducated, with the result that nobody any longer reads the Bible in a human way. But this is doing irreparable harm; the fact of the Bible acts as a fortification of all sorts of excuses and subterfuges by which men evade existence; for it is always a question of first going into a matter and always the excuse that first of all one must have a complete understanding of the doctrine before one begins to live it—which means that in the end people never do begin to live it."

"The Bible societies which are an insipid caricature of missionary activity, and which essentially work merely by the power of money, just like any other company, and which are just as busy in selling the Bible as other companies are in their enterprises—these Bible societies have done irreparable harm. Christianity has long since needed a religious leader who in fear and trembling before God would have the courage to forbid the people to read the Bible. This is just as necessary as it is to preach against what passes for Christianity."[25]

[24] X.2, 548.  [25] IX(A), 442.

*(g) Towards contemporaneity with Christ through the overleaping of the historical process.* "Luther's mistake was that he did not go back far enough and did not enter sufficiently into contemporaneity with Christ."[26] His dogmatic Biblicism prevented him from doing this, in spite of his occasional correct insights: "This is a true word of Luther: 'Experience also teaches that, for longer than is imaginable, the Gospel nowhere in the world has remained in a pure and undistorted form, but as long as those who set it in motion were alive, it remained firm and increased—when they were dead and gone, the light of the Gospel, too, had gone out. Then came along sectarians and false teachers.' This last observation is less important. The former one is completely true, though Luther himself does not seem to be really aware of its implications. Contemporaneity with Christ is what matters and is the essential truth of the situation. Then comes the derivative; contemporaneity with a true Christian in the stricter sense. Secondhand Christianity is idle talk; for it is Christianity apart from the tension of reality."[27]

Here Kierkegaard seems to allow a relative significance to the derivative, to "contemporaneity with a true Christian in the stricter sense." But he must go yet a step further and find a decisive break between the historical Jesus and all His followers, as he does with all desirable clarity in the following sketch of his views:

"The life of Christ is Christianity lived for God and His Will."

"At the very moment when He dies, Christianity becomes a religion lived in the interests of man. The Apostle changes essentially the figure of Christ our Example into the figure of Christ the Atoner. In so doing he establishes the difference between the God-man and any other man. The Atonement, or the view that the life and death of Christ accomplishes the Atonement, is a symbol expressing the difference between Christ and every other man. Discipleship to Christ implies a measure of equality with Him. The Apostle does indeed follow Him and is crucified—but he makes the Atonement central, for otherwise the Apostle himself would be a sort of Christ."

26 IX(A), 95.                    27 X.1, 595.

"And it is quite significant that it is precisely that one Apostle who was not a witness of the life of Christ and did not live with Him, the later apostle Paul who most strongly emphasises the atonement and almost completely overlooks the imitation of Christ."[28]

Thus the authority of the Apostle as a link with Christ fades away, for even he has already begun to fall away from original Christianity. "It is easy to see that Luther's preaching of Christianity distorts the Christian standpoint. He concerned himself one-sidedly with the Apostle Paul and then goes so far (and this often happens) as to use the Apostle retrospectively as a norm for testing the Gospels; if he does not find Paul's doctrine in the Gospels then he concludes, '*Ergo* this is no Gospel.' Luther seems to have been completely blind to the fact that the true situation is that the Apostle has already degenerated by comparison with the Gospel. And this mis-guided attitude which Luther adopted then continued in Protestantism, which made of Luther the absolute criterion; and if it was discovered that the Apostle was stricter than Luther (which he is), then it was inferred, 'Here the Apostle is making a mistake, this is no true Gospel.' In this way and systematically, step by step, God had been mocked and cheated of His Gospel, or rather it has been attempted to do so, and the whole situation has been reversed."[29] The whole history of Christianity now becomes a history of the continuous lapse from Christianity.

"Thus in the history of the Church, from generation to generation, Christianity has been ever more egoistically diverted to serve the interests of men: the Atonement does away with discipleship (or rather people delude themselves about discipleship). Thus more and more Christianity is getting a bad conscience, and the thought that fellowship with God means suffering has been entirely lost, and, on the contrary, it is assumed that the mark of fellowship with God is prosperity and success—and thus in effect Christianity is no more."[28]

(*h*) *The Church as an obstacle to the individual's becoming contem-poraneous with Christ.* With the removal of the various specific authorities—ordination, the Bible, and the Apostolate—through

---

[28] x.4, 499.  [29] XI.1(A), 572.

this sweeping aside of the whole of Christian history, naturally, too, the significance of the Church in which those authorities were rooted must also disappear. "In the definition of the Church which we find in the Augsburg Confession, namely that it is that communion of the saints where the Word is rightly taught and the sacraments correctly administered, it is simply the two latter clauses about doctrine and the sacraments which have been correctly understood (i.e., incorrectly), while the former clause has been overlooked: the communion of the saints, in which description the emphasis lies on the existential; in this way the Church has been turned into a communion where doctrine is correct and the sacraments correctly administered, but where the lives of individual members are a matter of indifference (or where the existential element is neglected): this is nothing but heathenism."[30] It is characteristic of Kierkegaard's argument that the emphasis on the Word and the sacraments as the factors which objectively constitute the Church *must* have as its consequence a disregard of the existential element. He no longer seems to realise the possibility that a qualification of existence might result *precisely from those factors*, in that doctrine would be dialectically understood as implying discipleship. At most, according to his argument, existence would follow from the description of the Church as the communion of saints, it is no longer a question of those who are sanctified by the Atonement but of those who are saints by their discipleship, which they can only be as individuals. This implies that the Church has altogether lost its significance and is become merely an obstacle on the path of discipleship.

"The two main factors as a result of which not only discipleship, but the very idea of it, has been lost, are:

(a) That one's whole attention is directed to something objective, doctrine or the sacraments and in haughty tones they speak with scorn of the subjective—yes, thank you very much, frauds that we are!

(b) That one's whole attention is directed to the community, the corporation, the Church, i.e., a collective, with the consequence that the category of the individual is lost sight of. Christ gives Himself to the collective, but not in the same way

[30] x.4, 246.

to the individual, and with the disappearance of the individual disappears also the idea of discipleship, for, categorically, the latter is relevant to the individual—and then in haughty tones they speak of individualism, calling it a stupidity or morbidity and vanity—frauds that we are! By what means did Thomas Aquinas, the greatest thinker of the Middle Ages, defend indulgences? By means of the doctrine of the Church as a mystical body through which as in a social game we all participate in the entail of the Church."[31]

Further, it is plain, in this connexion, why Kierkegaard's criticism of Luther does not signify a championship of Catholicism: "Accordingly to be received into the Catholic Church would be rather rash, and a step of which I would not be prepared to make myself guilty, even though it were expected of me. . . . For, finally, it is precisely the idea of the Church which constitutes the basic error of official Christianity both in the Catholic and the Protestant worlds; or rather I should say the idea of Christendom."[32]

(i) *The essence of the Luther-criticism: revelation becomes true for us only through discipleship.* "The development of Christianity has been a process of constant retrogression. First they did away with the God-man as our example; it was too exalted; but they still retained the Apostle, the disciple. Then they suppressed the Apostle and the disciple, it became the extraordinary which in practice they got rid of; nevertheless they retained the idea of the witness to the truth. Then that, too, they superseded, the decline went on increasingly, until at last the Christian representative is one who practises a trade.

"You can see from this picture that the fundamental sin of official Christianity is this decline in values, this trafficking in remissions. The imitation of Christ is finished and Christianity is sold at various prices. Such is the history of the Church or of Christendom. The depreciation had been going on long before it reached the pitch where Luther raised his objection; and at once, hardly was Luther dead, even while he still lived, Lutheranism was being exploited to depreciate Christianity further."[33]

[31] x.4, 369.      [32] *S. V.*, xiv.47-8; *Angriff*, p. 142.
[33] x.4, 340.

This sweeping-aside of Christian history is aimed at restoring the true situation for discipleship: "The genuine Christian point of view has been simply turned upside down. In the New Testament the thing is so very simple. Christ says, 'Do as I say, and you will learn.' Thus, first of all, a decisive action. By means of that your life will then come to clash with existence as a whole, and you will have something else to think about besides doubt, and you will need Christianity in both senses, you will need Christ as your example and His grace."[34] The demand of discipleship must humble men so that "they need Christianity," and "genuinely feel the need of 'grace.' " In no other way can doubts about Christianity be overcome. "True following of Christ (rightly understood, hence not the kind that becomes self-torment or hypocrisy and the cultivation of good works, etc.) really offers the guarantee that Christianity will not deteriorate into poetry, mythology, abstract thought—which is what it has almost become in Protestantism."[35] The usual relationship between faith and existence must be inverted.

"Generally the matter is so put that it is understood you must first have faith and then a way of life will surely follow.

"This also has contributed to the confusion by which it is supposed possible to have faith without existence. And people have become so obsessed by this idea and so overlooked the necessity of existential transformation that faith has become far the more important.

"The matter is quite simple. In order to get faith, there must first be an existential decision and a reorientation.

"It is this which I cannot sufficiently stress: in order to have faith, in order that faith should even be in question at all, there must be an existential situation. And such a situation must be brought about by the decisive action of the individual.

"This propaedeutic element has been completely forgotten. The individual is allowed to go on in his normal humdrum routine—and then it is supposed that he gradually acquires faith just as without needing to have an existential situation lessons can be learnt by heart.[36]

But consider the consequences of this introduction of the propaedeutic element of decisive action as the necessary

[34] X.4, 349.          [35] X.4, 354.          [36] X.4, 114.

preliminary in the *ordo salutis*, or rather consider what it means that by his removal of historical Christianity Kierkegaard has been compelled to push his position thus to its extreme conclusion: through his discipleship man discovers that he "needs" Christianity. Grace corresponds to a need realised through discipleship. And such discipleship at the same time "guarantees" that Christianity shall not degenerate into mere poetry, mythology, or abstract thought. This means that the truth of Christianity is referred exclusively to subjectivity. How serious the consequences are becomes clear when we ask what objectively corresponds to this subjective truth.

When, with reference to Socratic existence, it was said that "subjectivity is truth," the corresponding objective truth lay in the paradox. And because no other relation with this objective truth was possible except its passionate personal appropriation by the subjective thinker, the converse could also be said: "Truth is subjectivity." What is in question here is an eternal truth whose objective and subjective reality implies the being-in-truth of the existential thinker.

If we now ask what objectively corresponds to the subjective truth which the believer expresses in his existence, the answer must be, "The absolute paradox of the God-man." When man in his existence encounters this truth, he must recognise himself to be one whose whole being is rooted in untruth, i.e., a sinner, and if he faces up to such recognition in faith, then he is the forgiven man endowed with grace. But in what way does he become confronted by this absolute paradox?

Since it is at one and the same time an eternal and an historical fact, he must encounter it as an eternal fact which has entered history at a given point. Thus he encounters it in his confrontation by the historical Jesus, in which experience alone now there can be contemporaneity with Christ, since the whole of the rest of Christian history and historical media have been swept aside.

Here many difficulties and problems arise. In the first place, we need an introductory knowledge in order to be able to establish the historical fact at all. At this point already everything is imperilled precisely in consequence of what Kierkegaard says in the *Nachschrift* about the purely approxi-

mative character of the conclusions attainable by such prologo-
mena, and on which no certainty can be built. But let us
continue: what we can establish in this approximative way is
the fact of an historical man, Jesus of Nazareth, who by His
existence expresses the universally human and makes an absolute
demand on men to follow Him. Thus He embodies the ideal
of the universal human. "For this reason, everything that
Christ expresses belongs essentially to the life of a Christian.
He is really no true Christian whose life does not express this
*ecce homo*. But it depends on honesty that one shall not express
simply what is admirable according to the conceptions of the
prevailing environment, e.g., voluntary poverty and chastity
in the Middle Ages."[37]

But on what grounds does man know that the claim made by
this Jesus of Nazareth is justified? He can obtain this certitude
only by his decision to follow Jesus, even though he runs the
risk of making a mistake. Thus he certifies the claim as true
by his subjective decision. But in his discipleship he finds that
he is not capable of meeting the claim, and at the same time he
is told that to meet this case Jesus of Nazareth desires to be
gracious to him. How does he know that this is true? He
decides in faith to believe it to be true, because, confronted by
the demand of discipleship, the rightness of which he recognises,
he needs this grace and hence makes use of it. This Jesus of
Nazareth says furthermore, however, that He is not only this
particular man but at the same time God, implying that His
claim and His forgiveness mediate to man the claim and the
forgiveness of God. In Him God has become man in order
to show through His life and suffering and dying that a truly
human life can consist only in a dying to the world, as a result
of which man obtains the good pleasure of God.

What now are the implications of the fact that man the
disciple believes all this? In the first place, on the basis of his
experience existentially he believes in the significance of the
event in which the God-man is revealed, and only in the second
place, and in consequence of the first consideration, does he
believe in its historical factuality, and even then he believes it
in its aspect of "double potency," i.e., he accepts it as an histor-

[37] IX(A), 82.

ical fact which is also an eternal fact. Hence it is faith which through the existential fulfilment of the believer transforms a specific historical fact into a revelatory fact, and this change comes about through insight into the meaningfulness of that historical fact. Thus we have at last the figure of that Kierkegaard whom Rudolf Bultmann is said to have commented on in the form of an exegesis of St. John's Gospel.

But how is this self-understanding of the believer distinguished from a philosophical dialectic of existence, and how is the absolute paradox distinguished from a metaphysical speculation? It would be hard to show this. The historical form which the believer gives to the interpretatory principle of his existence cannot mark this difference since the philosopher will always be able to use a similar type of principle, i.e., derive his interpretatory principles from such a history. There could only be such a difference if the historical fact of primary potency, i.e., the man Jesus of Nazareth, concretely confronted the believer in the latter's historical situation as an historical phenomenon making the claim to be an "historical fact of double potency," i.e., the God-man. He could do this either Himself or through an authorised representative. But neither of these possibilities is here the case. Here, stepping beyond all historical mediation, the believer enters into relation with an historical phenomenon of the past. He becomes aware of its claim to be an historical fact of double potency not through the impact of the claim of anything present, but rather his faith—and why?—endows with this meaning an historical fact of the past.

For the authentication of this procedure he can only invoke the Holy Spirit, who has made clear to him this truth and say with Kierkegaard: "There is only one proof of the truth of Christianity: that inner proof, *argumentum spiritus sancti.*"[38] Yet while the Holy Spirit can indeed, when man encounters the historical fact of revelation, demonstrate that the truth of the latter lies in its factuality, and, *for that reason,* can disclose its significance, it cannot do the reverse, it cannot infer factuality from meaningfulness, if the effectiveness of the revelation—and this means its factuality—is to be preserved.

[38] X.1, 481.

The one who believes in this way might further claim that in practice Christ meets him not only in that questionable conclusion of introductory research, as the "historical Jesus," but —he is not allowed of course to quote Church authorities nor the Church itself—in individual Christians who through the demonstrative power of their existential representation would have the authority to confront him with the claim of Christ. We have already said above all that is needful about this kind of authority. But if we wished to investigate further in terms of Kierkegaard's own categories the only possible relationship between teacher and pupil in this connexion, we could classify it in no other way than as the missionary activity of the "one who is awakened" and quote all that John Climacus has said about such a one and his "immediate relationship with God."

Above (see pp. 166 f.) in elucidating the dialectics of Christian discourse as opposed to Christian preaching, we have expressed our doubts that the fact of scandalisation might be replaced by a theory of scandalisation. Now, in consequence of the radical sweeping away of the historical element, this doubtfulness is even plainer. Now there is really no more room for the fact of scandalisation. According to our earlier representations, the shock of offence arose because the historical fact of primary potency, Jesus as man, raises the claim to be an historical fact of double potency, to be the God-man, and so compels us to make a decision between offence and faith. But this no longer takes place. Now, through an ideal manifested in an historical process which like all historical facts, as such, is only of primary potency, man is invited to allow this ideal to germinate as a possibility in his own existence. He can either do this or fail to do it. But only after, for reasons of his own, he has done so, can he become aware of the importance of his decision through insight into the meaningfulness of the claim with which he has to do and through his consequent recognition of the fact underlying it. But what should now give him cause for offence? If, on the other hand, he does not adopt this decision, then he can never experience what he has missed by his neglect and thus is never confronted with the possibility of offence. In either event there is nothing therefore which might arouse scandal.

At most the claim in its absolute idealism might repel; but that is something quite different from the shock of offence.

### (iii) The question of the "real" Kierkegaard

We have now traced the consequences which Kierkegaard must have drawn from his Luther-criticism had he wished to complete his task according to the indication given in a diary of the year 1848: "What we have to do is nothing more nor less than a complete revision of Christianity, a removal of the effects of those 1800 years as though they had never been. That I shall succeed in this task, I firmly and confidently believe. The whole thing is as clear as daylight to me. Yet I realise all the more seriously that the slightest movement of impatience or wilfulness disables me and confuses my thoughts."[39]

As we have seen, in his published writings Kierkegaard *never did* draw these conclusions from his Luther-criticism. He did not undo the effects of those 1800 years as though they had never been, but to the end simply remained as a mere corrective to official Christianity and by means of a dialectical relationship to authoritative pronouncements of the Church tried to create a situation favourable to contemporaneity with Christ. He did so "without authority" and to the last declared that he would not dare to affirm of himself that he was a Christian—whereas, on the other hand, in his Luther-criticism the crux of the situation is that the only possible and necessary authority for the communication of Christianity is that which the communicator acquires through the reverberation of his message in his personal existence.

We might now ask which, then, is the true Kierkegaard whom we ought to accept, the Kierkegaard of the Luther-criticism, or the Kierkegaard whom we have learned to know through his published writings.

We may perhaps discover that this question is an illegitimate one from Kierkegaard's own point of view, because it diverts interest from intrinsic matters to the personality of Kierkegaard himself. But what we have to face here are two totally contrasting points of view which must have some connexion, and

[39] IX(A), 72.

N

the obvious thing would be to seek this nexus in the personality of Kierkegaard himself. When the question is put in this way we might pointedly answer that what Kierkegaard very much *wanted* to be was the Kierkegaard of the Luther-criticism, but what, against his will, he *had* to be was the Kierkegaard of the published writings. We must now prove this statement in detail without going further than may be necessary into a psychological analysis and estimate of Kierkegaard.

Let us picture this man who rightly says of himself that no one has such a sharp eye for the weaknesses of official Christianity as himself, whom in fact nothing escapes: no comical contradiction, no moral or intellectual dishonesty, no fault of logic, and who not only commands the most brilliant formal equipment as a writer but in addition has at every moment a mastery of ethos and pathos, imagination and passion, irony and humour, and a quite unusual degree of dialectical skill in order to express his ideas and realise his aims. Furthermore, he sees the weaknesses of official Christianity as one who suffers from them in a way beyond all imagination and description. He suffers as a Christian who lives his life according to the most decisive demands of the Christian conscience, and at the heart of a situation where Christianity is grossly falsified by the Church and society of his time. He suffers from the complete political failure of this society, from the inner corruption of its authorities, from the emergence of an avenging nemesis manifesting itself in 1848 on the stage of world politics. He suffers from the fact that with clear-sighted anxiety he foresees the downfall of Europe and nowhere finds any understanding for that which to him is luminously clear. And he suffers above all from the difficulties of his own nature, from his melancholy, from his incapacity to make himself understood and to enter into a direct relationship with the men of his own time. He cannot escape the conclusion that in this world one must suffer and that for himself as a human being there can be no other redemption from the world than by dying to it. For all these reasons what he expresses in his Luther-criticism he feels most intimately from a simple human point of view. This would have been the radical cure by which not only the world but he himself would have been helped. The height of the ideal cannot terrify one who has grown up under it. It has taught him humility. In any case mortification remains the hope of Kierkegaard. Here would be the way of reaching at last a bond of union and solidarity with all those who suffer in this world, whom he loves so deeply, and to whom he cannot show his love without being completely misunderstood and so deeply hurt by them. Here would he find an immediacy of communion by which at last the imprisonment of his own thoughts would be shattered: here would he enter into direct fellowship with all those who are known to each other by a secret sign as the brothers and sisters of Jesus Christ, as the companions of His suffering in this world yet united by the blessed assurance that they are sustained in their life of suffering by the love of God. And at the same time this would spell salvation for the world. We have only to read the last entry of Kierkegaard in his diary of 1855, on 25 September, to feel the heart beat pulsing behind such thoughts.[40]

Yet he felt compelled to do something quite different, to use his gifts in quite another way, to deal with his melancholy on quite different lines, to renounce any possibility of direct self-revelation to men and seek emancipation solely through the strongest discipline. He could not escape the course of his thought by taking refuge in the comfort of direct relationship with his fellow men, but rather, pressing forwards, he must seek its ultimate conclusions through the highest conceivable degree of dialectical existential interiorisation.

We said, he *must* do so. Who compelled him? Kierkegaard would have answered, *Providence*. What does this imply?

### (iv) Kierkegaard's training by Providence

"Providence had me now once for all in its grasp; perhaps as a suspicious person I have been put on a poor diet. I am accustomed to live in such a way that at most I count on a year; at times, not infrequently, when tension has to be extreme, I live with a view to eight, or indeed one day. And Providence has me bound by its chain in every respect. My aesthetic work could not deflect me from my course in such wise that finally I

[40] See Appendix III (below, 213 f).

might have found my life wholly absorbed in aesthetics.  That thorn in the flesh would have prevented this, even had the religious point of view not been in the background.  And in regard to my religious writings, Providence had me bound by its chain so that I presumed nothing and understood myself to be as it were in a large parish.'[41]

"If now I am to express as definitely as possible this interest of Providence in my work as an author, I know no more characteristic or decisive expression than the following: it is Providence which has brought me up and this educative process is reflected in the process of my creative activity."[42]

This does not merely mean that his work is a mirror in which is reflected the process of his education by Providence, but rather this work was the essential means of his education by Providence.  We recall the already-quoted programmatic indication in his diary: "Yet I realise all the more seriously that the slightest movement of impatience or wilfulness disables me and confuses my thoughts."  This means that his work has an immanent teleology and inner governing law from which he is not allowed to break free and which gradually discloses itself only as his work reaches completion.  What this implies we propose now to elucidate by a comprehensive retrospective survey of the dialectic of existence of Kierkegaard as a whole.

### (v)  Summary of Kierkegaard's dialectic of existence

In the work of Kierkegaard's existential dialectic it is not a question of a closed system which is unfolded from specific principles and which by the application of a particular method to a particular statement of the problem must inevitably reach a particular conclusion.  The rigidity with which we have interpreted the one Kierkegaard of the published writings might lead to this wrong impression and thus contradict Kierkegaard himself who causes John Climacus to say: "there can be a logical system, but there cannot be a system of existence."[43]  The unifying point at which the disparate elements are

---

[41] *S. V.*, XIV, 571;  *Ges. W.*, X, 61-2.
[42] *S. V.*, XIV, 562;  *Ges. W.*, X, 52.
[43] *S. V.*, VII, 88;  *Ges. W.*, VI, 193.

brought together does not here lie in any ultimate principle of thought but in the subject of the existence of a concrete man, this in a special way unique Søren Kierkegaard, who cannot escape his self-identity and who with concentrated passion wishes to master his life by thought.

(a) *The fulfilment of the universally human in the existence of one concrete particular individual.* Kierkegaard seeks to master his life by thought, as every man must do who as a particular individual is concerned to realise the values of universal humanity, to become the universal man which all must be yet within the concrete terms of his particular individuality which no other can or may express. In order to achieve this he must first work out the categories for this human existence and adhere to them. This determination of universally valid categories is the prerequisite for understanding oneself rightly, even when in a given instance one cannot and may not fulfil the universal, and for clarifying the question whether and in what sense one may be justly regarded as an exception.

Since in this matter it is a question of categories of existence, hence of conceptual abbreviations not of being but of existence, in principle they will cover the whole area of this existence in its intellectual, social, political, aesthetic, ethical and religious aspects. This does not mean to say that Kierkegaard has mastered all these aspects equally by the process of thought. Like any one else he could do so only in the degree to which the breadth of his humanity reached. This of course was considerable enough, but in principle there cannot in this connexion be any watertight compartments.

(b) *The relation of the dialectic of existence to theology and philosophy.* We have to note that for Kierkegaard life as a Christian is a decisive part of this existence, and hence he must work out the categories applicable to Christian existence. This does not simply mean dogmatic definitions, for the latter as such are not yet existential categories. For example, a dogmatically correct teaching about sin and grace or about the Law and the Gospel does not in itself express how the life of sinful man is concretely manifested in its tension between the demand of discipleship and the offer of grace so that the doctrinal statement is existentially realised. But the presupposition for the development of these existential categories is of course that the dogmatic teaching should be correct. The business of existential dialectics is neither to prove nor to dispute dogmatic definitions but to reckon with them as a given datum and to examine their correctness in the light of their own presuppositions. Thus, for example, existential dialectics is concerned to see whether dogmatics is not being unfaithful to its own proper task by elaborating its dogmas into philosophical truths or by deriving them or attempting to prove them from the latter.

Thus far Kierkegaard's work is indissolubly bound up with the discipline of theology without itself being a theology. Here, too, it remains simply a dialectic of existence covering the whole area of Christian existence. Nor is this dialectic a philosophy but is related to the latter in the same way as it is related to theology, in so far as it seeks to grasp the principles of philosophy, like the dogmas of theology, as categories of existence, and from this point of view examines their correctness. Thus indirectly it makes a contribution to the work of philosophy as to that of theology.

(c) *Kierkegaard's parody of speculation.* Since the dialectic of existence has as its object the one, indivisible existence of the Christian and in this cannot distinguish between the man and the Christian, we may not expect it to make any direct contribution to the determination of the relation between philosophy and theology. It is in fact not interested in this question at all. It must repeatedly be pointed out that the *Philosophische Brocken*, which might be understood as an attempt in this direction, not only work out on merely hypothetical lines an "experiment in thought," but imply in their very structure a parody of speculation (see above p. 54, n. 6) if all is not to be misunderstood and false conclusions drawn. The book was conceived by Kierkegaard as a parody on Hegel's attempt to mediate systematically between philosophy and Christianity. He is here pursuing no independent interest but is only concerned to show the mistakenness of such an attempt by pointing out, especially in the *Nachschrift*, how by this means both dogmatic definitions and philosophical thinking are equally ruined. To a large extent he does so by positive studies intended to clarify philosophical and dogmatic ideas, but the latter again are put forward only *ad hoc* and orientated by opposition to Hegel. Hence they are not merely fortuitous and incomplete, but constantly betray that they have their origin in the author's parodying intention. This applies, for example, to the central idea of the "absolute paradox," or faith as the organ for the apprehension of the historical. It is hardly conceivable that a thinker who had worked out independently the existential categories governing the attitude of man to the Christian revelation, without having had to do so in opposition to Hegel's philosophy, would have hit upon the idea of proceeding on these lines. In this respect Kierkegaard's arguments are determined by his adversary's position, in which he had to make a breach.

For this reason, we can hardly feel surprise that in his corrective elucidation of dogmatic ideas, important points are lacking. We need only recall, for example, that in discussing the relation of historical factuality and revelation, he causes John Climacus to say: "Had the contemporary generation left behind them nothing but the words, 'We have believed that in such and such a year God manifested Himself in humility as a servant of mankind lived and taught among us and then died,' it would have been more than enough." We can hardly consider this to be enough but see in it rather an abstract summary of the historical fact of Jesus of Nazareth in favour of a Christ-principle; in particular, we may demur to it on the ground that alongside the life and death of Jesus His resurrection is nowhere mentioned. But we should not forget that here we have no independent exposition of dogmatic ideas, but only observations *ad hoc* which are to be understood and appraised within their limited framework and intention.

If the whole argument is to be explained in the light of its polemic against Hegel, then certainly the old tag will apply to it: "*Victus victori legem dat.*" In this particular case it means that by allowing his opponent to force upon him a certain way of putting the question, Kierkegaard, even after he had victoriously overcome that opponent, was still in consequence impaired in his vision of the problems and unduly fettered in his solution of them. But Kierkegaard shares this fate with every thinker who lives and thinks not outside time but within a certain historical situation, especially when, like Kierkegaard, he stands in a tensely polemical relation to it.

(d) *Kierkegaard's indirect contribution to the determination of the relation between philosophy and theology.* Although, in spite of all this, Kierkegaard made no direct contribution to the determination of the relation between philosophy and theology, nevertheless he did so indirectly in so far as by his parody he reduced *ad absurdum* this whole attempt to establish systematically the character of this relation. And this applies not merely to his attack on Hegel.

The Christian, who believes the revelation of God in Jesus Christ, must certainly come to grips with it by all the resources of his thought. In this respect the fact of revelation claims his thinking powers no less than any philosophical principle accessible to his faculties of inherent reasoning. And through his thinking it also makes demands upon his existence which he must master by thought. As Kierkegaard shows, he has no other alternative but to revise the presuppositions of his thinking if he believes in the Christian revelation, but he is not called upon to give up thinking itself. And what remains the same in this process of revision is not any sort of unifying point between "philosophical" and "theological" thought—whether it is fixed by means of the *analogia entis*, or objectively by means of a doctrine of the paradox and subjectively by means of a corresponding theory of the offence of the paradox and its resolution, or again whether in the brutal manner of a *sacrificium intellectus* as a result of which thought remains self-consistent after as before—the unifying link can only be that it is the same subject of the existential thinker which in its indissoluble self-identity as Christian and as man thinks about its humanity and expresses in its existence the categories flowing from such a process of reflection.

From such a point of view it can no longer be a question of the difference and relationship between philosophy and theology as two separate or mutually related sciences, but only of whether man wills or does not will to incorporate into his whole existence the fact of revelation, which in effect means whether he is willing or not to subject himself to the qualification of his existence which is its consequence. All ways of putting the question are thus rendered irrelevant.[44]

(e) *The dialectic of indirect communication.* The dialectic of existence, as we have seen, has always two aspects: that which leads to the interior assimilation of thought in the whole process of existence and indissolubly connected with it, the aspect of communication by which the self-existent thinker stands in relationship with his environment. As regards this latter aspect also there are specific categories. The problems arising here spring from the fact that truth is not a process of thinking but of living: it is the life of the thinker who exists according to those categories, but a life which as such cannot be directly communicated and received. It can be communicated only obliquely through the dissolution of reality into possibility by the process of thought. The question is to find a form for such communication, which, on the one hand, prevents the communicated truth which is the whole life of the thinker from being received without challenging the existence of the recipient and, on the other, makes this truth strike home with maximum effectiveness.

A further considerable complication in this matter arises from the fact that the dialectic of existence as the right way to being in the truth cannot be assumed to be known and appreciated in its rightness and necessity. Rather we must reckon with the possibility that the recipient will be involved in the precisely opposite false way in that he will be seeking truth in an objective process of thought which is indifferent to the subjective existence of the thinker. Hence the dialectic of communication must both make him aware of the wrongness of the way in which he is engaged and recall him from it. But it cannot do this directly and undialectically by pointing out to him the right way of thought because this procedure would not make any impact on his existence, but it can explain and communicate the dialectics of existence only in so far as it practises the latter. In mastering all these tasks and problems Kierkegaard develops in his work his comprehensive dialectical method of oblique communication and at the same time applies it practically.

[44] See Appendix IV (below, 215 ff.)

(*f*) *The dialectic of oblique communication in its relation to the preaching of the Church.* For the dialectic of communication the entry into existence of the Christian factor denotes a fundamental change and broadening of scope. This is because, from the Christian point of view, it is not merely a question of communicating and realising eternal truths. Rather revelation as eternal truth is at the same time an historical fact, or, more precisely, it is such truth embodied in historical fact. The qualification of existence which follows takes place through the reaction to this truth enshrined in historical fact. This historical fact must therefore be drawn into the dialectic of communication.

Just as dialectic of existence, when broadened to include the Christian factor, had to make room in its categories for dogmatic ideas, so the dialectic of communication, when applied to revelation, has to deal with certain historical facts which claim to be of similar nature to the paradoxically historical fact of revelation itself, i.e., the Church as an historical factor manifesting itself in particular historical facts such as the Apostolate, the canon of Scripture, holy orders, preaching, and the sacraments. And just as the dialectic of existence has neither to prove nor disprove those dogmatic ideas, but to reckon with them and to examine them in order to see whether they are correctly framed according to their own presuppositions, so it is with the dialectic of communication and the historical fact of the Church, or the particular facts authorised by the latter. These do not merely exercise the function of communicating truth inasmuch as they communicate the fact of revelation, but as a result of their paradoxically historical character assume a specially qualified form of communication, namely communication with authority. Kierkegaard has shown this especially in his discussion of the character of preaching. This type of authoritative and therefore direct communication exercised by the preaching ministry of the Church and other paradoxically historical media must now be worked into the dialectic of communication in its oblique form so that it may make an impact on existence.

But the dialectic of communication cannot itself take over the functions of Church proclamation, because the resources at its disposal are lacking in the special authorisation flowing from the paradoxical-historic fact of revelation. Hence it is dependent on the fact that Church proclamation takes place at the same time as its own activities. But just as the dialectic of existence does in regard to the formulations of dogma, it must examine this preaching in order to see whether it is correct according to its own presuppositions, whether, for example, the preacher is exercising his authority rightly and is keeping to the correct categories. Likewise it will turn to the hearer of the preaching in order to enquire of him whether he is realising the proclaimed truth in his existence, and by its own technique to help towards the interior assimilation and practice of this truth.

(g) *The difficulty of plunging official Christianity once more into the stream of becoming.* The difficulty is that Kierkegaard, just as in regard to the dialectic of existence applied to general human existence, sees himself in his special work confronted by a partner who not only refuses to practice this interior assimilation but is seeking truth in the utterly wrong direction: Christianity is related to truth as to an objective doctrine, which may be assented to as correct without the believer receiving from it any existential impact, with the consequence that the transformation of existence which Christianity requires can no longer take place. And official Christianity, in all that it is, says and does, only serves to confirm its adherents in this false way.

But the most serious point is that the Church itself, especially through its alliance with the State, has become an integral part of this wrongheaded Christianity. Historically the Church understands itself to be the result of the fact of revelation, and will no longer allow itself to be challenged by the latter, i.e., made dynamic once more. Those paradoxical-historic facts in which the Church is recognisable as an historical factor of a unique kind and which mark a break with immanentist historicism, implying a total challenge to existence, can no longer fulfil this special function since they have been levelled down to the immanentist historical process. Ordination, for example, besides conferring on the ordinand that "paradoxical transformation of a teacher in time," confers on him a position in the social hierarchy and the ordained person from time to time invokes as his authority his official position in the state and his spiritual dignity sacramentally understood. Thus his true authority, which consists solely in the valid exercise of his preaching mission, is no longer manifest. For the same reason he can no longer preach, and what he claims as preaching is not such, for it makes no impact either on his own existence or on that of the hearer. It serves only to justify the existing condition of organised Christianity. Baptism has become simply a rite of initiation into this organised Christianity, etc.

The Church authorities can no longer fulfil their peculiar task of marking the break with immanentist historicism, but, on the contrary, by their false objectivising attitude which secures them against dialectics, serve only to prevent such a break and thereby to prevent the interiorisation of truth in existence.

The Lutheran Reformation, which aimed at checking this process and restoring the situation on the right lines, had as its final result a far greater aggravation of the evil. Since the external visible manifestation of discipleship was opposed in the interests of combating medieval errors, the assimilation of the Church to the State was only made easier. Since everyone could now appeal to his hidden inner life and hence could no longer be challenged, the Reformation had the effect of making the situation far more difficult to handle for every future reformer.

(*h*) *The attempt to give spiritual support to organised Christianity.* In this situation Kierkegaard attempts by his work to impart to official Christianity fresh inspiration and spiritual support. Once again he cannot do so directly, because such aid cannot be directly received, but only through that shock by which the individual is thrown into existence and Christianity into the process of becoming. Hence this work must be carried out in such a dialectical way that it can be equally taken to be either an attack or a defence, and it is for official Christianity to decide by the mode of its reaction to this shock whether in fact it becomes an attack upon it or a defence of it. The right reaction would be the confession of failure by which both it and Kierkegaard himself would be driven to flee to divine grace.

(*i*) *The categorical possibilities for an attack.* For long Kierkegaard had to reckon with the possibility that such a confession
would never materialise and that an attack would therefore
be unavoidable. Nevertheless he still waits for it and works
with it in view, because he must keep to his own categories
which compel him to tread this path to the very end. He has
no "programme" from which it might have been logically
deduced from the start what the next step must be. He has
only the categories. These are no doubt of general validity
and have logical interconnexion and logical consequences,
because thought must be logically consistent. But the consequence of action is something very different. The subject of
action is he himself as this particular concrete man who has to
master this unique and to a large extent eccentric existence
by means of the universally valid categories. These categories,
however, have room also for the exception, not of course without
a precise categorical definition of this room. Thus he thinks
through his categories in order to discover the justifiable
exception and within the framework of the categories seeks to
define his own place: that of Apostle, witness to the truth,
martyr prophet, corrective. But it is he himself who must
decide into what class he should fit and which categories he
should realise. No doctrine of categories can relieve him of
this decision.

(*k*) *The attempt to break free from the situation.* The decision
must be taken in a concrete situation and in consequence a
new situation created. For this an interpretation of the
situation is required, which results from an application of the
categories that have been attained, though it cannot simply be
read off from the latter. Here various courses are open,
between which not the categories but the individual living
within them has to decide in the light of his specific self-
understanding.

And there is still a further possibility: namely the possibility
of breaking free, i.e., not to make the decision at all under the
pressure of the given categories, not to accept the situation, and
in view of its inextricable difficulties to seek another issue from
the hardness of the decision required and the burden which
humanly is no longer supportable.

*(vi)* *The Kierkegaard of the Luther-criticism as showing a possible attempt to break free*

We might regard the Kierkegaard of the Luther-criticism as representing such an attempt at escape, or rather the consideration of such an attempt. In this respect one thing stood immovably firm for Kierkegaard: the justification for the one who acts as an extraordinary individual can only follow from the sacrifice of his life. Precisely that end, however, could be most easily and effectively attained by following out this path.

"What we have to do is to remove the effects of those 1800 years as though they had never been." At the same time will be removed those dogmatic definitions by means of which Christianity has transformed revelation into a system of objective doctrine indifferent to existence. And at the same time the Church is eliminated together with all the historical media which it authorises and by means of which existing Christianity maintains those illusions on which it lives. What remains after this destructive work is Christ Himself and His individual followers who passing beyond the historical decline of Christianity fulfil the claims of discipleship in contemporaneity with their Master, and, mortified by the height of the ideal, live by divine grace, and through the reverberation of the Gospel in their personal existence gain the authority openly to oppose official Christianity and to allow themselves to be slain by it.

This is the path which Luther really ought to have trod and which now his true follower must tread. "The true follower of Luther will arrive at exactly the opposite result to Luther himself, because Luther reacted to the fantastic exaggeration of asceticism, whereas his followers will react to the terrible deception which Lutheranism has given birth to."[45]

It is clear that, like everything that Kierkegaard says and does, this way is logically consistent and that to one in Kierkegaard's situation it might seem an attractive issue. Moreover, at first sight, it is not so easy to understand why such an issue should not be consistent with the trend of his work as a whole. It is not so easy to dispute the justification of his Luther-criticism, and—because the problems are not so much derived

[45] x.3, 153.

from this criticism itself as from the conclusions which Kierke-gaard inferred from it—the thought seems obvious that these conclusions show only the one-sidedness imposed on a corrective view.

But it could not escape a dialectician such as Kierkegaard that this issue represents an attempt to shirk the problem just because it abandons the path which had been so carefully secured by the most complex dialectics, and simply cuts the Gordian knot.

Hence Kierkegaard did not take this path but followed the other road to the very end, along which he also and equally sacrificed himself, in intention for the good of Christianity, but in a much more modest way. Along this road, he could have no follower, as he had no predecessor, nor could he contrive his sacrifice as something catastrophic. Here his sacrifice could not possibly become an attitude for others, nor could he, who had at heart the fate of Christianity, know or even reckon with the possibility that he would thus succeed in changing this fate.

### (vii) The connexion of the two ways

It should be noted that these two ways do not run alongside each other as completely separate and mutually exclusive. Apart from intrinsic reasons we have distinguished them by noting that Kierkegaard followed the one way in his published work, whilst the other is to be found in his unpublished diary. From the point of view of method this mode of discrimination is not in itself free from objection, since Kierkegaard wrote his diaries, too, for publication (even if only posthumous), and often enough we have made use of his diary for the understand-ing of his published work. The inner intrinsic reasons for the distinction are alone decisive.

Moreover, from time to time, it is not so certain that in his published work the other tendency has not manifested itself. The cancellation of the Foreword in the second edition of the *Einübung des Christentums* may be so explained as we have done above, for it disclosed the trend of his previous work. It might also be said that he now wishes to expound that other relation of discipleship and grace which we know from his

Luther-criticism, and therefore no longer wishes to acknowledge this Foreword. The same applies to those passages of the articles during his last attack where he represents discipleship in a way which makes one wonder whether it is only the one-sidedness of a corrective view, or whether he thus wishes to exclude his earlier thought that God is still willing to have to do with an existence which puts grace first. That a neat and exclusive discrimination between these two tendencies is not possible is essentially shown by the consideration that generally it is only the conclusions themselves which make clear which tendency Kierkegaard is following up. But for the most part these conclusions are not drawn in particular instances. And from the point of view of the personality of Kierkegaard such a discrimination is not possible, since in both cases we have to do with the same Kierkegaard, who according to his own confession was disciplined by his published work and possibly sought from time to time to escape this discipline. Who is to say in each individual case which of these tendencies is in operation?

Here we can only judge in so far as the facts and the criteria given by Kierkegaard himself are recognisable and verifiable by us. Such are, above all, the categories which Kierkegaard worked out, both those of his published work and those which are inferred from his Luther-criticism. We may quite plainly state that the former are not only far more profound and more thoroughly thought-out than the latter, but that also, according to our theological judgment, they are correct, whereas we would have to consider the other Kierkegaard to be a visionary, a fanatic, which he himself under no circumstances wished to be.

### (viii) Providentia specialissima

We would like once more to insist that not only in his literary work but with the involvement and sacrifice of his whole personality Kierkegaard followed the one and not the other path. And we recall once again the notice in his diary which runs: "Merely the slightest movement of impatience or wilfulness disables me and confuses my thoughts." We might add that in view of the situation and his personality it was, humanly speaking, an only too understandable "impatience and wilfulness" which led him astray on the other path. And the fact that his thoughts grew confused on this way was surely because the inner truth of the matter opposed him and prevented him from following this tendency to its conclusion with existential inwardness. But we must guard ourselves against saying too much in this respect. We must not forget that not even the categories could relieve him of the necessity for personal decision, and that secondly the correctness of these categories was questionable. The compulsion of Providence to which he appeals cannot consist merely in the compulsion of insight into the correctness of the categories.

There remains here an opening for decision which is filled by the prayers of the active subject, Søren Kierkegaard, and through which he seeks to come to an understanding of and surrender to Providence considered as *providentia specialissima*.

Under the heading "*Providentia specialissima*," we find in one of the last entries in Kierkegaard's diary: "To be a Christian means to believe in a *providentia specialissima*, not *in abstracto* but *in concreto*. Only he who has this belief *in concreto* is an individuality; every other is really only an example of a certain type, he has neither courage nor humility; he is not tormented, nor is he sufficiently helped to be an individuality."[46]

Thus the question of the real Kierkegaard has become pointless. What the man Søren Kierkegaard really wanted is not our concern; we are only concerned with what Providence wanted to say to us through him and has thus set us as our specific task. But we shall not be able to gather this so simply and directly from Kierkegaard's work, and still less from any interpretation of his personality. That there are clearly two possibilities here forces upon us also a decision. And we, too, shall not be able to deduce simply from any doctrine of categories what is demanded of us, but we shall have to come to realise in which path we have to tread through submission to our *providentia specialissima*, above all when perhaps we suppose that we ought to go that way which Kierkegaard, after all, and in spite of everything, did not go.

[46] XI.2(A), 259.

## (ix) *Kierkegaard and posterity*

In the last diaries there are certain entries which reveal what thoughts Kierkegaard entertained concerning his influence on posterity. After he has reached certainty about the fact that he is being sacrificed as a corrective to what passes for Christianity, it becomes at the same time clear to him that in his work he has no predecessor and can have no legitimate successor. He writes in the year 1854: "My task is so new that there is literally no one in the 1800 years of Christianity from whom I can learn how I should proceed."

"For all that has been seen so far in the sphere of the unusual and extraordinary has had the effect of spreading Christianity; and my own task lies rather in checking a spread of false Christianity, and probably also will have the effect of making Christianity strike off its roll a large number of merely nominal Christians."

"Hence none of the extraordinary personalities has stood so literally alone as myself, still less has he understood it to be his special task to defend his right to remain solitary—for if I am to check the false process it can easily be seen that the task will the more quickly be performed the fewer the persons engaged in it."

"Yes, I am glad that when once I am dead there will be something here for the lecturers to talk about. Those pitiful rascals! And yet it will be of no use, not even if it were printed and read over and over again—however, the lecturers will make profit out of me, they will lecture about me perhaps even adding, 'His characteristic is that it is not possible to lecture on him.'"[47] The hope of being better understood by future generations seemed to Kierkegaard a false subterfuge:

"Talk of being better understood by posterity—i.e., a posterity in which admiring professorial rascals and a pack of parsons make profit for themselves and their families out of the life and work and papers of the deceased. Is that a better posterity, do you call that being better understood?" "And yet it has always been thus with these *men* who have struggled, of whom I have read (Socrates alone excepted) that they are inspired by the thought of better appreciation from posterity."

[47] XI.1(A), 136.

"This thought does not inspire me and in my opinion to need the inspiration of such an illusory thought shows indirectly that one is not satisfied with one's inspiration in and for itself. In any case such a thought does not create any enthusiasm in me, on the contrary, what stirs me most is when I come to think of this rascally posterity. The misunderstanding of one's contemporaries is not nearly so embittering, nor, if you like, so hopeless; no, all is hopelessly lost only when one's life is smothered in misunderstanding, and when the misunderstanding is characterless, empty, insipid admiration."[48]

In such sentences one should not read merely the deep embitterment of the man who was not understood by his contemporaries and could not even hope for a better understanding from posterity. In this respect it is not merely a question of personal moods and pessimism, but rather for Kierkegaard the whole question as to what his work will mean for posterity belongs essentially to the material estimate of that work itself. This becomes especially clear from an earlier note of 1852:

"If a lecturer could steal my thoughts from me, he would be very fortunate. I know that very well, and understand that this too is a reason for stiffening my examination. For I am very far from trumpeting about a better posterity, although I realise that future generations will come along who will judge me otherwise than my contemporaries, but I only deny that their judgment will therefore be better. No, if I could reach out to posterity, as I wish, it would be in order to baffle, if possible, the false lecturing that will batten on me. But this is not possible; if it were possible, the considered opinion of my life would be different. No, it is not possible; in my own time, envy and mediocrity—repulsive vermin!—will eat me up; and after my death lecturers will just as horribly live on me."

"There have perhaps been men who have harassed themselves to despair to see whether they could not succeed in driving away the vermin among their contemporaries: but it cannot be done if you do not wish to elude the truth and become vermin yourself. Most of these men have no doubt comforted themselves, as people say, with the hope of better appreciation

---

[48] XI.2(A), 32.

from posterity. It has probably occurred more seldom to a person to see whether he could not take measures to strike at the lecturers of the next generation: but it cannot be done..."[49]

We break off the quotation at this point in order to ask why Kierkegaard considers it impossible to forestall the misuse of his work by the lecturers of posterity. He was of course unable to prevent his contemporaries from reading his works without paying attention to the obliqueness of his method of communication, and thus disregarding their dialectical nature and taking the ideas to be something capable of direct exposition. In the *Nachschrift* he causes John Climacus to say: "Only he who realises the obstinacy of a misunderstanding which attempts to assimilate the most strenuous attempt at explanation and yet remains a misunderstanding, will understand the difficulty of a type of writing in which every word has to be carefully noted and every word has a twofold bearing. By direct teaching about existence and inwardness the only result will be that the thinker will take a keen interest in the matter and yet miss the essence of it."[50]

During his lifetime Kierkegaard could to some extent protect himself from the enthusiasm of the lecturers both by his own personal attitude and the whole apparatus of pseudonymity which intensified the obliqueness of his literary method. But with his death this obliqueness ceases. One is no longer confronted by the spectacle of his own personal life as a challenge and a shock. The mystery of the pseudonyms is pierced. It is no longer necessary to pay heed to Kierkegaard's own requirement that his writings should not be cited under his own name but under that of the pseudonyms in order to guard the obliqueness of his communication as an essential part of his whole work, for it can concern nobody if this is not done, and, moreover, the lecturers regard the failure to do it as a scholarly proceeding. On the contrary, the position now is that the pseudonyms can be utilised in order to probe the personality of the author underlying them, and the main interest is centred on that personality.

Thus the modern critic need no longer subject himself to the ultimate intention of Kierkegaard's work and is in a

[49] X.5(A), 18.          [50] *S. V.*, VII, 210; *Ges. W.*, VI, 321.

position to make a judgment on the work and its method and purpose. And thus we are in a position to analyse the work into its component parts and so to exploit it as we will. It will be found to yield an enormously rich store of material for lecturers of all the faculties: aesthetic critics, psychologists, philosophers, and, not least, even theologians. And this misuse will be especially subtle and hard to deal with when it seizes on Kierkegaard's dialectic of existence. Instead of engaging in a dialectical approach to this work in its passionate concentration and wholeness—an approach which requires the involvement of the critic's personal existence—existence will rather be made the object of academic exposition, and philosophers and theologians will take from Kierkegaard's work the cornerstones for the construction of a system of "existential thought." And they will completely overlook the small distinction, so momentous in consequences, namely the fact *that Kierkegaard speaks not of "existential thought" but of "the existing thinker."*

How will Kierkegaard hinder all this? He is aware that there is no means of doing so; and under the heading "Melancholy" he writes therefore in his diary:

"Somewhere in one of the Psalms it is said of the rich man that he heaps up riches in vain disquiet and cannot tell who shall gather them: thus from an intellectual point of view I shall leave behind me a not inconsiderable capital: ah, yes, and I know also who will inherit my wealth, he whose figure is so monstrously repulsive to me, he who so far has inherited all the better things and will go in inheriting them: the lecturer, the professor."

"But this also is part of my suffering that I should realise this and yet go on quite calmly in my struggle, which will bring me toil and heaviness and trial and all the yield of which will in one sense be monopolised by the professor—in one sense; for in another sense I shall take it with me."

And in a postscript Kierkegaard adds:

"And should the professor read this, it would not stop him nor have the effect of rousing his conscience. No, this again would be solemnly expounded. And again this very remark, should the professor chance to read it, would not check his activities, no, it would be professorially expounded.  For the professor is longer than the tape-worm (the length of which has recently been seen to be 100 yards in consequence of a letter of thanks in which a husband expresses his gratitude for his wife's being freed from it and he gives the length as 100 yards) yes, longer: and no man can cut someone free in whom the tape-worm of the professorial character dwells: that only God can do, if the man so wills."[51]

For these reasons Kierkegaard forbids himself to entertain the hope of better appreciation from posterity, and continues in his notes of 1852:

"Hence only one thing remains:  see that you stand your test well—and thus judgment will come both to him who has loved the truth and to the lecturer, that noxious vermin, who hypocritically lives on the sufferings of a dead man.

"Hypocritical!  Yes, indeed, that is why Christ says that the guilt is the same, to slay the prophets and in the next generation to build their graves and to say, 'Had we lived when they did, such a thing would not have happened.'

"It is possible when a man suffers from his contemporaries that he should, as it were, reach forward to the next generation in the hope that there justice will be done to him: but that point of view shows a limitation and enslavement of thought, for such a one cannot see that the next generation, the academic people are as disgusting as the most bestial of one's contemporaries.

"No, no, let everything else slide, think not of your mishandling by your contemporaries and still less of the horror of academic persons, no, only see that you stand your test well.

"If you do that, you are doing something infinitely important. Perhaps it will turn out thus, perhaps not, that some individual in the next generation will be inspired by your life to examine his life also and stand his test.  His experience will be just the same as yours—the testing of the life cannot and must not be hindered, but perhaps many a time it will encourage him to think of you, as you too have experienced in relation to someone or other dead and gone."[49]

[49] x.5(A), 18.                          [51] x.4, 627-8.

# APPENDIXES

Geismar, moreover, objects: "In the sketch of his essay on Adler, it did not escape Kierkegaard's notice that there was a real danger lest the Apostle should come to be regarded as on a level with Christ; but he tried to obviate this danger by a note which explains nothing."[2] Geismar does not see why Kierkegaard supposes that he need only say something which goes without saying and need not explain anything, because Geismar has quite another unanswered question to put to Kierkegaard. He thinks, in fact, that when in the *Nachschrift* a paradoxical-dialectical existence is ascribed to the Apostle by which he possesses authority, this must be "utterly impossible, according to the *Brocken*; such a teacher, endowed with such authority, would teach truth in the same way as Christ, even though he were a man."[3] We have seen (above, 91, n. 14) that the *Nachschrift*, in its historical form, treats exactly the same problem as was abstractly treated in the *Brocken*. Hence there can be no question of any contradiction, rather the authority of the historical orders, the Apostolate, and the priesthood, is of decisive importance, for it prevents that dissolution of time in eternity as a result of which the historical fact of revelation would become simply an eternal truth. Geismar says that this theory of the Apostle "would lead straight to Catholicism if it were worked out"; and if, as Kierkegaard wants, "it applies also to the ordained clergy, then we are half way to Catholicism."[4]. No, for if that in itself were a forbidden Catholicism, then there would be no Church and no preaching ministry at all; and all dogmatics would be dissolved in existential philosophy. Kierkegaard has seen this point more clearly than Geismar. Geismar is right in saying that then the hearer, in regard to the recognition of the truth, stands over against Apostles and clergy in the same position as contemporaries stood to Christ. But it is just this which Kierkegaard means and which he regards as of such decisive importance.

The equation of the Apostle and clergyman, in this respect,

---

[1] See above, 140, n. 18.  [2] Geismar, *S. K.*, 321 ; cp. also 362.
[3] *Op. cit.*, 321.  [4] *Op. cit.*, 320-1.

which at first sight does not seem to fit into Kierkegaard's thought, quite understandably arouses doubt and repulsion again and again. Thus Lögstrup recently has occupied himself with this question.[5] Unlike Geismar, he finds, however, that what is said about the Apostle is consistent with Kierkegaard's thought—though in his view it stands in complete contrast to Luther's position—but he does not think that the statements about the ordained clergy fit in and considers that "no room is made for the ministry of proclamation in general."[6] He mentions the passages which we have quoted, but comments: "These and similar observations are neither supported nor closely examined—the reference to ordination is neither the one nor the other—they stand as pure assertions. The essential presupposition for the authority of the Apostle, namely that his existence is subsumed in his commission, does not apply to the pastor. But on what then rests that parallel between the call through revelation and the call through ordination which constitutes both the Apostle's authority and the pastor's? There is no answer to this question. Nor can it be otherwise, because the ministry of proclamation lies outside Kierkegaard's categories."[7] We may grant simply that Kierkegaard nowhere uses the idea of ecclesiastical office, but his many remarks about ordination are there, and because we trust that Kierkegaard, with his systematic thoroughness, knows what he means by them, we have not just eliminated them as unintelligible contradictions but have investigated them and have thus reached conclusions quite different from those of Lögstrup. We have found that those questions which the latter has put as unanswerable can well be answered and that the idea of ordination is not a foreign body in the thought of Kierkegaard, but is of decisive importance for his whole dialectic, so much so that it would emerge from the system of his thoughts even if he had not mentioned it so repeatedly and emphatically. Almost everything that Kierkegaard has written both in criticism of current preaching, and especially in supplying positive norms for true preaching, proceeds from just this assumption of the authority of the preacher. It would be relevant to ask whether according to all that Lögstrup himself says "the decisive presupposition for the authority of the

---

[5] Lögstrup, "Die Kategorie und das Amt der Verkündigung im Hinblick auf Luther und Kierkegaard," in *Ev. Th.*, 1949, 249 ff.

[6] *Op. cit.*, 263.　　　　　　　　　　[7] *Op. cit.*, 263 ff.

apostle" is in fact for Kierkegaard "that his existence is subsumed in his commission." So far we have found that this
presupposition is rather his call which confers on him the essential authority. And in that respect he can be classed along
with the pastor. We have yet to enquire how, in regard to
both, absorption in their commission works itself out.

Lögstrup has allowed himself to be led astray thus by Kierkegaard's researches into the nature of authority in the essay
"Concerning the Difference between a Genius and an Apostle."
There Kierkegaard says that all secular authority is only
"ephemeral," a "transitory thing," in contrast to that of the
Apostle, of whose commission it is said that "by this paradoxical
fact the Apostle is different to all eternity from other men."[8]
Lögstrup comments: "This is certainly metaphysics! Why
does not the authority of the Apostle vanish in eternity like that
of governors and parents? The answer is: 'Because the
authority of the Apostle is divine.'"[9] From this he draws
very far-reaching conclusions and says: "This metaphysics
can be explained from Kierkegaard's attitude towards profes-
sional and official life; it springs from his disqualification of life
in its secular forms of authority as something merely immanent
and relative."[10] According to his theological presuppositions
Lögstrup may well describe it so, but we might ask whether
Kierkegaard as a result does not stand nearer to Luther than a
certain Lutheran doctrine of these authorities.[11] But, in any
case, it is incorrect of Lögstrup to describe these thoughts of
Kierkegaard's as metaphysical. We must therefore make clear
what Kierkegaard understands by "divine authority." For
Kierkegaard, the divine character of authority does not reside
in any metaphysical qualification—as, would, for example, the
divine authority of the King which Lögstrup finds missing—
but it comes about because through the commissioning of
the Apostle the eternal is enshrined in the historical and so
transforms him paradoxically that his being marked-out and
resultant qualitative distinction from other men cannot now
be re-absorbed in immanentist thought, which is only able to
conceive of differences among men against the background of
their essential equality. It is this which Kierkegaard means
when he says that the distinction of the Apostle will remain
eternally—not a speculation as to whether the Apostle will play

[8] S. K., S. V., xi, 97; Ges. W., x, 144.       [9] Lögstrup, op. cit., 265.
[10] Ibid.                                       [11] Cp. above, 125, n. 2.

a special role in the beyond also.  And exactly the same distinction of a historical fact as an eternal fact applies to the pastor through his ordination—and this Kierkegaard especially emphasises in this very connexion.[12] But to give this authority to the King also, Kierkegaard has neither occasion nor dogmatic grounds.

[12] *S. V.*, xi, 101 n.; x, 147 n.

# Appendix II [1]

## Lögstrup's comparison of Luther and Kierkegaard

K. E. Lögstrup[2] has a different interest in his comparison of Luther and Kierkegaard. As a systematic theologian, he asks what answers Kierkegaard and Luther give to the question concerning the category of ecclesiastical office and proclamation, and comes to the conclusion that their answers are different and irreconcilable. One can of course pose this question, but one should be clear from the outset that a systemisation of Luther's theological position, is also possible which would render it at some points more discriminating and not so undialectical as Lögstrup makes it.[3] But in the case of Kierkegaard it would be more difficult, because he does not develop these categories as dogmatic positions, it is rather that with him their corresponding dogmatic ideas have been worked into an existential-dialectical procedure. Even though they have their place within this scheme and are consistent and coherent, yet a dogmatic position and a dialectical proceeding are incommensurable and cannot be so simply compared and contrasted as Lögstrup does when he concludes: "It is the task of systematic theology to give an account of the fact when their answers to certain fundamental questions are not only different but irreconcilable."[4] But such a method ought to be excluded by the historical fact that Kierkegaard does not develop his dialectic as an independent system in opposition to Luther's dogmatic position or without taking it into consideration but only in constant dialectical relatedness to it, as he found it in the Lutheranism of his Danish Church. It seems rather unintelligent to confront Kierkegaard with the dogmatic positions of Lutheranism as though he had not himself been aware of the latter, and without considering the question which especially preoccupied him, namely what would become of Lutheranism when subjected to existential dialectics.

---

[1] Cp. above, 159, n. 2.　　　　　[2] *Op. cit.*

[3] See above, 125, n. 2, and Appendix I.　　[4] Lögstrup, *op. cit.*, 269.

# Appendix III[1]

## The Supreme Grace of the Christian Life[2]

The characteristic of this life is that it is led to the point of uttermost weariness and disgust and satiety. He who, brought to such a pass, can nevertheless hold fast (or whom God enables to hold fast) to the faith that it is God who out of love has brought him to such a situation, is one who has stood the test from a Christian point of view and who is sealed for eternity.

I have arrived at this point through a fault and against the will of God. The fault, which in one sense is not mine, but which nevertheless makes me guilty in the sight of God, is that of giving life. The punishment fits the crime; that punishment is to be deprived of all joy in life, and led to the supreme degree of weariness and satiety. Man wished to dabble in the handiwork of the Creator and, although not wishing to create man, yet to give him life. You are to atone for this fault; for the characteristic of this life is—yet through my grace, for it is only those who are being saved to whom I show my grace—that I lead you to the utmost degree of weariness with life.

The majority of men however are so unspiritual, and so utterly abandoned by grace, that the punishment simply does not strike them. Lost in this life, they yet cling to it, and starting from nothing, they return to nothing, their life is a continuous process of degeneration (i.e., it is something superfluous).

Those who are more spiritual and are not overlooked by grace, are led to the point where life reaches a supreme degree of weariness and ennui. But they cannot be satisfied with this, they revolt against God and so on.

Only those who, brought to this stage of life-weariness, are by the assistance of divine grace held firm in the belief that God does this through love, so that there is no lurking doubt in the inner chambers of their soul about the fact that God is love—only *they* are sealed for eternity.

And God is concerned about them in eternity too. What does God want? He wants a soul which can praise, adore and give thanks to Him (which is the business of the angels). For

---

[1] Cp. above, 187, n. 40.    [2] Taken from *S. K. P.*, XI.2(A), 439.

this reason God is surrounded by angels. Those beings of whom there are thousands in so-called Christianity, who howl and shout in praise of God for a penny—those He does not care for. No, the angels please Him. And what pleases Him even more than the praise of the angels is the spectacle of a man who, when God, as it were, becomes for him disgusting cruelty, and seems to do everything with the most refined cruelty in order to rob him of all joy in life, nevertheless holds fast to the belief that God is love and does all this from love. Such a man becomes then an angel. And in Heaven it is easy for him to praise God, but the time of testing and trial is always the most severe. As though it occurred to a man to travel round the globe in order to hear a singer who had a perfect voice, so God sits in Heaven and listens. And whenever He hears praise from a man whom He has brought to a supreme degree of life-weariness, He says to Himself: "That is the authentic tone I wanted to hear." He says this as if He were making a discovery. But He was prepared for the fact since He Himself was with this man all the time and helped him in so far as God can help in what is after all the sole work of freedom. Only freedom can do this; and does it indeed with surprise at what she achieves, thanking God as if it had been a work which God Himself had wrought; and such a man is so joyful at being able to achieve this and feels so happy about it that he will not hear it ascribed to his own doing, but in thankfulness traces it all back to God, and asks God that it may be accepted as God's own work. For he does not believe in himself, he believes only in God.

## Kierkegaard and the Relation between Philosophy and Theology

In his article "Christlicher Glaube und existenzielles Denken,"[2] Krüger, as a philosopher, considers the old question of the relation between philosophy and theology, which has a personal rather than a purely academic interest for him. He says: "If in philosophy there is achieved a personal union of faith and philosophic thought, the problem then arises as to how the admitted limit of philosophy shall be observed, without the independence of thought being given up, or rendered merely apparent with the consequence that either thinking in general or its genuineness is sacrificed."[3] He adds: "In our time this problem is concentrated in that type of existentialist thought inaugurated by Kierkegaard. Here it has been shown with unusual force how near philosophy and theology can come to each other, and how difficult it is to determine correctly the distinction between them."[4] Hence it seems remarkable that the founders of the philosophy should reject the Christian revelation. "Whether it be that the Christian character of existentialist thought was already doubtful in Kierkegaard, or whether in the philosophers of today that type of thought has undergone an essential change; the fact remains that here there is discussion of things which are also contained in the Christian creed, though it is expressly forbidden us to understand them in a Christian sense."[5] Krüger illustrates this with reference to Heidegger and Jaspers, and thus gives a good account of the problems of their philosophy, elucidating their connexion with Kierkegaard. As regards direct point of contact, there is not much more than the fact that in both, as in Kierkegaard, the ideas of care, guilt, anxiety, conscience, temporality, are the distinctive notes of human life, though, unlike Kierkegaard, they explain these emphatically without taking the Christian revelation into account and in antithesis

---

[1] Cp. above, 193, n. 44.
[2] In *Festschrift Rudolf Bultmann*, Stuttgart 1949, 168-89.
[3] *Op. cit.*, 169.     [4] *Op. cit.*, 170.     [5] *Op. cit.*, 171.

to the latter.  Also, from the point of view of method, their proceeding has nothing in common with Kierkegaard's dialectic which is all the more important since with Kierkegaard the dialectical procedure is the essence of the matter, and it yields no separable truths which, as results, might be compared with the conclusions of other thinkers attained in different ways. Hence we would not be able to say with Krüger: "The teaching that truth is subjectivity and inwardness brings the existential concept of Heidegger into line with that of Kierkegaard. For the latter also, truth is present only in the process of self-evolving freedom, only in becoming, only in the movement of personal appropriation where there is no distinct result."[6]  But for Kierkegaard all this is just not a directly communicable doctrine, and presented as such is not correct.  He is not concerned with any doctrine about the right way of being, but with this way of being itself, i.e., the dialectical proceeding by which such a way of being is to be attained and imparted.  If this dialectical procedure is neglected, then we have nothing more to do with Kierkegaard essentially.  In particular we could not continue to say with Krüger: "With Kierkegaard, too, man is sovereign, in so far as he alone can really make true all that is objectively true.  For him this applies not only to human life but also to Christianity."[7]  The fulfilment of truth in subjective existence does not create truth but presupposes truth as something objectively given: for the Socratic existence in "paradox," for Christian existence in "absolute paradox." Krüger himself moreover draws attention to this decisive difference between Heidegger and Kierkegaard in what follows and quite rightly points out that "the project of the *Philosophical Fragments* shows in the way it is carried out that it does not spring from human invention."[8]  Krüger's question, then, is characteristic: "Perhaps Kierkegaard as a thinker stopped halfway along this road because for him his existential thought only served to show 'how man becomes a Christian.'"[9]  This is what one is inevitably led to ask when the starting-point is the relation between philosophy and theology, both of which as personified sciences agitate about the line of demarcation between them, and when as a thinker one is compelled to observe "the admitted limitation of philosophy."  This whole presentation of the question is not applicable to Kierkegaard. Perhaps Krüger himself would have become aware of this if in

[6] *Op. cit.*, 177.          [7] *Ibid.*          [8]*Op. cit.*, 178.          [9] *Ibid.*

observing the method of the *Brocken* he had also noticed that it was intended to be a parody of speculation, and had asked how Kierkegaard had the freedom to handle the "admitted limits of the sciences" with such masterly ease—for the reason, namely, that he knows so much more about the limits of human thought in its existential realisation, as also about the positive significance of this thought in its existential relation to revelation.

The trouble which Krüger then takes to investigate the thinking of Jaspers and Heidegger to see whether here too there is not the possibility "that existence constantly involved in becoming might not be pushed beyond itself,"[10] yields some very interesting insights into the problematics of this philosophy. Krüger considers that "if this did happen, then there would arise for theology also (and perhaps even for the believer as such) quite a new situation." We think, on the contrary, that this would hardly have any significance for theology.

Characteristic is Krüger's question whether the reason for the rejection of the Christian revelation is that "the Christian character of existentialist thought was already doubtful in Kierkegaard, or whether in the philosophers of today that type of thought has undergone an essential change." It is just as impossible to speak of an "existentialist thought" in Kierkegaard as it is to enquire about the Christian character of this thought. Hence it is not surprising that Krüger finds no answer to his question.

[10] *Op. cit.*, 170.

# BIBLIOGRAPHICAL NOTE

## A. Danish Editions

*Søren Kierkegaards Samlede Vaerker*, edd. A. B. Drachmann, J. L. Heiberg and H. O. Lange, 14 vols., Copenhagen 1901 ff. Cited as *S. V.*

*Søren Kierkegaards Papirer*, edd. P. A. Heiberg and V. Kuhr, Copenhagen 1909 ff. Cited as *S. K. P.* (The first published edition of S. K.'s papers was entitled *Eftirladte Papirer*. Selective English translation of *S. K. P.*: K.'s *Journals, A Selection*, ed. and tr. A. Dru, Oxford 1938.)

## B. German Translations

*Sören Kierkegaard: Gesammelte Werke*, edd. and tr. H. Gottsched and C. Schrempf, 12 vols., Jena 1922 ff. Cited as *Ges. W.*

*Leben und Walten der Liebe*, tr. A. Dorner and C. Schrempf, Jena 1924. Eng. trans.: *Works of Love*, tr. D. F. and L. M. Swenson, Princeton 1946.

*Der Begriff der Ironie*, tr. W. Kütemeyer, Munich 1929.

*Der Begriff des Auserwählter*, tr. T. Häcker, Innsbruck 1926. Cited as *B. A.*

*Kritik der Gegenwart*, tr. T. Häcker, Innsbruck 1922. Cited as *K. G.*

*Angriff auf die Christenheit*, Sören Kierkegaards agitatorische Schriften und Aufsätze 1851-5, tr. A. Dorner and C. Schrempf, Stuttgart 1896. Cited as *Angriff*.